The
Fence
and the
River

Cultural Studies of the Americas

Edited by George Yúdice, Jean Franco, and Juan Flores

Volume 3 *Latin Americanism*
    Román de la Campa

Volume 2 *Disidentifications: Queers of Color and the Performance of Politics*
    José Esteban Muñoz

Volume 1 *The Fence and the River: Culture and Politics at the U.S.–Mexico Border*
    Claire F. Fox

The
Fence
and the
River

Culture and Politics

at the U.S.–Mexico

Border

Claire F.
Fox

Cultural Studies of
the Americas
Volume 1

University of Minnesota Press
Minneapolis
London

An earlier version of chapter 2 titled "The Fence and the River: Representations of
the U.S.–Mexico Border in Art and Literature" was published in
Discourse 18, nos. 1–2 (fall/winter 1995–96): 54–83.
Copyright Wayne State University Press, Detroit, Michigan 48201.

An earlier version of chapter 5 titled "The Portable Border: Site-Specificity, Art,
and the U.S.–Mexico Frontier" was published in *Social Text* 41 (winter 1994): 61–83.
A portion of chapter 5 titled "Mass Media, Site Specificity, and the U.S.–Mexico Border:
Guillermo Gómez-Peña's *Border Brujo* (1988, 1990)" also appeared in
The Ethnic Eye: Latino Media Arts, Chon A. Noriega and Ana M. López, editors
(Minneapolis: University of Minnesota Press, 1996), 228–43.

Published by the University of Minnesota Press
111 Third Avenue South, Suite 290
Minneapolis, MN 55401-2520
http://www.upress.umn.edu

Library of Congress Cataloging-in-Publication Data

Fox, Claire F.
    The fence and the river : culture and politics at the U.S.–Mexico border /
Claire F. Fox.
        p.   cm. — (Cultural studies of the Americas ; v. 1)
    Includes bibliographical references and index.
    ISBN 0-8166-2998-6. — ISBN 0-8166-2999-4 (pbk.)
    1. Mexican-American Border Region—Civilization. 2. Mexican-American
Border Region—In art. 3. Mexican-American Border Region—In literature.
4. Mexican-American Border Region—In mass media. 5. Popular culture—
United States—History—20th century. 6. Mexican-American Border Region—
Politics and government. 7. United States—Relations—Mexico. 8. Mexico—
Relations—United States. I. Title. II. Series.
F787.F69   1999
972′.1—dc21   98-50312

Printed in the United States of America on acid-free paper

The University of Minnesota is an equal-opportunity educator and employer.

10 09 08 07   10 9 8 7 6 5 4 3 2

Contents

List of Illustrations   vii

Acknowledgments   ix

Introduction   1

1. Cultural Exemptions, Cultural Solutions   15

2. Establishing Shots of the Border: The Fence and the River   41

3. U.S.–Mexico Border Conflict in U.S. Popular Culture:
   Recodifications of the Revolution and the Porfiriato   69

4. Narratives of Cross-Border Migration during
   the Revolution's Developmentalist Phase   97

5. Mass Media, Site-Specificity, and Representations
   of the U.S.–Mexico Border   119

Appendix: Videos about Free Trade and Related Issues   139

Notes   143

Bibliography   169

Index   183

Illustrations

1. Karl Beveridge and Carole Condé, *Free Expression,* 1989

2. Karl Beveridge and Carole Condé, *Shutdown,* 1991

3–6. Lynn Schwarzer, *Images of Labor* (detail), 1993

7–10. Terry Allen, *a simple story (Juarez),* 1992

11. Malaquías Montoya, *Undocumented,* 1981

12. Peter Goin: "Because of careful ranch management, grasses survive in the Animas Valley on the United States side of the line (to the right)."

13. Peter Goin: "Today, no federal, state, or local governments have any concerted policy regarding the border fences."

14. Peter Goin: "View of the border line and fence at the port-of-entry at San Ysidro and Tijuana, looking west."

15. Peter Goin: "The westernmost marker, Monument No. 258, rests in Border Field State Park at the Pacific Ocean."

16. Don Bartletti, *Uneasy Neighbors,* 1988

17. David Avalos, Eriberto Oribol, and Michael Schnorr, *Border Realities III,* February 1987

18. Michael Schnorr, *Fence "Border line boundary,"* January 1987

19. Sara Jo Berman and Michael Schnorr, *Border Realities II,* February 1986

20. Michael Schnorr, *Burning Fence,* 1991

21. Jeffry D. Scott, Waterfill Colonia, Ciudad Juárez, Chihuahua, Mexico, 1994

22. Jim Saah, Ciudad Juárez, Chihuahua, Mexico, 1991

23. Cal Osbon, "U.S. and Mexico State Line," 1915

24. Unidentified photographer, "Detained at the Refugee Camp"

25. Cal Osbon, "Trenches on the Border at Douglas, Arizona," 1915

26. Unidentified photographer, "International Line at Nogales"

27. Cal Osbon, "Long Distance Telephone to President Wilson," 1916

28. F. C. Hecox, "American Sightseers near Madero's Camp"

29. Unidentified photographer, "Americans and Insurrectos at Rio Grande"

30. Alexander, "Americans in El Paso watching Mexican Insurrectos from across the Rio Grande"

31. Walter H. Horne, "Triple Execution in Mexico #2"

32. Walter H. Horne, "Identifying Soldiers"

33–35. Publicity stills from *Espaldas mojadas,* 1953

36. The Bordertown series

37. Director Isaac Artenstein and Guillermo Gómez-Peña during the *Border Brujo* shoot

Acknowledgments

The preliminary research for this project was conducted during the 1992–93 academic year with funds from a Luce/ACLS Doctoral Dissertation Fellowship in American Art. The grant permitted me to travel to El Paso, where I was a visiting research fellow at the Center for Inter-American and Border Studies on the campus of the University of Texas at El Paso. I would like to thank Dr. Samuel Schmidt, Teresa Nevárez, and Mary Genest of the Center, who welcomed me and provided a pleasant environment in which to conduct my investigations. I am also grateful to Marta Estrada and the staff of the El Paso Public Library's Southwest Collection, where I camped out for several weeks while working on chapter 3. Scholars from El Paso and Juárez were extremely kind during my stay and went to great lengths to introduce me to the city and to other border scholars. I would especially like to thank Debbie Nathan, Eduardo Barrera Herrera, María Socorro Tabuenca, and Pablo Vila for their friendship and hospitality.

As I worked on the manuscript, I received generous response and support from my professors and colleagues. At the University of Iowa, Dudley Andrew, Charles A. Hale, Tom Lewis, and Steve Ungar provided invaluable feedback. Kathleen Newman read the manuscript carefully several times, and it has benefited greatly from her suggestions. Several other scholars also read all or part of the manuscript. I would like to thank George Yúdice, Andrew Ross, Chon Noriega, Cynthia Steele, Rolando Romero, and the anonymous reader for the University of Minnesota Press for their insightful comments and criticism. I also thank Neil Larsen, who offered advice and encouragement to me at a key moment in the early stages of this project. At Stanford, I would like to thank my chair, Mary Louise Pratt, and my colleagues in the Spanish and Portuguese department, as well as the undergraduate and graduate students of my two border studies classes for their lively, thought-provoking discussions about U.S.–Mexico border issues.

I am very grateful to Lisa Freeman, Micah Kleit, and Jennifer Moore at the University of Minnesota Press and the series editors, George Yúdice, Jean Franco, and Juan Flores, for their support of my work. In addition, many artists, writers, and activists consented to be interviewed, provided research materials, and granted permission for their work to be illustrated in this book. Their names are listed in the body of the text, and I would like to extend a special thank-you to them for their generosity and time.

My deepest gratitude goes to those close to me who, like it or not, became involved for several years in the everyday struggles of my work on this project, and who had the patience and devotion to put up with me through some rough times. My friends never tired of encouraging me. Many thanks to Germaine, Shari, Anne-Marie, Sheila, Wheezi, Gail, and Lora; to my dad and mom, for the weekly packets of newspaper clippings about U.S.–Mexico border issues; and most of all to Peter, for all those little things.

Introduction

The Border Is Fashionable.
—*BAW/TAF[1]*

We look at the material solidity of a building, a canal, a highway, and behind it we see always the insecurity that lurks within a circulation process of capital, which always asks: How much more time in this relative space?
—*David Harvey[2]*

This study is about representations of the U.S.–Mexico border that have appeared in literature, art, and mass media in the twentieth century, focusing especially on texts from the past three decades. Although intended as a critique of the current fashion in postnational, non-site-specific border imagery in contemporary cultural theory, my work is no doubt also symptomatic of that trend and indebted to it for much of its source material. Some artists and writers, such as Guillermo Gómez-Peña, argue that border art had already peaked in the 1980s and that its current popularity can be attributed to opportunists promoting mannerist derivatives of earlier images.[3] Others argue that due recognition of the border region has not occurred yet. Even in Chicano/a studies, where the idea of "borderlands" is an overarching metaphor in much fiction and criticism, Charles Tatum recently noted the scarce appearance of the geographical border: "It is unusual that although the United States–Mexican border plays a dominant role in the history of Chicanos in this country, it has not become an important literary space in contemporary Chicano letters."[4] I believe that an accurate description of the current situation lies somewhere in between these two arguments. While the border has received a great deal of attention in recent literature and art, this body of work has not yet been fully acknowledged by scholars and critics. Meanwhile, an abstract, metaphorical "border" has gained widespread currency

I

in academic writing, particularly in cultural studies, but this usage is rarely tied to the U.S.–Mexico border region.

The recent rise in border imagery in both mass media and academic writing is directly connected to the development of "transfrontier metropolises,"[5] or twin cities along the border. Some of these cities, such as San Diego/Tijuana and El Paso/ Ciudad Juárez, have become huge industrial centers and received a great deal of media attention in the latter part of the 1980s and the early 1990s, as the North American Free Trade Agreement (NAFTA) was negotiated. Because free trade was introduced on a limited scale through the *maquiladora* industries in the border region, U.S.–Mexico border cities became an emblem in the media of all that free trade implied for inhabitants of the future trade bloc.[6]

The media spotlight that was so abruptly cast upon the border during NAFTA coverage calls attention to a dynamic between the short- and long-term views of history that run throughout this study. On the one hand, I am eager to emphasize the century-long process whereby the U.S.–Mexico border developed at the crux of two very strong nationalist tendencies. On the other, I often refer to the border generically and structurally, as a region shaped by a set of circumstances occurring simultaneously in other parts of the world.

Other scholars have also confronted the border's duality of "space" and "place," ephemerality and permanence, and have argued that each of these categories is fundamental to study of the region. Historian Robert Alvarez reconciles patterns of border migration and settlement, for example, by stressing the mutual interdependence of these processes. Traditionally, the social sciences have viewed international border zones as culturally diluted and marginal to the interests of the nation-state. This attitude, according to Alvarez, has prevailed in U.S.–Mexico border studies, where immigration issues have been emphasized to the almost complete exclusion of the Chicano/a and Mexican populations that have occupied the region for centuries. He writes, "These people are placed in a direct relationship to the marginal status of the border region and are often perceived as transitory and marginal participants in both [national] systems."[7] Instead of privileging either migration or settlement, Alvarez argues that both phenomena are aspects of a border "social system" that has been characterized by a northward orientation since the colonial period. Beginning in the seventeenth century, hundreds of years before the existence of the present U.S.– Mexico boundary, Spain used its northernmost settlements in North America as hubs from which to launch exploratory, missionary, and military expeditions. In the eighteenth and nineteenth centuries, migration northward was encouraged by mining, trade routes, and foreign capitalist expansion. In the twentieth century, U.S. cities and transnational investment in the border region continue to lure migrants northward. Throughout these historical periods, layers of kinship and economic networks became established in border cities, which have continually assisted north-south migratory flows. Following Alvarez, I argue throughout this study that the border as it appears in literature and art must be understood as polyvalent, as a place where urban and rural, national and international spaces simultaneously coexist, often in complex and contradictory ways.

The rise in urbanization of the U.S.–Mexico border in the twentieth century is matched by similar growth in other border regions around the world. Lawrence Herzog, a geographer of the San Diego/Tijuana area, argues that such transformations distinguish the post–World War II era:

> In essence, a new territorial order emerges in the post–World War II period, one in which boundaries are no longer simply militarized, isolated wastelands at the edge of nation-states; boundary regions have developed autonomous and viable economies; permanent boundary population centers are no longer the exception but the rule.[8]

For Herzog, the incorporation of border zones into the national and regional economies of Latin American countries in particular has involved two courses of action: first, changing land-use practices around border zones, and second, encouraging "cross-border trade and cooperation in economic development."[9]

Besides the U.S.–Mexico border's obvious importance to NAFTA and its similarities to other industrialized border regions in the European Union and Pacific Rim countries, the growth of the border region may also be understood within the context of changing spatial and economic formations in Latin America, where regional trade blocs have quickly gained momentum in this decade. In 1991, Mercosur, or the Southern Cone Common Market, was formed, uniting the economies of Brazil, Argentina, Paraguay, Uruguay, and most recently Chile. In 1991 the Andean Pact countries of Bolivia, Colombia, Ecuador, Peru, and Venezuela formalized a plan to create an Andean common market by the year 1996 (Peru left the Pact in 1997). Two older trade units, the Central American Common Market (CACM), founded in 1960 and consisting of Costa Rica, El Salvador, Nicaragua, Guatemala, and Honduras, and the Caribbean Common Market (CARICOM), founded in 1973 and consisting of fourteen Caribbean countries, have likewise lowered tariff barriers in keeping with the present climate of trade liberalization in the hemisphere.

Together with NAFTA, Mercosur, the Andean Pact, CARICOM, and CACM represent the strongest trade blocs in the Americas; however, numerous bilateral and trilateral agreements are also in effect or currently being negotiated (including several involving the European Union). The Group of Three founded in 1994, for example, includes Colombia, Venezuela, and Mexico, and intends to eliminate trade barriers among those countries by the year 2005. When expansion of NAFTA seemed to stagnate in 1995 due to gridlock in the U.S. Congress, many Caribbean governments grew distressed at the prospect of losing transnational operations to Mexico. Twenty-five Caribbean and Latin American nations, including Cuba, formed the Association of Caribbean States (ACS), a free-trade and regional development group based in Trinidad.

The combined force of neoliberalism in Latin American countries and anti-protectionism in the United States is tending toward the formation of the single hemispheric trade zone that George Bush once fantasized, although the road to achieving such an entity is widely debated and subject to political and economic vicissitudes within constituent countries. So far, five inter-American summits have been held (Miami, December 1994; Denver, June 1995; Cartagena, March 1996; Belo Horizonte, May 1997; and Santiago, April 1998) in order to formulate plans for the eventual implementation of a Free Trade Area of the Americas (FTAA), which ideally would go into effect by the year 2005.[10]

Although the U.S.–Mexico border is more industrially developed than other border zones in the Americas, as the epigraphs to this Introduction indicate, one day the border's built environment, along with the current vogue in border images, will succumb to the need for "creative destruction" in order to circumvent overaccumulation.[11] A common observation in much border scholarship is that border regions are growing as the power of nation-states relative to transnational capital is decreasing.[12] Now that NAFTA is in effect, who is to say that industrial development will stop at the border, especially when there is even cheaper labor to be had in the Mexican interior and elsewhere in Latin America? Transnationals are also investing in other Latin American countries, and in recent years the United States has signed framework agreements for reducing trade barriers with many Latin American and Caribbean countries.[13] Chile was invited to join the NAFTA bloc in December 1994, the same month that the General Agreement on Tariffs and Trade (GATT) won Congressional approval in the United States. The status of Chile's incorporation into NAFTA is temporarily on hold; in the meantime, Canada and Mexico have negotiated bilateral agreements with Chile as a first step toward NAFTA incorporation. Because Chile also holds associate membership in Mercosur, that country promises to become a strategic link in terms of uniting the Americas' two largest trade blocs.[14] In the immediate post-NAFTA era, however, the Mexican border region is still the preferred site for foreign capital investment in Mexico; 82 percent of maquiladoras are located there and employ over eight hundred thousand workers, bringing the total number of maquiladoras in the six Mexican border states to over twenty-three hundred in the four years following NAFTA's passage.[15]

I conducted research and wrote this study during the years 1991–97, an extremely volatile period for the border and for U.S.–Mexico relations in general. Every time I turned on the radio or picked up a newspaper, it seemed, I was learning something that was to have an impact on my research. The decade began with former President George Bush's Enterprise for the Americas Initiative, which called for the establishment of "a free trade zone from the North Pole to Tierra del Fuego."[16] NAFTA was the first step toward attaining his goal; the treaty was ratified in the United States in 1993 and went into effect in 1994 under the Clinton administration. All three of the original NAFTA countries underwent major changes of leadership during the first half of the decade, which at various points seemed likely to jeopardize the treaty's future.[17] The Republican administrations of Reagan and Bush ceded to the Democratic Clinton administration in November 1992. Canadian Prime Minister Brian Mulroney resigned at a critical moment in February 1993 and was succeeded by Jean Crètien. But events in Mexico were the most dramatic. On January 1, 1994, the first day of NAFTA implementation, the Ejército Zapatista de Liberación Nacional (EZLN) began its rebellion in the southern state of Chiapas. Two months later, the country was rocked by the assassination of the Partido Revolucionario Institucional (PRI) presidential candidate Luis Donaldo Colosio in Tijuana, and in September, PRI Secretary General José Francisco Ruiz Massieu was assassinated in Mexico City. These events ultimately led to a national scandal involving the Salinas family that reached epic proportions. Carlos Salinas's brother Raúl was arrested on murder charges in connection with the Ruiz Massieu slaying under the regime of newly inaugurated President Ernesto Zedillo. Meanwhile, former President Carlos Salinas de Gortari, whose successful shepherding of NAFTA had made him the prime candidate for head of the newly founded World Trade Organization, was obliged to flee Mexico in early 1995 under growing suspicion over the Ruiz Massieu affair and widespread corruption during his administration; he remains in exile.[18] Finally, in July 1997, the PRI's seventy-year reign over the Mexican political system received a serious blow. Former presidential candidate Cuauhtémoc Cárdenas, of the Partido de la Revolución Democrática (PRD), won the Mexico City mayoral election (traditionally a stepping stone to the presidency), while the PRI lost its majority in the lower house of Congress and also suffered defeats in numerous regional elections. The future of NAFTA is therefore still in question, as Cárdenas has stated that he would like to revisit the terms of the treaty.

The early 1990s also witnessed renewed attacks on immigrants to the United States from Mexico, Central America, and Caribbean nations such as Haiti and Cuba. Beginning in 1993 with El Paso's "Operation Blockade" (renamed "Operation Hold the Line"), the Border Patrol went on to set up similar blockades in other border cities such as San Diego ("Operation Gatekeeper") and Nogales ("Operation Safeguard"). Anti-immigrant sentiments were further accentuated by California's passage of Proposition 187 in 1994 and Proposition 209 in 1996, which sharply curtailed the rights of immigrants and their children to basic social services and affirmative action, and inspired a host of copycat initiatives in other states. (A court order, however, has indefinitely suspended the implementation of Proposition 187 in California.) At present, the crackdown on undocumented immigration in the United States continues through federal legislation passed under the Clinton administration, which promises to increase dramatically the number of Border Patrol agents stationed along the U.S.–Mexico border. Finally, the sharp devaluation of Mexican currency in the winter of 1994–95 and the $47.5 billion "bailout package" assembled by Clinton with funds from the United States, the International Monetary Fund (IMF), the World

Bank, and other countries evoked memories of Mexico's previous crisis of 1982, because it drastically reduced the standard of living for average Mexicans while simultaneously precipitating a flood of investment capital from the United States and other countries to maquiladoras.[19] Ironically, the 1982 crisis had served as a major catalyst for foreign investment in the border region in the first place.

I encountered several other uncanny historical returns as I conducted my research, including the reappearance of Porfirian and Mexican Revolutionary imagery (see chapters 2–5). The mercurial political and economic climate of the contemporary period made me hesitant to speculate broadly about the future of the border, and I elected instead to present case studies with specific historical parameters. I decided to explore three major areas of inquiry: artistic production about the border; the work of political activists on the border; and the writings of U.S. and Mexican intellectuals about the border. Above all, I wanted to investigate the relationship between regionally based texts and political and economic transformations taking place at the global level. By presenting local and national phenomena from an internationalist perspective, I have attempted to demonstrate that arguments both for and against free trade shared common emphases and blind spots, particularly regarding the role of culture in relation to economic and political changes. This approach proved challenging, but it was also appropriate, given that at the current historical juncture, celebratory metaphors of border-crossing and migration are in common use among groups with widely divergent political, national, and class affiliations.

The texts I selected—from literature, film, video, photography, plastic, and performance art—align this study with the tendency in cultural studies to juxtapose heterogeneous source material in order to stress the manner in which discourses are formulated socially and across genres. Indeed, my intention was to explore relationships among the arts and to problematize the categories of "high" and "low" culture, considering that representative texts from both categories find themselves distributed across national and linguistic boundaries through mass communication networks. More important than these considerations, though, was the fact that the works discussed registered significant historical turning points in the representation of the border region.

As I selected these case studies, I was also trying to synthesize historical periodizations inherited from related academic disciplines, some of which themselves have been constituted as interdisciplinary fields. For Chicano/a studies, the La Raza movement of the 1960s and 1970s has traditionally been the major watershed mark, although scholars are increasingly focusing on both earlier and later moments in Chicano/a history, from the precursors of the Chicano/a movement in the World War II era and the early history of Mexican populations in the U.S. Southwest, to more contemporary forms of cultural production that critique the "cultural nationalist" tendencies of the 1960s and 1970s. Whereas border geographers have tended to posit a major shift in U.S.–Mexico border development dating from the Border

Industrialization Program of 1965, historians, on the other hand, have cited the beginning and conclusion of the Mexican Revolution as the milestones of significant transformations in the border region.[20] More recently, in the 1980s and 1990s, the burgeoning interest in transnationalism has given rise to a prominent group of pundits who specialize in NAFTA and trade-related issues.

Unfortunately, while today's border has drawn much scholarly attention from social scientists and natural scientists, it has received relatively little from humanists, despite the substantial body of literature and art that exists about the border region. I do not attribute this to a lack of interest, talent, or production on the part of scholars in the humanities, but to institutional divisions and differing degrees of access to resources, which perpetuate a split between the humanities and the sciences, devaluing the former and generously promoting the latter. While Cold War area studies are declining in many academic fields, their post-NAFTA counterparts are steadily increasing in strength in border studies. Of the region's two most prominent research institutions, the Center for U.S.–Mexican Studies at the University of California, San Diego, explicitly excludes study of the arts and literature from its grant programs, while the Colegio de la Frontera Norte primarily encourages the study of cultural phenomena through social science disciplines such as communications, sociology, and anthropology.[21] Both institutions nevertheless have sponsored qualitative social science research projects about the border region that closely resemble cultural studies work currently being done in the humanities. In addition, many U.S. universities in the border region house research centers that function as maquiladora start-up organizations or information clearing houses for promoting free trade, while academics at border colleges and universities often serve in an extracurricular capacity as consultants for transnational corporations.[22]

The marginalization of the humanities by major research institutions on the border, however, does have the happy effect of promoting collaboration among intellectuals outside of the academy. The region's strong cultural centers, such as the Guadalupe Cultural Arts Center in San Antonio, The Bridge in El Paso, the Centro Cultural de la Raza in San Diego, and the Centro Cultural Tijuana, have become magnets and meeting places for artists, writers, activists, and scholars. In Mexican border cities, the roles of the *cronista* and *bellaletrista* literary traditions remain strongly centered around local newspapers, magazines, and social events such as the *tertulia* and the *presentación del libro*. Furthermore, north of the border, a humanities-inflected current of border studies has established itself in U.S. universities, where the field is often associated with Chicano/a studies and interethnic approaches to literature and expressive culture.

Given my desire to see further development of cross-disciplinary dialogue among border scholars, I am indebted to several earlier studies that served as guides for my project. Norma Iglesias Prieto and David R. Maciel each compiled ambitious, annotated filmographies about the representation of the border in U.S. and Mexican cinema.[23] Aurelio de los Reyes catalogued U.S. newsreel coverage of the Mexican Revolution in his *Con Villa en México.*[24] Paul J. Vanderwood and Frank N. Samponaro edited and assembled two volumes of early-twentieth-century photography chronicling U.S. military presence in the border region.[25] The large group of writers, critics, and *cronistas,* including Sergio Gómez Montero, Gabriel Trujillo Muñoz, Rogelio Reyes, and Harry Polkinhorn, all of whom are associated with the Editorial Binacional in Calexico/Mexicali, have worked for many years to promote the work of border authors and artists and to develop critical approaches to the study of their work.[26]

The projects of pioneers such as Américo Paredes, who fused sociology, literary analysis, and ethnomusicology in his important 1958 study, *"With His Pistol in His Hand": A Border Ballad and Its Hero,* continue in the work of several innovative interdisciplinary scholars of the border region such as José E. Limón and Pablo Vila.[27] Gloria Anzaldúa's 1987 collection of essays and poetry, entitled *Borderlands/La Frontera: The New Mestiza,* is a recent landmark in border studies that has played a key role in encouraging interdisciplinary dialogue in fields such as women's studies, queer studies, religious studies, and ethnic studies.[28] The fact that several of these scholars were trained in fields outside of the humanities indicates the capacity of border studies to accommodate synthetic projects involving the arts, literature, and critical social theory, despite institutional restrictions.

The idea for this book began with my reaction to an image of the border that appeared at the end of the 1989 Hollywood movie *The Old Gringo.*[29] The shot is an aerial view of a horse-drawn cart crossing an antique bridge that spans a verdant river valley. Aboard the cart, the movie's protagonist, Harriet Winslow (Jane Fonda), sits next to a coffin containing the body of Ambrose Bierce (Gregory Peck). Each had come to Mexico in search of something: she, an alternative to spinsterhood in the United States; he, an elegant death. Now, thanks to one man, Villista General Tomás Arroyo (Jimmy Smits), their wishes are fulfilled, and they return home. As the music swells and the credits begin to roll, the camera pulls back until the cart moves out of frame, and on either edge of the screen the flags of Mexico and the United States become visible—that of Mexico perched high on a bluff to the left, that of the United States below on the right.

The shot caught my attention because of the subtle geographical trick that it played on viewers, at least on those of us who stay for the credits. It was unclear exactly where in the state of Chihuahua previous scenes were supposed to have taken place; several were set in Ciudad Chihuahua, about four hours south of Ciudad Juárez. But suddenly there we were on the U.S.–Mexico border for the first time. Apart from the fact that this did not look like any part of the Texas/Chihuahua border I had ever seen, it seemed remarkable to me that a movie whose main theme was cultural contact managed to avoid a border-crossing scene until the very end. Saving the shot of the border for last, though, converted it into a pensive, minitreatise on U.S.–Mexico relations. In the context of *The Old Gringo*'s collaboration between

Mexican writer Carlos Fuentes and U.S. producer and actress Jane Fonda, this is a present-minded tale stressing the need for cultural understanding and national sovereignty.[30] Like so many other contemporary mass media texts, *The Old Gringo* mines earlier stories of the Revolution for material from which to construct its own utopian vision, the politics of which are suggested in this final shot. Here there is no repressive border apparatus, no massive flow of poor immigrants, but rather tranquillity, stasis, and mutual respect between nations.

As I did further research on the movie, however, I began to think that the shot was tricky in another way, in that it cleverly belied the political and economic circumstances surrounding the movie's twenty-five-year production history. In light of this information, rather than being a story about a haughty Yankee schoolmistress who broadens her cultural horizons after an encounter with a fiery Mexican rebel, *The Old Gringo* became a story about two gringa producers who turned the Estudios Churubusco into their own maquiladora in order to get the most for their dollar. As the *New York Times* reported in 1990, citing Fonda's coproducer, Lois Bonfiglio, "Low production costs, spectacular settings, skilled local technicians and proximity to the United States have combined to 'push Mexico to the forefront any time people think of making a movie outside the United States.'"[31] *The Old Gringo*'s peculiar mixture of liberal humanism and free-trade production profile made me feel that NAFTA-era movies were not to be viewed as mere epiphenomena to political and economic transformations, but as prime locations in which to study these transformations as they were occurring.

After that, I began to look closely at representations of the border in other examples of visual culture. The technique of concluding with an overcoded "parting shot" of the border would be repeated in several movies of years to come, as in the 1994 Mexican-Canadian (Québec) production, *El jardín del Edén (The Garden of Eden)*.[32] Set in the present day, this movie is also about a diverse set of characters from north and south who converge on the border, where their destinies collide. Instead of presenting an argument for national sovereignty, however, the utopian vision we see at the conclusion of *El jardín del Edén* is that of a borderless continent.

The Mexican and Canadian anti-imperialist politics that inform this feature make its portrayal of the border richly complex.[33] The concluding scene begins with a long shot of a deserted beach in late afternoon. Then the camera tilts down to reveal two familiar icons: a mint green Border Patrol wagon and a portion of the corrugated steel fence that separates San Diego from Tijuana. We are on the Mexican side of the border looking north at the United States. On this side of the border, a *conjunto* plays traditional music, while families enjoy picnics, vendors sell their wares, a few figures stand around a campfire, and people play along the shore.[34]

The camera comes to rest behind two men standing on a bluff overlooking the ocean. The older, taller one is Felipe (Bruno Bichir), who comes from the rural interior of Mexico and now appears to be preparing for his second trip to the United

States. Gone are the vaquero shirt, hat, and boots that he wore at the beginning of the movie. Now he sports tennis shoes, a T-shirt, jeans, and a duffel bag. The young man next to him is presumably the younger brother whom he had mentioned earlier in the movie. We cut to a close-up of their faces as they stare at the sea. Felipe rustles his brother's hair, puts his old cowboy hat on him, and throws his arm around his shoulders. They smile. The final shot of the movie reveals what they had been look- ing at—schools of dolphins in the distance swimming northward.

This final scene does not stigmatize south-to-north border crossing as national betrayal, a common theme in a certain, older tradition of Mexico City–based popu- lar culture. Instead, it contrasts the artificiality of the fence and Border Patrol to natural migratory patterns. By concluding with the shot of the dolphins, the movie turns one of the favorite symbols of the Mexican pro-free-trade movement on its head. The monarch butterfly, whose migratory circuit also extends from Canada to Mexico, had been a logo of the movement prior to NAFTA's passage, and was invoked to "naturalize" the idea of a continental trade bloc.

One troubling aspect of the "nature versus culture" dichotomy as it is employed in the *El jardín del Edén,* however, is the manner in which transnational migratory circuits of indigenous peoples seem to fall on the "nature" side of the balance, along with the dolphins, rather than being presented also as "cultural" phenomena. In fact, all of the movie's non-Mexican characters undergo highly charged encounters with either aestheticized versions of nature or indigenous people. While Frank (Joseph Culp), a gringo recluse, ponders the inscrutable language of the whales, his sister Jane (Renée Coleman) experiences two epiphanic moments at the beginning and end of the film upon seeing quasi-hallucinatory images of indigenous girls. The fact that indigenous languages are not subtitled in the movie, while English and Spanish are, reinforces the enigmatic quality ascribed to indigenous people.

Jane's friend Liz (Rosario Sagrav), a Chicana who has come to Tijuana to curate an art exhibition and search for her identity, also experiences epiphanic moments while viewing photographs and videos dealing with indigenous themes, but in con- trast to Jane, who wishes to possess or pursue indigenous women, Liz sees her own reflection in them. She identifies with a portrait that appears in Graciela Iturbide's famous photo essay about the women of Juchitán.[35] Later, she weeps while viewing a video depicting a therapy session in which a Chicana comes to terms with the fact that she has repressed her indigenous identity in favor of a cultural self-identification as "white." Through Liz's encounter with indigenous imagery, an older nationalist version of *mexicanidad* reveals itself, recalling a tradition in Mexican popular culture that deems Chicanos/as to be culturally inauthentic until they return to the mother country and learn proper Spanish (see chapter 4).

This nationalist conceit aside, the border in *El jardín del Edén* is a kaleidoscopic world of mutually unintelligible linguistic registers and sexy, surreal juxtapositions.[36] This is a predominantly celebratory view of border culture that was popularized on the eve of free trade by artists such as Guillermo Gómez-Peña (who, not surprisingly, has a cameo in the movie) and progressive academics such as Néstor García Canclini in his 1990 book *Culturas híbridas (Hybrid Cultures)*. The latter work concludes with a chapter about San Diego/Tijuana in which the author tidily dismisses nationalist myths of the border as a deracinated zone in opposition to the traditional cultural center of Mexico City, and instead celebrates Tijuana's innovative, synthetic cultural processes.[37]

Despite their differences, it is clear that both movie images I have discussed invoke the border both literally and metaphorically in order to "ground" an ethical argument about the management of national space.[38] In his foreword to D. Emily Hicks's *Border Writing: The Multidimensional Text,* Neil Larsen points to an irony in the author's usage of border metaphor that could well apply to a whole generation of cultural studies texts of the past decade—namely, that national space reemerges in the very figure that is supposed to signify its absence, the border.[39]

I noted a similar tendency in contemporary political and social theory to rely upon the national, however "outmoded," as an interface between local (identified as urban) and global (identified with the economic and trade blocs) spatial registers. Recent calls for a federative, supranational model of government in Latin America, for example, often appropriate existing industrialized countries as their geographic imaginary. At the close of his study of the Latin American left in the post–Cold War era, *Utopia Unarmed,* Jorge Castañeda argues that the left should avail itself of the best features of Germany and Japan in setting its agenda for the next millennium.[40] At the outset of his study *Consumidores y ciudadanos* (Consumers and citizens), Néstor García Canclini argues that the market and consumerism have replaced the power of nations as shapers of identity. In his conclusion, however, he returns to the notion of an enlightened, democratic state as protector of public interests:

> El desafío es más bien revitalizar al Estado como representante del interés público, como árbitro o garante de que las necesidades colectivas de información, recreación e innovación no sean subordinadas siempre a la rentabilidad comercial.

> (The challenge is rather to revitalize the State as a representative of the public interest, as arbiter or guarantor, so that collective needs for information, recreation or innovation are not always subordinated to commercial profitability.)[41]

Carlos Fuentes's proposal for a "Federal Ibero-America" (excluding the United States and Canada but including Spain and Portugal and eventually Pacific Rim countries), explicitly recalls nineteenth-century dreams for the newly independent Latin American republics, such as Bolívar's *patria grande* and Martí's *Nuestra América.*[42]

An inquiry into how contemporary representations of the U.S.–Mexico border may be read as evidence of the persistence of the national in the postnational thus became my theoretical point of departure for this work. The first two chapters are concerned with debates about national identity and culture that were waged during the simultaneous negotiation of NAFTA and GATT in the early 1990s. Chapter 1 is a study of arguments concerning the "cultural exemption"—the idea held by progressive and nationalist sectors during this period that culture industries (defined by the treaties as mass media) should be exempted from trade agreements entirely and left to state or national capitalist supervision. The fight for the exemption was waged differently in Europe and North America, but on both continents it elicited strong reactions from artists and intellectuals, including such well-known figures as Régis Debray, Mario Vargas Llosa, Octavio Paz, and Carlos Monsiváis. Many of these intellectuals proposed theories of "cultural intervention" and "cultural resistance" as antidotes or buffers to the socioeconomic transformations signaled by free trade and neoliberal economic policy.

Meanwhile, in the three decades leading up to the free-trade debates, unobtrusive "establishing shots" of the U.S.–Mexico border in visual media were registering a significant change, which not only announced the arrival of urbanization, industrialization, and a host of social problems in the border region, but also the overall transformation of nationally coded space. During the early 1990s, both protectionists and free-traders foregrounded the U.S.–Mexico border in their arguments as a prototype of what would occur throughout the North American continent after free trade went into effect. Chapter 2 is a study of representations of the border in contemporary art and literature produced by Chicano/a and Anglo artists who feature the region prominently in their work. I contrast their portrayals of the border to those found in the many videos about border issues produced by grassroots and labor organizations. Throughout this chapter, I argue that the changing valence of two common border icons—the fence and the river—attests to the persistence of nationalism in the contemporary era, although older representations of the border as a unitary "line drawn in the sand" have given way to a more dispersed spatial construct.

Chapter 3 relates current representations of the border to ones dating from the beginning of this century, when the U.S.–Mexico border was also a free-trade zone. I argue that picture postcards and silent movies produced during Pershing's Punitive Expedition into Mexico following Pancho Villa's raid on Columbus, New Mexico, gave rise to a system of representing the border in U.S. popular culture that drew heavily upon notions of citizenship and militarism. Later in the chapter, I turn to more recent versions of the Columbus raid, in order to speculate upon the fact that, although the border still lends an extremely Manichaean dynamic to these narratives, they have converted the Mexican Revolution into an innocuous, entertaining spectacle for gringo adventurers.

Chapters 4 and 5 consider the themes of movement and migration that pervade narratives about the border region. Chapter 4 examines Luis Spota's novel, *Murieron a mitad del río* (They died in the middle of the river) (1948) and Alejandro Galindo's movie *Espaldas mojadas* (Wetbacks) (1953), two of the first works to deal with the bracero program of mid-century, the predecessor of today's maquiladora program. In

Chapter 5, I discuss the recent work of performance artist Guillermo Gómez-Peña in order to criticize the current tendency on the part of postmodernist intellectuals to universalize the phenomenon of "border crossing." This is based upon a close analysis of a major turning point in Gómez-Peña's career, roughly from 1988–91, when he ceased to work primarily on the U.S.–Mexico border and adopted a bicoastal orientation that afforded him access to a broader national and global audience. I discuss Gómez-Peña's fin de siècle apocalypticism in relation to similar currents in U.S. popular culture, as in the speculative fiction of the Borderlands group.

At the outset, I would like to advise the reader of certain biases and limitations of this book. I began my research with a conceptual framework based upon the pregiven cultural identities of various social groups rather than one based upon processes or events through which identities are invoked by various social actors. I quickly abandoned the former approach in favor of the latter because I felt that the isolation of discrete social groups underestimated the complex reality of the border as a "contact zone" with a long history of transculturation.[43] Following Mary Louise Pratt's use of these terms in her work on colonial travel literature, such a perspective recognizes that imperialist expansion creates dominant and marginal groups, geographic centers and peripheries, but also that under circumstances of prolonged interaction, mutual influences among peoples are inevitable. Intellectual production and expressive culture are arenas where the impact of transculturation becomes manifest. The work of sociologist Pablo Vila on identity and subject formation of border dwellers confirms that while border identities can be loosely systematized according to a variety of factors such as social class, age, place of birth, current residence, linguistic ability and education, terms of self-identification are also extremely relative in the border region, shifting according to social context, location, and relation of the speaker to listener.

Rather than promote a single frame for studying the border, I found it more useful to consider the border as subject to multiple spatial registers of analysis, ranging from the international to the regional and the urban. These registers in turn may be traversed interchangeably by individual and collective subjects, much in the same way that linguists speak of code-switching. The geographical imaginary that I have privileged in this study runs along a north-south axis, in keeping with the concern about national space that informs this project. It would be equally interesting and fruitful to examine the border according to an east-west axis, thus stressing the diversity and uneven development of the region in this era of accelerated industrialization. The texts that would form the basis for such a study are plentiful; there are numerous travelogues in which the narrative consists of picaresque, journalistic encounters along the length of the border.[44] In contrast, a host of border writers have produced works strongly rooted in a sense of place—for example, the Tijuana of Federico Campbell and Luis Alberto Urrea, the Mexicali and Tijuana of Rosina Conde, the Juárez of Rosario Sanmiguel, the Presidio of Aristeo Brito, and the fictitious Lower Valley town of Klail City of Rolando Hinojosa.

By focusing my analysis primarily on images of El Paso/Juárez and San Diego/Tijuana, I have replicated an archetypal view of the border that Carlos Monsiváis has criticized in his Mexican compatriots—a view that reduces the border to its two largest and best known cities.[45] For me, these sites of investigation represent a point of departure rather than a goal; in future research, I look forward to examining other dimensions of the border region.

In conclusion, I would like to impress two points upon the reader throughout the following chapters: the first is to caution against a hasty dismissal or underestimation of the nation-state as a category of analysis. As much as I, for one, would like to see national(ist) obstacles to internationalist movements disappear, one cannot make this happen by writing it so. Rather, the only way to the postnational and post-capitalist is through what Larsen has aptly called the "slow and tortuous route of revolutionary political movements."[46] My second point follows from the first: we need to question the consequences for cultural workers of isolating the "cultural" as a privileged category or entity independent from other sectors of economic production, which is becoming an increasingly common presupposition in current debates about the role of intellectuals. Most cultural workers, regardless of their national or transnational orientation, still operate as relatively free agents with regard to the political and economic struggles with which they express solidarity. The large-scale integration of cultural workers into continental organizations remains an important task of cross-border organizing.

Though the current wave of enthusiasm for the border in the mainstream press may in fact turn out to be its swan song, the U.S.–Mexico border's media visibility should not blind one to the materiality of this "constructed space" and the power it has to affect and structure the lives of those crossing it and divided by it. In spite of disturbing trends in U.S.–Mexico relations and U.S. border policy, the work of border geographers, historians, artists, writers, and activists has been very inspiring to me. In the border cities, the "international division of labor" may be a matter of several hundred yards rather than thousands of miles. This facilitates communication and participation in cooperative political struggles among people on both sides of the border, and it has given rise to distinctive forms of visual and literary expression. I hope that this study will promote these movements.

Chapter 1

Cultural Exemptions,
Cultural Solutions

In a dark, smoky theater, Mexican performance artists Jesusa Rodríguez and Liliana Felipe lie in side-by-side caskets as skeleton marionettes dance over their bodies. After a group of bored and uncomfortable mourners file by to pay their last respects, the two corpses rise from their coffins and turn to read the names inscribed on the funeral wreaths beside them; suddenly both recoil in shock and horror, bolt from their caskets, and run offstage. According to the wreaths, PRI and Televisa were the "beloved" deceased. This is the final scene of *Cielo de abajo (Heaven Below)*, a play directed by Rodríguez, which had its U.S. première at Chicago's Mexican Performing Arts Festival in April 1994.[1] The organization of *Cielo de abajo*'s cabaret-style acts was inspired by indigenous Mesoamerican cosmology, which held that "[t]he underworld consisted of nine places or steps full of hazards which the dead had to cross and finally arrive to the ninth and last step, called *Mictlán*."[2] The play follows Rodríguez and Felipe on a cyclical journey of death and rebirth, culminating in this last vignette set in contemporary Mexico. Clearly the Chicago audience, which was on its feet applauding and cheering wildly even before the performers had returned for their bows, understood the scene as a satirical comment on the final and necessary death that the Mexican nation must undergo if it is ever to be transformed.[3]

I had been studying literature about free trade and cultural policy when I saw this play, and I was struck by what a departure Rodríguez's two-pronged attack on Mexico's ruling political party and its largest media conglomerate was from the stance of left intellectuals in other countries, and even from those in her native Mexico. Since Rodríguez and Felipe founded the Teatro La Capilla in Mexico City in 1991, they have insisted upon its being an alternative space, independent of both state and corporate funding, where nontraditional attitudes about sexuality, morality, politics, and religion could be freely explored.[4] As NAFTA and GATT were simultaneously negotiated in the early 1990s, many European and Canadian intellectuals in contrast not only supported nationally based media producers, but also advocated a close, protective relationship between the state and private capital on issues of cultural policy.

In part, the specificity of the Mexican situation rests in the fact that the relationship between the state and cultural industries has undergone drastic transformation in recent years.[5] Traditionally, the centralized and peremptory Mexican government controlled a large share of publishing, film production, newspapers, museums, and other arts institutions. Though state supervision of cultural industries had been the dominant configuration since the Mexican Revolution, all of this began to change rapidly with the turn toward neoliberal economic policies in the 1980s. In the last fifteen years, many social welfare programs were reorganized, and the large, state-run industries once central to Mexican nationalist discourse, such as the petroleum industry, were privatized. For the cultural industries, these changes have meant that large corporations increasingly act as patrons of the arts or collaborate with the government in joint ventures, in much the same way that arts patronage functions in the United States.

Jean Franco has argued that the new wave of privatization has not only thrown the older version of Mexican nationalism into crisis, it has also had a profound effect on everyday life:

> [B]oth on the level of representation and on the social, privatisation has remapped the boundaries between the public and private spheres. What was formerly thought of as a separate affective sphere (the family, personal life) is now collapsed into this other "private" space of aggressive market forces.[6]

In the case of many cultural commodities such as music, television, video, and magazines—goods that are often consumed privately in the home—the old and new senses of the term *private* described by Franco come into direct collision. Several prominent Latin American intellectuals, including Octavio Paz, welcomed this reorientation. Paz had previously criticized the Mexican state as a "philanthropic ogre" that curbed artistic expression.[7] For him, increased economic competition implied more choice, and more choice in turn, implied greater freedom of expression for individuals.

The distinction of Jesusa Rodríguez's conclusion to *Cielo de abajo* lies in the fact that instead of promoting either the state or the free market, she rejects both. Her performance asserts that the neoliberal Mexican state has not lessened its control over its citizenry but has entered into a new type of partnership with private enterprise. The greatest question of her play however, remains unanswered: What, or who, rises from the ashes of the PRI and Televisa? Is the last stop of the journey heaven *(cielo)*, hell *(abajo)*, or both?

The rather exceptional case of *Cielo de abajo* notwithstanding, certain broadly defined affinities characterized debates about free trade and cultural policy on both sides of the Atlantic. Though the issues of globalization and trade liberalization pro-voked sharp divisions among left intellectuals in Western Europe and North America, the divisions tended to express themselves in terms of two main tendencies: one ad-vocated a progressive populist nationalism and supported the exemption of cultural industries from trade agreements as a means of safeguarding national identity; the second generally promoted and celebrated cultural contact, described through vari-ous liberatory metaphors such as border-crossing, migration, deterritorialization, and hybridity. Both positions were similar in that they ascribed a great deal of agency to cultural processes, and envisioned "cultural solutions" that would serve as potential antidotes to the dislocations brought about by global economic restructuration. In this chapter, I concentrate on the groups described by the first tendency—that is, the advocates of the "cultural exemption"—and the manner in which intellectuals from Europe, Canada, the United States, and Mexico became spokespersons on matters of cultural policy during the late 1980s and early 1990s.

Aside from the work of a handful of scholars, most discussions of NAFTA and culture that have appeared in mainstream media have tended to rest on grandiose assertions about national character rather than on substantive analysis.[8] One reason for this is that the treaty says very little directly on the subject of culture in the first place. The cultural industries were exempted from the U.S.–Canada Free Trade Agreement of 1988 (USCFTA), and this exemption has been carried over to govern the U.S.–Canadian relationship under NAFTA.[9] In the case of U.S.–Mexico trade re-lations, many important cultural commodities such as published material and sound recordings were already free from tariffs prior to the treaty. Other cultural industries were affected immediately upon the treaty's passage, such as commercial cinema and trade in fine arts and antiquities, both of which saw tariff elimination effective in January 1994.[10] The difference among these cases calls for an individual rather than collective treatment of impending transformations in the cultural industries.[11]

Another reason why scholarship about NAFTA and culture has been limited is that very few trade barriers remained for mass media industries on the continent prior to NAFTA. In the decades preceding the passage of the treaty, U.S. mass media had already developed quite a strong presence in Canada and Mexico. A 1992 study estimated that U.S. interests controlled 93 percent of Canada's movie and video busi-ness, 90 percent of the recording industry, and 92 percent of book publishing, as well as a substantial share of the country's television programming.[12] In Mexico, U.S. movies and music, along with other U.S. consumer goods, have a strong presence, a situation which is more acutely noted in the border region and in urban areas.[13] In 1992, Néstor García Canclini placed the percentage of U.S. movies on Mexican screens at 62 percent, and estimated that this figure would increase to 70–76 percent with the elimination of Mexican tariffs on U.S. films.[14] Echoing his projections, the U.S.–Mexico Free Trade Reporter found that the five top-grossing movies in Mexico City during 1993 were all U.S. productions, accounting for 87 percent of ticket sales.

(*Jurassic Park* topped the list; I discuss the significance of this movie later in this chapter.) Even though the Mexican government attempts to limit the popularity of U.S. movies by dubbing only a select few "family entertainment" titles into Spanish while subtitling the rest, Hollywood productions are still extremely successful in Mexico.[15] Among Mexicans, the consumption of U.S. cultural products tends to rise according to social class, and some Mexican scholars have even welcomed the challenge posed to Televisa by such U.S.–based corporations as Turner Broadcasting and Blockbuster Video.[16] On average, only 13.5 percent of the videos carried in Video Visa, Televisa's own chain of video rental outlets, are Mexican in origin.[17] Thus, the choice for Mexican consumers on the eve of NAFTA was not so much between "nationalist" and "imperialist" media providers as between economic monopoly and competition.

The sustained incursion of U.S. mass media into the Canadian and Mexican markets prior to NAFTA has led many scholars and activists of divergent political orientations to view the treaty as the mere standardization of already existing trade arrangements and trends, rather than as a qualitative change in trinational relations. Pro-NAFTA economist Paul Krugman added, correctly in my opinion, that the treaty's less-than-dramatic changes in tariff structures should not be viewed as its sole purpose; rather NAFTA is a tool of foreign policy on the part of the United States, indicating its pledge to continue backing neoliberal regimes in Mexico through future presidential administrations.[18]

Much research on NAFTA and culture, consequently, has tended to avoid pinpointing a "big change" effective January 1, 1994, based on the literal interpretation of the treaty's few articles about the cultural industries per se in favor of more exploratory studies about how the elimination of trade barriers may have "cultural" effects, understood here in a much broader sense than the sense of the term in the treaty. This is the basic approach established by Mexico-based scholars Néstor García Canclini and Gilberto Guevara Niebla in their noteworthy anthology about free trade and culture in Mexico, *La Educación y la cultura ante el Tratado de Libre Comercio (Education and Culture before the Free Trade Agreement)*.[19] Departing also from this perspective in the U.S. context, George Yúdice coined the phrase "transnational culture brokering" to describe the manner in which artistic texts and cultural industries in general have come to play significant, even hyperbolic, roles in representing the potential gains and losses associated with hemispheric economic integration.[20]

I concur with the tendency of the scholars mentioned above; I view NAFTA as a signpost in an ongoing historical process that has immediate precursors in the establishment of the Border Industrialization Program in 1965 and the financial crises of the early 1970s and 1980s and has antecedents in the limited free trade zones that have existed intermittently along the U.S.–Mexico border since the late nineteenth century. The following sections briefly trace the history of oppositional movements to GATT and NAFTA that sought to exempt culture from trade negotiations. Then

I discuss how pro- and anti-NAFTA political forces drew upon existing understandings of the word *culture*—often preceded by silent modifiers such as *high, low, popular,* and *national*—during the debates about free trade.

A Brief History of the Cultural Exemption

On the eve of NAFTA's passage in Mexico, journalist and essayist Carlos Monsiváis identified two predominant reactions to NAFTA: the "utopian" and the "apocalyptic."[21] In his typical fashion, he adopted an ironic and critical distance from both positions, while declining to outline any alternatives to them (as we have seen in the case of *Cielo de abajo*). In the Mexican context, the utopian and apocalyptic positions loosely corresponded to the official PRI stand on the issue, on the one hand, and a broadly defined populist oppositional view on the other. The position of the late poet and essayist Octavio Paz is a good example of what Monsiváis labeled the utopian perspective. In an interview that appeared in the *New Yorker* just after the U.S. Congress approved the treaty, Paz stated,

> NAFTA will be important for Mexicans because it is a chance finally for us to be modern. . . . We have failed to be modern for centuries. We only started trying to be modern at the end of the eighteenth century, and our conscious model of modernity has tended to be the United States. This is the first time in the histories of our two nations that we are going to be in some ways partners with each other.[22]

An even greater benefit of NAFTA, in Paz's view, was that it would accelerate existing processes of cultural interchange between the United States and Mexico. His unnamed interviewer agreed and went on to conclude that cultural voluntarism might have preceded economics when it came to laying the groundwork for NAFTA:

> Today, we observed, a young North American poet would need to discover Octavio Paz in order to complete his or her education—and by doing this would assimilate, among other things, the Aztec past. Wasn't this proof that free trade had already existed in our hemisphere in the realm of the imagination?[23]

As we shall see, this basic assertion, that free trade was "imagined" by privileged sectors (in much the same way that Benedict Anderson described Latin American creole elites "imagining" nations on the eve of Latin American independence[24]) is a constant motif in the debates surrounding the cultural exemption.

Although Monsiváis reserved his sharpest criticism for those like Paz, who viewed NAFTA as Mexico's entrée to the First World, he concurred that a "cultural dream" on the part of Mexican elites preceded easy acceptance of the treaty by Mexico's ruling class. Monsiváis wrote,

> La formulación ensoñadora o utópica es, de hecho, la renuncia a cualquier problematización, es dar por sentado que el solo acto de la firma liquida los siglos de atraso y escasez. Mucho antes de que sepamos en qué consistirá el TLC, el sueño

cultural le declara el fin de sitio arrinconado de la nación (léase su clase diri-
gente) en el mundo. A la globalización, a la prosperidad, al Primer Mundo por
vía del Tratado de Libre Comercio.

(The dreamy or utopian formulation is, in fact, the renunciation of any prob-
lematization; it takes as a given that the single act of the signature liquidates
centuries of backwardness and scarcity. Long before we know what NAFTA will
consist of, the cultural dream declares it to be the end of the nation's (read the
ruling class's) marginal place in the world. To globalization, to prosperity, to the
First World, by means of the Free Trade Agreement.)[25]

Also misguided in Monsiváis's estimation, however, was the apocalyptic point of view
that opposed NAFTA in the name of a nostalgic desire to preserve a pure Mexican
culture. According to Monsiváis, this position could only lead to censorship. The real
issue, he argued, was not the "virginity of cultures" but "the destruction of economies,
and the subordination of the nation to the sole rank of being a producer of raw materials and exporter of cheap labor."[26] Perhaps because it belonged to the underdogs,
Monsiváis's taxonomy held the apocalyptic view of NAFTA to be a lesser evil than
the utopian one. There may be another reason, however, why he was loathe to push
his critique of the apocalyptic point of view any further, for it was this very argument
that captured the commitment of broad segments of progressive intellectuals, grassroots, populist, and labor movements throughout North America—from the Ejército
Zapatista to Ralph Nader and Margaret Atwood.

Many who opposed free trade on the grounds outlined by Monsiváis had comprehensive political goals that informed their position. According to Ricardo Hernández
and Edith Sánchez, the basic principle of most popular anti-free-trade groups was in
fact, "democratic participation in the definition of new commercial relationships between the three countries of North America."[27] In the United States, culture took a
back seat to other issues such as the environment and wage scales in the opposition
movements to NAFTA. It became a more prominent issue in Canada and Mexico,
where it was tied to traditions of anti-imperialist sentiment against the United States.
Activists in those countries raised important points concerning cultural policy. They
argued for the rights of linguistic minorities to buy products that would be produced
in their native languages and express local traditions. They also cautioned against the
potential for limited ideological perspective and restricted access to media that arises
when production is concentrated in one geographical location.

As Monsiváis's critique suggests, the apocalyptic view of free trade presumes a
certain symbiotic relationship between cultural identity and national sovereignty,
while it casts transnational capital and the United States in general as interlopers. In
order to protect the cultures of nations with smaller economies from being wiped out
by a vast homogenizing wave of U.S. mass media and consumer goods, many anti-
free-trade organizations argued for a "cultural exemption" that would leave the cultural industries out of treaty negotiations altogether. Implicit in this argument was

the idea that the state should enforce protective measures in order to encourage or sustain existing cultural industries. A watershed event for the cultural exemption in NAFTA negotiations occurred in October 1991, when three organizations, the Mobilization on Development, Trade, Labor, and the Environment (MODTLE; U.S.–based), Action Canada Network (ACN), and the Red Mexicana de Acción Frente al Libre Comercio (RMALC), convened a conference called "Alternative Agenda to the Free Trade Agreement" in Zacatecas, Mexico. The "Foro de Zacatecas" was attended by delegates from 112 North American organizations.[28] RMALC, itself a coalition of about one hundred groups founded in April 1991, issued a platform for the conference that was subsequently distributed on video and addressed many issues that the organization felt should be included in international trade agreements, among them the rights of workers and women, environmental protection, and re-duction of the Mexican national debt. Culture, however, was one of three items to be excluded from any treaty: "Cultura, educación, y comunicación deben considerarse afuera de cualquier acuerdo commercial" ("Culture, education, and communications should be considered outside of any commercial agreement").[29]

RMALC's call for a cultural exemption in 1991 actually had a brief but rich his-tory that predated NAFTA negotiations. It first became a rallying cry of Canadian activists in 1987–88 prior to the ratification of the USCFTA. *MacLean's* magazine reported that "[i]n 1990, the European Community (EC) actually had snubbed Canada's proposal to push jointly for a cultural exemption within GATT."[30] But by 1993, the successful Canadian effort to exempt cultural industries was held up as a model by the French for their own victory in exempting cultural industries from GATT negotiations. In December 1993, one month after the Clinton administration had successfully mustered up enough votes for NAFTA to win Congressional ap-proval, GATT negotiations came to a close in Geneva. In December 1994, the U.S. Congress had approved GATT as well.

The oppositions that grew around NAFTA and GATT were not always easily distinguishable from one another, especially when it came to the exchange of ideas among public intellectuals, who freely published and appeared on television on both sides of the Atlantic. A spirited debate took place on the pages of Madrid's news-paper, *El País,* between Peruvian author and erstwhile presidential candidate Mario Vargas Llosa, an advocate of neoliberal economic policy and foe of state subsidies for the cultural industries, and French writer, bureaucrat, and erstwhile national libera-tion theorist Régis Debray, who supported the exemption.[31] The exchange was subse-quently reprinted in Latin American newspapers, where it drew strong reactions from Latin American intellectuals.[32] The *New York Times* editorial section also regularly featured letters and columns from international commentators who alternately re-ferred to both trade agreements. Professor Jagdish Bhagwati of Columbia University wrote a letter citing certain double standards in U.S. trade policy toward France and Japan, respectively, that was challenged by Jack Valenti, President of the Motion

Picture Association of America (MPAA), a lobbying group for the U.S. film industry.[33] William Safire's *New York Times* editorial, in which he asserted that "the French
public prefers the American product," was in turn challenged by Seth Fein, a graduate student living in Mexico (now Assistant Professor of History at Georgia State
University), who related the GATT debate to NAFTA by citing historical examples
about the growth of the Mexican film industry during various phases of U.S.–Mexico
trade policy.[34]

By 1993 if not earlier, the two trade agreements had been assembled under the
umbrella of "global free trade." This was made explicit in the title of consumer advocate Ralph Nader's anthology, *The Case against Free Trade: GATT, NAFTA, and the
Globalization of Corporate Power,* which featured several articles that addressed cultural
policy.[35] Nader was one of several leaders who emerged to form a broadly defined
anti-free-trade movement in the United States, a role that he shared with independent
presidential candidate Ross Perot and conservative Republican Patrick Buchanan,
as well as the AFL-CIO and some environmental groups. In his chronicle of the
Uruguay Round, Ernest H. Preeg, a U.S. delegate to the GATT negotiations, confirms that for a brief period, the fate of GATT seemed to depend upon the outcome
of NAFTA and that a great deal of sensitivity existed among the Uruguay Round
participants toward the anti-free-trade movement in the United States.[36]

As the varied profiles of the anti-free-trade protagonists in the United States attest, it was not just left and liberal groups who championed the cultural exemption,
but also national capitalists, who often made for strange bedfellows in free-trade
opposition movements. In Canada, where the struggle for the exemption first took
root, one of the biggest advocates of the movement was Harold Greenberg, the president of Canadian pay-TV and production giant Astral. Greenberg chaired a group
called the Canadian Cultural/Communications Industries Committee, composed of
executives from large Canadian mass media corporations, the purpose of which was
to lobby for the cultural exemption from NAFTA. At stake was not so much protection for the existing 60 percent quota of Canadian content in television programming, but the protection of a law, known as C-58, that allowed Canadian advertisers
to write off ads if they appeared on Canadian TV stations. It was estimated in 1990
that the law was worth about $76 million in tax write-offs to Canadian broadcast-
ers.[37] Greenberg couched his arguments in strong nationalist and anti-imperialist
rhetoric, in which he demanded the right of Canadians to define themselves through
their own media. In one interview, he stated, "My concern is that the U.S. wants to
turn our country into what they always thought it was—an extension of the United
States."[38] This mode of argumentation closely resembled that of Canadian labor
leaders and served to reinforce the idea that all Canadians must unify in order to
confront U.S. expansionism.

Canadian author Margaret Atwood foregrounded the gendered image of U.S.
"penetration" of the Canadian market in her essay "Blind Faith and Free Trade," in

which she argued that "Canada as a separate but dominated country has done about as well under the U.S. as women worldwide have done under men; about the only position they've ever adopted toward us, country to country, has been the missionary position, and we were not on top."[39] Her portrayal of a Canada raped by the United States resonates with the *malinchista* imagery mobilized by "apocalyptic" anti-free-trade forces in Mexico in order to attack those who would sell the nation to the gringos.[40] Thus, in their allegations of cultural imperialism on the part of the United States, the Canadian anti-free-trade arguments tended to position Canada as Mexico's third-world peer, rather than as a first-world country with a gross domestic product lower than that of the United States, but significantly higher than that of Mexico.

Across the Atlantic, France took the lead in demanding a cultural exemption from GATT, and the pragmatic alliance that evolved between national capitalists and progressive intellectuals in that country was even more accentuated than in Canada because both of these groups also supported the French government. Alain Carignon, then France's communications minister, hailed the GATT accord as "a great and beautiful victory for Europe and for French culture."[41] The idealistic invocation of culture as a realm unsullied by commerce did not obscure the fact that a great deal of money was riding on the cultural exemption for both U.S. and French industries. France's film and TV industry is the largest in Europe and the world's second largest export producer after the United States. According to the *New York Times,* then French Minister of Culture Jacques Toubon hinted at the eventual creation of a large, state-supported film production consortium, along the lines of Airbus Industrie, which would produce Hollywood-style blockbusters for the European Union.[42] As for the United States, the entertainment sector is the country's second largest export industry in terms of profits after aerospace. The U.S. film industry has traditionally used foreign markets as a lucrative dumping ground for its films, after it recoups most production expenses on the domestic market. According to the MPAA, in 1992 U.S. entertainment industries received $4 billion in revenues from Western Europe out of $18 billion total revenues.[43] But by the time of the GATT negotiations of 1994, the pressure was on to maintain Hollywood's success abroad. California was experiencing a severe recession, and the Clinton administration was especially eager to protect the Hollywood film industry, one of its traditional bases of political support.[44]

In order to compensate for the strong presence of U.S. mass media, many Western European countries levy taxes on cultural products and use the funds to subsidize their own national entertainment sectors. In comparison to the United States, most European governments allocate five to fifteen times more funds per citizen for cultural institutions and events.[45] As Nataša Ďurovičová has argued, it is this prominent "public" space traditionally accorded to national culture within European countries, rather than any set of shared characteristics, that underlies contemporary references to "European culture."[46] To provide a concrete example of how such policies functioned at the time of GATT negotiations, French subsidies for filmmaking and TV were fueled by an 11 percent surcharge on movie tickets and a 5 percent tax on television advertising revenues, respectively. Furthermore, French media producers compensated for losses due to piracy through a tax on sales of blank audio- and videotapes. MPAA President Jack Valenti repeatedly asserted that a portion of the antipiracy subsidies should rightfully be funneled back to the U.S. industries that distribute their products for sale on the European market.[47]

The majority of countries in the European Union entered GATT negotiations seeking to preserve a quota system for European-produced movies and television, to continue state subsidies for national cultural industries, and to allow for the future renegotiation of audiovisual trade policy in line with new technological developments.[48] France spearheaded an effort to exempt culture from the agreement entirely, after having made concessions on other sensitive issues such as agriculture. When negotiations threatened to fail altogether, the United States finally withdrew the subject of audiovisual services from the table, relegating it to the realm of future trade agreements.

High, Low, and Mass Culture in the European Union

Proponents of the cultural exemption often invoked the word *culture* in a holistic anthropological sense, defined by Néstor García Canclini and Guevara Niebla as "the collectivity of practices in which the meanings of social life are elaborated, processed, and communicated."[49] The pro-exemption forces used the term in this manner to combat the narrowly commercial designations ascribed to the cultural industries in the treaties. The idea of culture as a "way of life" is a relatively recent one, as Raymond Williams has argued,[50] yet when compared to the manner in which the term *culture* has been repositioned within recent international trade discourse, it seemed positively timeworn. According to the text of NAFTA, the products implicated in the treaty's definition of the "culture industries" are books, periodicals, newspapers, movies, videos, audio recordings, printed music, radio, television, and cable TV.[51] Some scholars, such as George Yúdice, also include "intellectual property" with this group, a "grab bag into which all kinds of technical innovations are deposited," from copyrights to computer programs, because the items under that heading have received treatment similar to the cultural industries under recent trade legislation.[52]

In spite of these two very different invocations of culture, even anti-free-trade forces often ended up designating the narrow spectrum of arts and entertainment as representing their enormous cultural field, which led to contradictions in the argumentation of the cultural exemption itself. A central assumption of the exemption argument was that mass media products had a more palpable impact on the formation of identity than did other consumer goods such as clothing, cars, and food, and by extension, that cultural workers were somehow more important to the integrity of the nation than other workers. Arguments for the exemption exhibited a strong "culturalist" perspective, a term defined by anthropologist Virginia Dominguez as "that propensity to employ culture (to think, act, and fight with it)."[53] I share her suspicion of the tendency to define culture ontologically, as an entity that can be catalogued according to attributes. Instead, she argues, it is time to start asking *"what is being accomplished* socially, politically, discursively when the concept of culture is invoked to describe, analyze, argue, justify, and theorize."[54] One thing that the arguments for the cultural exemption certainly accomplished was the reinforcement of already existing, debilitating hierarchical distinctions between mental and manual labor, between those workers who create "ideas" and those who create "things."

The supreme communicative power of mass media's words and images over other consumer products was often cited in writings about the exemption. For example, Guillermo Bonfil Batalla, writing of NAFTA, stated,

> Las industrias culturales no pueden manejarse con los mismos criterios que la industria del calzado o la fabricación y venta de pantaletas. Los productos de las industrias culturales transmiten *mensajes* (pedestres o no, ese aquí no es el punto); esos mensajes corresponden a sistemas precisos de significación, reflejan jerarquías de valores claramente establecidas y surgen de (y proponen) modos de vida y formas de concebir el mundo que expresan una cultura particular, definida, única.

> (The cultural industries cannot be handled with the same criteria as the footwear industry or the manufacture and sale of underpants. The products of the cultural industries transmit *messages* (pedestrian or not, that is not the point here); those messages correspond to precise systems of meaning, reflect hierarchies of clearly established values, and arise from (and propose) lifestyles and ways of conceiving the world that express a particular, defined, unique culture.)[55]

A similar idea was expressed by Régis Debray in his debate with Mario Vargas Llosa about GATT:

> Tú lo sabes bien: uno no se parece a lo que come, pero siempre acaba pareciéndose a lo que lee, y ahora a lo que mira. Vivir es contarse historias. Hace cuatro días estaban sobre papel; hace nada, sobre celuloide, y ahora en soporte electrónico. Según que un joven se cuente *Easy Rider* o *Morir en Madrid*, *El acorazado Potemkin* o *Ciudadano Kane*, variará su destino. La imagen goberna nuestros sueños, y los sueños nuestras acciones. Nunca se ha visto una conquista gastronómica del mundo: ¿cuál es el desafío moral del *chop-suey*, del *camembert* o de la paella? Pero una hegemonía política supone siempre la extinción de las miradas diferentes.

> (You know very well: one does not resemble what one eats, but always winds up resembling what one reads, and now what one sees. To live is to tell oneself stories. Four days ago they were on paper; a little while ago, on film, and now they're on electronic media. According to whether a young person tells him or herself *Easy Rider* or *To Die in Madrid*, *The Battleship Potemkin* or *Citizen Kane*, he or she will change his or her destiny. The image governs our dreams, and dreams, our actions. A gastronomic conquest of the world has never been seen: What is the moral challenge of chop-suey, camembert, or paella? But a political hegemony always assumes the extinction of different views [gazes, looks].)[56]

Several key ideas inform these statements. The first, which seems obvious, is their assertion that cultural texts are internalized by human beings as "scripts for life," while other consumer products may be used and discarded at will, as in the case of clothing and food. Thus, they argue that human subject formation hinges upon self-emplotment or identification within externally produced narrative structures and, more important, that communal identity formation (understood at the default level of the nation in these arguments) occurs by the same mechanism. Second, the autonomy ascribed to the cultural industries relative to other industries is pronounced. Though cultural products may have an exchange value, according to Bonfil Batalla and Debray, their special function as messages and stories makes them easily and self-evidently detachable from the rest of economic production, per se. Cultural imperialism consequently replaces intercapitalist rivalry between the United States and the European Union as a rationale for opposing U.S. market domination of mass media industries; in fact, the cultural imperialism argument replaces more comprehensive theories of imperialism altogether.

Many of the pro-exemption arguments furthermore implicitly overturn the rigid base/superstructure model associated with orthodox Marxism, in which the economic base is privileged over ideological forms as a site of intervention. Ironically, they retain the schism between economy and ideology, except that now they posit that ideology directs the shape of the economy. This concept of "cultural determination" was perhaps most clearly acknowledged by François Mitterrand, who in the context of GATT negotiations, declaimed a global *cultural* takeover by the United States, waged under the "false ideology" of *economic* expansion: "Who can be blind today to the threat of a world gradually invaded by an identical culture, Anglo-Saxon culture, under the cover of economic liberalism?"[57]

Glib references to cultural difference permeated mainstream coverage of GATT. The symbolic oppositions that the international press coined during GATT negotiations, tellingly, were not of workers in competition for one another's jobs or of warring corporations, but rather of cultural icons: the triumph of I. M. Pei's billion-dollar addition to the Louvre, for example, was contrasted to the failure of Eurodisney.[58] It would be tempting to view the pervasiveness of such caricatures as evidence of vulgar nationalist retrenchment in the face of global economic integration, but the arguments of intellectuals were more subtle than that, especially when it came to defining the proposed role of the nation within the emerging trade blocs.

In his debate with Vargas Llosa, Debray argued that the French supported the cultural exemption not in order to promote or preserve a unitary French culture, but to ensure pluralism in a world that was becoming increasingly homogeneous. Europe, with its small, distinctive national cinemas, was already a model of cultural diversity in Debray's view. Like Monsiváis in Mexico, Debray saw French culture as a hybrid mixture of many influences, and he strongly dissociated French identity from racial or ethnic qualifiers. Free trade threatened French media quotas and subsidies, however, which in turn threatened France's cultural uniqueness. Debray compared the situation of France at the hands of U.S. cultural industries to that of the working class at the hands of capital:

> El dogma del libre intercambio de las imágenes debe universalizar el antiguo "que se callen los pobres," ese pobre cuyo imagen sube hasta Dios, tal vez, pero tan pocas veces hasta nuestras pantallas. Porque allí donde hay débiles y fuertes, "la libertad oprime y la ley libera." La fórmula no es de un marxista, puedes estar tranquilo, sino de un católico francés del siglo pasado, Lamennais. Cuando pidió una ley para prohibir que los niños trabajaran in las minas del carbón, hubo gente bien pensante que denunció en ella una traba policial a la libertad: la que les gusta tener los zorros en los gallineros.

> (The dogma of free trade in images should universalize the old "let the poor be silent"—that poor person whose image rises up to God perhaps, but so rarely up to our movie screens. Because there, where there are weak and strong, "liberty oppresses and law liberates." The formula is not from a Marxist, rest easy, but rather from a French Catholic of the last century, Lamennais. When he asked for a law to prohibit children from working in the coal mines, there were well-thinking people who denounced it as a crackdown on liberty: the same liberty that foxes like to have in hen houses.)[59]

It is difficult to read the allusion to nineteenth-century French labor reforms in the above passage without thinking of a movie that was released just one month before the publication of Debray's essay. *Germinal* (dir. Claude Berri, 1993) found itself at the center of another grand symbolic opposition during GATT negotiations. Adapted from Emile Zola's novel about the labor struggle of coal miners, the film was the highest-budget ($30 million) French film made to date.[60] Its release was scheduled strategically at the very end of September 1993, so that it would precede that of U.S.-produced *Jurassic Park*. The media seized upon these two movies, finding in them the epitome of a European "art film" on the one hand, and a U.S. high-tech blockbuster on the other.[61] In the final scene of *Germinal,* a long and brutal strike has been crushed, but several miners have learned enough from their experience to carry on the struggle. They exchange knowing looks with the strike's principal organizer as he departs on a journey through newly sown fields of French countryside. In light of Debray's transposition of the terms of class struggle to contemporary rivalries among industrialized nations, it is tempting to read this final scene as an allegory of France sowing the seed of "European identity" and solidarity in other European Union nations.[62]

Jean-Jacques Beneix, director of the movies *Betty Blue, Diva,* and *La Femme Nikita,* had vowed on French television to destroy his French passport if the cultural exemption was not passed.[63] Later he lauded news of the GATT decision as "the birth of a second Europe which is acquiring a spiritual dimension."[64] Indeed, if there was a "poster child" for the cultural exemption in Europe, it was the figure of the director. As audiovisual issues threatened to become the final stumbling block of

GATT negotiations, directors gained increasing prominence in media coverage of the treaty. U.S. directors Martin Scorsese and Steven Spielberg both issued statements in early October criticizing France's effort to uphold quotas for European film programming. Scorsese argued, "Closing the borders would not guarantee a rise in creativity in the local countries or even a rise in interest on the part of local audiences."[65] According to rumor, the root of Spielberg's and Scorsese's irritation was a speech critical of U.S. movies that was delivered by former French Minister of Culture, Jack Lang, in front of Spielberg, Scorsese, and other U.S. directors at that year's Venice Film Festival.[66] The European response to the U.S. directors was swift and angry. A group of them, including Pedro Almodóvar, Stephen Frears, Wim Wenders, and Bernardo Bertolucci, printed a letter presenting their side of the story in the film industry trade papers. "We are only defending the tiny margin of freedom left to us," they wrote. "We are trying to protect European cinema against its complete annihilation." Referring ironically to Spielberg's *Jurassic Park,* they continued,

> The dinosaurs of 1993, that's us. We are facing extinction, and we are merely fighting for survival, our backs against the wall. Work with us and inform yourselves who is "locking out borders" and who is truly "not welcome." Or do you seriously think that our European films are really so bad that they only deserve to reach one percent of American audiences, while American films fill more than 80 percent of European screens?[67]

As the debate heated up by mid-October, European Community trade chief Sir Leon Brittan interrupted talks with U.S. trade representative Mickey Kantor in Brussels in order to meet with a delegation of European directors, including Wim Wenders, Coline Serreau, and Andrei Konchalovsky;[68] meanwhile other directors and actors, such as Isabelle Huppert and Gérard Depardieu, participated in pro-exemption rallies in France.[69]

The clash of the directors was not a substantive intellectual debate as the one between Vargas Llosa and Debray was, but it did reveal certain assumptions about the different types of cultural products associated with Europe and the United States. For the purposes of the GATT debates, European national cinemas were equated with auteur cinema. As Thomas Elsaesser has pointed out, this conflation tends to mask certain tensions that exist within national film industries—namely, that auteur cinema often finds itself opposed to commercial cinema in its own country of origin.[70] Nevertheless, it was the U.S. cinema, synonymous with Hollywood, that became the imaginary opposite of European cinema for both sides of the debate. The U.S. film industry's position on GATT rejected this opposition, however, insofar as it was not so much concerned with Europe's art cinema and auteurs as it was with European forays into its own brand of commercial film and TV.

In statements by U.S. government and business officials, one sees repeatedly an appeal to the theory of comparative advantage used to assign a specialization in "elite culture" to Europe, and one in "commercial culture" to the United States. This principle of free trade, elaborated by classical economist David Ricardo, holds that a given producer should export those goods for which its "productivity disadvantage" is the least; a nation will thus profit by taking advantage of available resources that may be less plentiful in rival countries.[71] In the GATT context, it often seemed that cultural sensibility itself was the infrastructure to be exploited for export. At one point during the trade talks, Valenti was quoted as saying, "The negotiation has nothing to do with culture unless European soap operas and game shows are the equivalent of Molière."[72] Carla Hills, trade representative under President Bush, agreed in her advice to the French: "Make films as good as your cheeses, and you will sell them!"[73] Finally, *New York Times* economic columnist Peter Passell paraphrased an argument made by Eli Noam of Columbia Business School when he wrote, "It's one thing . . . to sweeten the pot for the best of the domestic product: Virtually every government subsidizes high culture. It is quite another to put a quota on an American cop show so that French studios can crank out their own car chases."[74] Clearly, one of the underlying messages of the U.S. opposition to the cultural exemption in Europe was that it was all right for European states to subsidize any cultural product that catered to a small elite public, while U.S. corporations would draw upon their "natural talent" for popular culture in order to serve mass audiences. It did not necessarily matter whether European subsidies underwrote low-budget art movies or other fine arts; what mattered was profitability. For the French, on the other hand, to distinguish between popular and elite forms of entertainment in itself implied capitulation to the terms of debate put forth by the United States.[75]

High, Low, and Mass Culture in North America

The fact that European debates about free trade and culture took mass media as their arena differentiated them from their counterparts in North America. In Europe, opposition to GATT came from actors within cultural industries and the government, and it was apparent that progressive artists and intellectuals felt their interests to be well served by the state.[76] Though nationalism informed the arguments of the free-trade opposition in Canada and Mexico, the Mulroney and Salinas governments were cast in villainous roles by grassroots movements and nongovernmental organizations as collaborators with Reagan, Bush, and U.S. corporations. This was particularly true in Mexico, in light of that country's long history of one-party rule and the government's intermittent persecution and censorship of cultural workers.[77]

Another major difference from the European context is that in North America, art museums and galleries played a greater role in promoting free trade, and opposition in turn arose from the margins of these institutions—from politically minded gallery and performance artists whose milieux were not directly targeted by NAFTA and whose work had relatively small viewing publics. Although these oppositional artists shared some goals in common with groups that favored the cultural exemption, they tended not to affiliate themselves directly with those movements. I will

1. Karl Beveridge and Carole Condé, *Free Expression, 1989*, cibachrome print, 27 ⅓ × 39 inches. Photograph courtesy of the artists.

briefly mention a few such oppositional artists before considering larger issues concerning trade liberalization and the arts in North America.

Toronto-based collaborative artists Karl Beveridge and Carole Condé had worked closely with trade unions and community groups for fifteen years prior to making art about free trade.[78] They became involved in the campaign for the cultural exemption during the negotiation of the USCFTA in the late 1980s, when they created several works of public art about the treaty. The photocollage entitled *Free Expression* was commissioned in 1989 by the Toronto arts magazine *Fuse,* which like other Canadian magazines, was concerned that special postage subsidies would be threatened by the trade agreement (figure 1).[79] The artists describe this piece as "a reversal of the 'Radio Free Europe' advertisements sponsored by the U.S. Information Service in the 1950s and 1960s."[80] It depicts a group of people in the foreground protecting Canadian publications from an entourage of anthropomorphic U.S. corporate icons, such as *Time, Fortune,* and George Bush, while a video image of Brian Mulroney stares blankly from the wall. In the background, a U.S.–based radio signal emblazoned with the words "FREE TRADE" blankets the globe. The billboard and collage entitled *Shutdown* (also 1989) were commissioned by the alternative arts center Artcite, in Windsor, Ontario, a border town hit hard by the decline of the automotive industry (figure 2). In this piece, a factory worker stands before an empty assembly line, while at home she throws up her hands in despair as she hunts for a job in the classified ads. In both of these pieces, the picture planes are strongly divided between "public" and "private" spaces; the besieged private or domestic space is identified with that which is Canadian, and the public with the United States and U.S.–owned corporations. Because both of these pieces are public works of art themselves in terms of the nature of their exhibition, one may read them as an attempt to reclaim public spaces for Canadian media and locally produced images.

It is interesting to compare *Free Expression* and *Shutdown* with other projects that

2. Karl Beveridge and Carole Condé, *Shutdown*, 1991, handpainted billboard, 7 × 24 feet, Windsor, Ontario. Photograph courtesy of the artists.

the artists have done for Canadian labor unions, in which the major conflict portrayed is that between workers and management.[81] The free-trade pieces, in contrast, mute class conflict in favor of foregrounding nationalist and anti-imperialist sentiments. The team has recently held an artists' residency in Argentina in conjunction with a labor arts festival there, and they are considering embarking on a new project about Chile's incorporation into NAFTA.[82] I am eager to see whether the motif of clearly delineated national borders continues to be such a prominent structuring device of their work as they continue to forge their own cross-border alliances.

In contrast to Beveridge and Condé's nationalist, site-specific pieces, New York–

based artist Lynn Schwarzer concerns herself with the need for international workers' solidarity in the face of growing economic globalization. Often dealing with events in labor history from the past two centuries, her work charts the gradual shift in concentration of unsafe manual labor jobs from the United States to developing countries. Inspired by the testimonies of women workers and the writings of Emma Goldman, Schwarzer's emphasis on social transformation from the bottom up closely resembles some of the videos about free trade that have been produced by labor and religious groups (see chapter 2).

An ongoing dynamic in Schwarzer's work is the juxtaposition of texts by women about their working and living conditions to texts from the corporate perspective, in which women are discussed as consumers and employees. Using simple visual forms associated with public signs and monuments, such as the (religious) icon painting, the banner, and the road sign, Schwarzer produces serial images that emphasize the aggregate effects of the events that she depicts on vulnerable populations. Her current work, for example, is a series of 198 five-by-seven-inch formal oil paintings on wood panels, each of which depicts a detailed rendition of a Dalkon Shield IUD. Each painting in turn represents one thousand women who were injured as a result of using the shield and who sought compensation from its manufacturer, A. H. Robbins. These birth control devices were shipped throughout the world, particularly to developing countries, where many women were unable to claim damages from the company. The icon paintings are accompanied by textual and documentary evidence, such as first-person narratives, records of congressional hearings, and official company statements about the safety of the product.[83]

An earlier (1993) multimedia project by Schwarzer entitled *Images of Labor* also consists of multiple components about women workers. In one section, Schwarzer made large, silk-screened images of modern-day work implements, based upon the designs of early-twentieth-century trade union banners. Another series consists of ex-voto–like portrait/narratives of nineteenth-century U.S. and twentieth-century Third World women workers. A third component of this project is an artist's book, in which testimonies by women workers are collated with statements by multinational corporations that do business in export-processing zones, including the U.S.–Mexico border region (figures 3–6).

In the field of performance art, Guillermo Gómez-Peña and Maris Bustamante each associate NAFTA with a fin de siècle malaise that is affecting the North American continent. Bustamante is a pioneer of feminist performance art in Mexico City, and her *Naftaperformances* are brief, highly spontaneous and physical sketches that broadly address issues of contemporary urban life for "intercontinental citizens."[84] The connection of her performances to NAFTA is purposely left vague. Bustamante has stated that the treaty is a great unknown and should be met with bravery and spontaneity by North Americans.[85]

California-based Gómez-Peña is more openly critical of the treaty in his ongoing

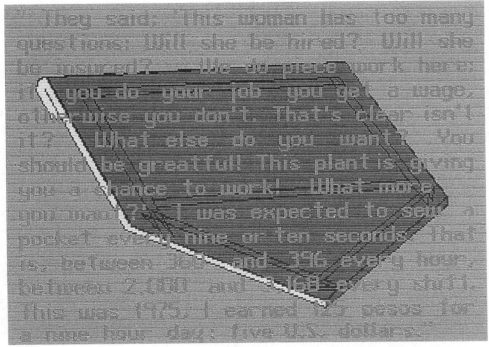

3. Lynn Schwarzer, *Images of Labor* (detail), 1993, artist book. Photograph courtesy of the artist and John Michael Kohler Art Center.

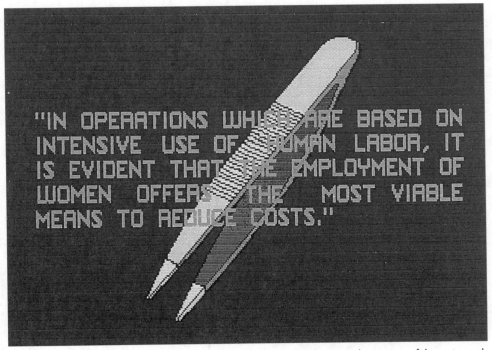

"IN OPERATIONS WHICH ARE BASED ON INTENSIVE USE OF HUMAN LABOR, IT IS EVIDENT THAT THE EMPLOYMENT OF WOMEN OFFERS THE MOST VIABLE MEANS TO REDUCE COSTS."

4. Lynn Schwarzer, *Images of Labor* (detail), 1993, artist book. Photograph courtesy of the artist and John Michael Kohler Art Center.

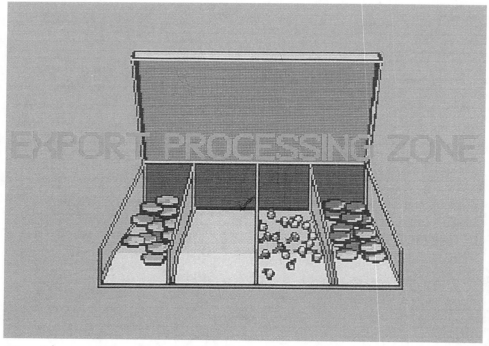

In 1986, electronics workers challenged the worker's compensation laws which, in California and New Mexico held that women could not recover for the loss of their reproductive organs because a hysterectomy did not affect their ability to work. Among those involved were women working in GTE's department 320 in Albuquerque. They had been exposed to carcinogenic substances, and 49 of them had had their uteruses removed. GTE responded by moving department 320 to Juarez, Mexico.

5. Lynn Schwarzer, *Images of Labor* (detail), 1993, artist book. Photograph courtesy of the artist and John Michael Kohler Art Center.

6. Lynn Schwarzer, *Images of Labor* (detail), 1993, artist book. Photograph courtesy of the artist and John Michael Kohler Art Center.

art project entitled "The Free Art Agreement/El Tratado de Libre Cultura" (FAA, 1993–94), the purpose of which is to create a supplementary, albeit oppositional, network of artists in order to call attention to NAFTA's lacunae.[86] The FAA is an attempt on the part of Gómez-Peña and his collaborators to valorize those aspects of intellectual and creative activity that were excluded from the treaty. He writes, "If formed, the tasks of this network of thinkers, artists, and arts organizations from Mexico, the U.S., Canada—and why not the Caribbean?—would consist of developing future models of multilateral cooperation, crosscultural dialogue, and interdisciplinary artistic collaboration."[87] Gómez-Peña's "free idea zone" does not purport to be NAFTA's antithesis. Rather, it is a parallel structure to the treaty that appropriates many of NAFTA's favorite metaphors, such as "the borderless continent." Thus, through strategies of imitation, parody, and alternative cultural circuits, Gómez-Peña proposes a "third way" that would avoid the twin traps of nationalist chauvinism, on the one hand, and homogenizing global consumerism on the other (Gómez-Peña's work is discussed further in chapter 5).

While Gómez-Peña was promoting his version of a free idea zone, pro-free-trade forces also staged their own cultural exchanges in major arts institutions as part of their promotion of the treaty. As stated previously, the only self-identified cultural aspects that were ever slated for tariff reduction or elimination during NAFTA negotiations were the mass media industries, and trade in fine art and antiquities. Other strata of aesthetic cultural production, such as the performing arts, certain types of ephemeral and public visual art, folk art, and artisanry, never went to the table.[88] Though the art forms of these fields have widely divergent social roles, they share certain qualities, such as ephemerality or functionality, that make them difficult to commodify, isolate, or distinguish from other consumer products. It is interesting to note the manner in which pro-free-trade forces appealed to this type of aesthetic production in order to wage their own publicity campaign in favor of the treaty. While anti-free-trade groups focused on mass culture, pro-free-traders could and did point to examples of "fine art" and "material culture" in order to demonstrate that national cultures would be completely unaffected by, and were in many cases already exempt from, any trade agreement. A statement that has by now attained the status of a free-trade one-liner, illustrates this point. When asked by a Canadian journalist whether Mexican cultural industries would be included in free trade negotiations, then Mexican Secretary of Trade and Industrial Development Jaime Serra Puche responded, "[La cultura] no es tan relevante para México. Si tiene tiempo debería ir a ver la exhibición 'Treinta siglos de esplendor' y se dará cuenta de que no hay mucho por qué preocuparse" ("[Culture] is not so relevant for Mexico. If you have time, you should go see the exhibition *Splendors of Thirty Centuries* and you will realize that there is not much to worry about").[89]

The exhibition to which Serra Puche referred was *Mexico: Splendors of Thirty Centuries,* organized in 1991 by the Metropolitan Museum of Art in New York. The show traveled to museums in Los Angeles and San Antonio and was well-attended and praised by critics. In his analysis of the exhibition, however, Néstor García Canclini pointed out that the event was manipulated by the Salinas administration as part of the "political cultural diplomacy" that accompanied the NAFTA nego-tiations.[90] By positing a historical continuity of *mexicanidad* extending from pre-Colombian civilizations to the Mexican muralists, *Splendors of Thirty Centuries* skill-fully managed to combine two seemingly contradictory themes: Mexico's unswerving millenarian drive toward national cultural self-definition *and* its desire for binational exchange. In this respect, the show implicitly asserted a mutual exclusivity between national culture and the global economy, similar to the one that characterized the logic of the cultural exemption.

The *Splendors of Thirty Centuries* show is but one example of a growing effort on the part of large North American arts institutions to redefine the art world according to a north/south continental axis, rather than one that stresses continuities with his-torical developments in European art. This is occurring during a period in which Latino/a artists in the United States have gained increasing recognition within main-stream arts institutions, and some Latino/a arts have become popular on a mass level, ranging from the transformation of Frida Kahlo into a cult figure, to the feature-film productions of *Selena* and *Evita* and to widespread dissemination of Day of the Dead iconography.[91]

Particularly in the field of contemporary art, there is a tendency to include Latin American, U.S., and Canadian artists within the same geographical imaginary. The United States is witnessing perhaps the largest resurgence of interest in Latin Ameri-can art among major arts institutions since the World War II era, when the Museum of Modern Art (MOMA), under the directorship of Alfred H. Barr, Jr., instituted the Inter-American Fund for the acquisition of modern Latin American art.[92] At that time, MOMA's cultural initiative was spurred on by the U.S. government's attempt to deter Latin American countries from siding with the Axis powers, but the rhetoric of discovery and recognition of "our neighbor to the south" is similar to what we in the United States are hearing today in the era of free trade.[93] Today, U.S. magazines such as *Art in America* and *Art News* have begun to feature pieces regularly on "north/ south" issues, while many Latin American journals, such as Mexico City's arts maga-zine *Poliester* and the literary review *Mandorla,* have taken a pan-American approach since their inception. In terms of exhibitions, the best example of this phenomenon is the 1991 blockbuster exhibition, *Mito y magia en América: Los ochenta,* organized by El Museo de Arte Contemporáneo in Monterrey. The show included artists from both North and South America and was organized around the theme of "regional inspira-tions and personal mythologies" in American art.[94] In the same vein, the Art Institute of Chicago decided to revive its traditional "American" show in 1994; but instead of showcasing U.S. artists, the revamped exhibition, entitled *About Place: Recent Art of the Americas,* included artists from Canada and Latin American countries.[95]

The exhibitions and periodicals that I have mentioned do not necessarily draw attention to the socioeconomic inequalities within the NAFTA bloc or among the different countries of the Americas. Instead, they posit the existence of a cosmopolitan arts "community" bound together through the museum-gallery nexus of such major cities as São Paulo, Mexico City, New York, Los Angeles, Toronto, and Vancouver. This recent wave of hemispheric cosmopolitanism is obviously facilitated by numerous factors, including large populations of Latin Americans and Latinos/as living in North America; however, the use of hemispheric art both as state- or multinational-supported propaganda and as a "bandwagon" marketing approach by major arts institutions is also influenced by developments in economy and trade policy. Los Angeles–based writer Rubén Martínez dubbed the new wave of blockbuster exhibitions "free-trade art," and Guillermo Gómez-Peña has further elaborated it as an attempt "to use art as conservative diplomacy and as a means to create a conflict-free image of a country for the purpose of seducing investors and promoting cultural tourism."[96]

There are indeed strong connections between multinationals and arts patronage, which may in part account for the vogue of "free-trade art" in the present era of privatization. To give one example, Televisa not only controls a vast share of Mexico's broadcast television and video rental outlets, but also has amassed a substantial collection of contemporary painting and sculpture, housed in Mexico City's Centro Cultural Arte Contemporáneo. García Canclini commented that Televisa's "multiple politics" is one way in which the corporation symbolically presents itself as a guardian of free expression in opposition to the state:

> A través de esta política múltiple, que abarca lo culto, lo popular y lo masivo, Televisa se presenta como benefactora y legitimadora de la producción cultural de todas las clases; como defensora de la libertad de creación cultural y de la información política frente a cualquier "monopolio" estatal; como articuladora interna de la cultura nacional y enlace con el desarrollo internacional moderno. La iniciativa privada compite así con el Estado para sustituirlo como agente constructor de hegemonía, o sea como organizador de las relaciones culturales y políticas entre las clases.

> (Through this multiple politics, which encompasses high, popular, and mass culture, Televisa presents itself as the benefactor and legitimist of cultural production of all classes; as defender of the freedom of cultural creation and political information before any state "monopoly"; as internal articulator of the national culture and tie to modern international development. Private initiative competes in this manner with the State in order to replace it as a constructive agent of hegemony, or as an organizer of the political and cultural relations among the classes.)[97]

Just as Jesusa Rodríguez had warned in *Cielo de abajo,* the corporate "alternative" is illusory in a country where partnerships between the government and large corporations are also increasingly common. Even Televisa's former director, Emilio Azcárraga

Milmo, sat on the board of the "society of friends" (a corporate fundraising body) of the state-run National Museum of Anthropology in Mexico City.[98]

Mexico's largest art sponsors at present are a sampling of both national and foreign-owned corporations; besides Televisa, they include IBM de México, Banamex, Pepsico, Pedro Domecq, AT&T, and Colgate-Palmolive. Some of these companies are also known for their patronage of the arts in the United States. As NAFTA was about to go into effect, the magazine *Business Mexico*, which caters to U.S. corporations, speculated that the treaty would bode well for the arts, in that growing U.S. influence in Mexico would prompt Mexican corporations to "develop a keener sense of their national heritage," at the same time that it would encourage more U.S. companies with subsidiaries in Mexico to sponsor binational art projects.[99]

As the preceding examples suggest, a strong national culture is not anathema to economic neoliberalism. In fact, a certain amount of nationalist pride may even be welcomed as a positive by-product of free trade. In this respect the arts, especially those in dialogue with cosmopolitan trends, hold a peer relationship with their counterparts in other countries. Those artists and activists who attempt to protest trade liberalization through the adoption or invention of nationalist aesthetics, therefore, may face an unintended obstacle in the very category of national culture that the exemption seeks to preserve, because the arguments of free-trade proponents also benefit from the dissociation between national and economic markers.

The study of representations of the U.S.–Mexico border region is useful in developing an understanding of how cultural nationalist and economic transnationalist ideologies coexist in the current historical period. Based upon his research on the maquiladora industries, British sociologist Leslie Sklair has theorized the emergence of a new type of bourgeoisie, formed out of elements of the older indigenous bourgeoisie and the comprador bourgeoisie, and concentrated especially in developing countries. He refers to this new group as the transnational capitalist class (TCC). Members of the TCC are not necessarily dependent upon transnationals; in fact they may even own their own transnational corporations with investments in other countries. What distinguishes them, according to Sklair, is that the TCC "sees its interests bound up not with transnational corporations or foreign capital as such, but with the global capitalist system. It sees its mission as organizing the conditions under which the interests of the system can be furthered within the national context."[100] Despite the global orientation of the border ruling class, Sklair continues, "this does not necessarily make it any less patriotic or even chauvinist in its practice or ideology."[101] The U.S.–Mexico border is certainly not the "origin" of this particular ideological and economic orientation—indeed, we have seen that it characterizes much pro-free-trade discourse. The border, however, is one geographical area in which unique factors, namely, the paradoxes of contiguous urban and divided national spaces, create an ideal environment for the expansion of U.S. and foreign capital in Mexico at the same time that they present huge contradictions and problems at the local and regional levels for inhabitants of border communities. For these reasons, identification with the global capitalist system in the border region is the occupation not only of ruling elites, but also of working classes that find themselves affected by the slightest fluctuations in U.S. and Mexican currencies as well as shifts in binational relations.

I have argued that the act of detaching culture from other spheres of production enables social actors to support cultural nationalism and free trade simultaneously. Yet, as far as the national register is concerned, it remains difficult to conceive this perspective without positing some theoretical or spatial point of alternation, some marker of difference that would regulate the coherence of one national identity as opposed to another. When talk of free trade was at its height in the early 1990s, so was anxiety about the stability and sovereignty of national borders (an anxiety that has escalated since the treaty's passage). For Mexican advocates of the cultural exemption and a protected national economy, the border represented the vulnerability of the Mexican nation before U.S. imperialism; from the U.S. perspective, conversely, it represented the loss of U.S. jobs to Mexican workers and another blow to the already moribund American Dream. Bonfil Batalla nervously posed these questions about NAFTA to his readers from a vantage point still at a safe distance from the fast-eroding frontier:

> ¿Cuál es la nueva concepción de soberanía nacional; en qué campos y sobre qué bases? ¿Qué separación marca nuestra frontera norte? . . . ¿Qué pasa cuando todo el país es frontera libre?

> (What is the new conception of national sovereignty? On what grounds and what bases? What separation marks our northern border? . . . What happens when the entire country is a free border?)[102]

At the very same time that the border served as a marker of difference, the spatial contiguity of binational cities and the fluidity of their respective populations called into question the notion that there was indeed a discrete national identity to be protected on one side or the other.

Thus, depending upon the political orientation of a given source and its spatial register of analysis, during the late 1980s and early 1990s border cities were alternately cast as NAFTA's best- or worst-case scenario, as a model of cultural hybridity and symbiosis, or as a great cultural chasm dividing the First and Third Worlds. For obvious reasons, the border also became a common meeting place for North American nongovernmental organizations, as well as a home base for many regional activist groups (some of whom, ironically, advocated the cultural exemption).

Chapter 2

Establishing Shots of the Border: The Fence and the River

For the first time the world is completely divided up, so that in the future only redivision is possible, i.e., territories can only pass from one "owner" to another, instead of passing as ownerless territory to an "owner."

—V. I. Lenin, 1916[1]

In spring 1992, Terry Allen, a multimedia artist known for his exploration of the mythology of the U.S. Southwest, was invited to do an installation at The Ohio State University's Wexner Center for the Arts as part of that institution's artist-in-residence program. The Wexner Center installation, entitled *a simple story (Juarez),* was the continuation of a project begun over twenty years ago, which has included record albums, a radio play, photographs, video, sculpture, collages, prints, and drawings. At the Wexner Center the artist constructed three sets: a cantina ("Melodyland"), an airstream trailer encased in the wooden hull of a ship ("The Perfect Ship"), and a gas station ("Stations") (figures 7–10). These sets loosely correspond to episodes in *a simple story*'s scripted narrative, which tells of four characters, Sailor, Spanish Alice, Chic Blundie, and Jabo, whose destinies become intertwined.[2] *A simple story* traces the journeys of the quartet from Southern California to Cortez, Colorado, where Jabo and Chic murder newlyweds Sailor and Alice in a trailer, and eventually part ways after they escape to Juárez.

Allen does not fix *a simple story*'s characters or their location in time or space. Instead, the fragmented episodes of *a simple story*'s narrative function as traces of memory that forge a connection among the depopulated sets of the installation. Allen built the sets at two-thirds human scale and theatrically illuminated them with the flicker of video monitors and neon signs. In her afterword to the published script accompanying the exhibition, Curator Sarah Rogers-Lafferty described the video images projected at "Stations" as "hypnotic." She wrote, "These images capture what is perhaps the most pivotal characteristic of this circular tale—the sense of endless journey, and escape to find oneself that haunts all the details of the story."[3] Rosetta Brooks, the reviewer for *Artforum,* also perceived Allen's border to be atmospheric and psychological; for her, *a simple story* was a nostalgic fantasy about the western U.S. frontier:

7. Terry Allen, *a simple story (Juarez),* 1992. Installation detail: *Melodyland.* Courtesy Wexner Center for the Arts, The Ohio State University, Columbus, Ohio. Commissioned project as part of an artist residency with funds from the Wexner Center Foundation. Photograph by Richard K. Loesch. Photograph courtesy of the Wexner Center.

> The installation recalled the kinds of buildings seen in many small, formerly frontier towns across the West. The frontier has always had a special force in the American psyche; the dream of surviving it, of passing through the wilderness to the promised land, seems to strike a chord in the hearts of this continent's Anglo population.[4]

It is telling that these critics stress the installation's existential antiheroes and overlook images of other bodies depicted in one of the videos projected at the "Stations" set, which features 360-degree pans taken from El Paso/Juárez's pedestrian bridge.[5] The bridge is crowded with people, while below, through chain-link fence, the viewer sees *indocumentados* crossing the river on makeshift inner-tube rafts.

The bodies of border residents and panoramic views of urban El Paso/Juárez are nagging reminders that photographic "evidence" of the contemporary U.S.–Mexico border can rarely support the mythological vision of the border as a no-man's land sparsely populated by deviants and drifters. This latter border nonetheless appears to have been the early inspiration for Allen's project. Honky-tonk songs, written and recorded by Allen in the early 1970s, were the first installments in the *Juarez* cycle,

8. Terry Allen, *a simple story (Juarez)*, 1992. Installation detail: *The Perfect Ship*. Courtesy Wexner Center for the Arts, The Ohio State University, Columbus, Ohio. Commissioned project as part of an artist residency with funds from the Wexner Center Foundation. Photograph by Richard K. Loesch. Photograph courtesy of the Wexner Center.

songs like "Texican Badman": "in Juarez / Gonna meet me a fine señorita / Gonna tip her my hat when I meet her / Gonna take her out / And dine her on tortilla / And if you love her / You bought her / If you didn't you oughta / Get a little off that daughter / In Juarez."[6]

I begin with this example from Allen's *Juarez* project because it so vividly stages the extreme polarization of border images in U.S. popular culture that evolved during the project's own twenty-year history. The border featured in Allen's video is a familiar visual accompaniment to descriptions of the gnawing social issues affecting today's border cities, such as pollution, rapid urbanization, and immigration. The border of fiction and fantasy evoked by Allen's sets is the highly eroticized milieu of outlaws and whores, where embattled individuals confront themselves through confrontations with "the Other."

Many artists who explore U.S.–Mexico border issues have critiqued both of the stereotypical image repertoires captured by Allen's installation, often through repetition, hyperbole, parody, and other formal devices. "Border art" has become a common phrase to describe projects like Allen's, though it is difficult to define border art as a movement, because the term does not posit a shared political tendency, aesthetic project, or site of production. Some artists and critics, for example, celebrate the

9. Terry Allen, *a simple story (Juarez)*, 1992. Installation detail: *Stations*. Courtesy Wexner Center for the Arts, The Ohio State University, Columbus, Ohio. Commissioned project as part of an artist residency with funds from the Wexner Center Foundation. Photograph by Richard K. Loesch. Photograph courtesy of the Wexner Center.

U.S.–Mexico border's capacity to juxtapose and absorb disparate cultural elements, while others criticize the former perception as an appropriative fascination with the daily life and experience of border dwellers. Both the cosmopolitan and the regionalist position have played a role in the complex process of setting criteria for this genre. In exhibitions, curators formulate various responses as to whether border art describes art about the border, art by people living on the border, or simply art located on the border. In the case of *La Frontera,* an exhibition about the U.S.–Mexico border experience co-organized by the Centro Cultural de la Raza and the Museum of Contemporary Art, San Diego, concerns about the organizing role of the latter mainstream art institution led several prominent artists working in the region to decline representation in the show.[7] In comparison, artists from around the world are invited along with local artists to submit projects for *inSITE,* a large-scale exhibition of site-specific art that has taken place in 1992, 1994, and 1997. Playing upon the "sister cities" trope so prevalent during NAFTA negotiations, the exhibition is held in Tijuana and San Diego, with sponsorship coming from a combination of corporate-funded regional arts institutions as well as government sources.[8] The result, as George Yúdice has commented, "is an almost ironic combination of artworks that

10. Terry Allen, *a simple story (Juarez),* 1992. Installation detail: *Stations.* Courtesy Wexner Center for the Arts, The Ohio State University, Columbus, Ohio. Commissioned project as part of an artist residency with funds from the Wexner Center Foundation. Photograph by Richard K. Loesch. Photograph courtesy of the Wexner Center.

raise political issues about immigration, race, and national and cultural identity, and that garnish, so to speak, a celebration of dubious economic arrangements brought about by NAFTA."[9] Border art has also commonly found itself included as one tendency within much larger geographic or cultural frames, such as multicultural, Chicano/a, folk, Mexican, and pan-American art.[10]

For the purpose of this chapter, I use a content-based approach to border art because I am interested in examining recent permutations of two stereotypical "establishing shots" of the border: the fence and the river. In narrative film and video the establishing shot is typically a two- to three-second take of a building exterior or landscape that is inserted at the beginning of a scene. Rarely are establishing shots imbued with special meaning; in fact they are meant to be unobtrusive keys that help the viewer to locate action within a larger space, before the ensuing scene systematically fragments that space into smaller units through medium shots and close-ups. I use the phrase *establishing shot* liberally in the analysis that follows, referring to how the border as a place has been registered not only in film and video, but also in photography, literature, and other media.

In many recent images of the border, such as those featured in videos about NAFTA, corporate chain-link fences and waste-water canals have become prominent aspects of the mise-en-scène, indeed much more so than the low-key establishing shots typical of mainstream narrative film and video. Both chain-link fences and waste water can be related to more conventional establishing shots of the border that U.S. audiences have come to know through commercial cinema and popular culture—namely, panoramic views of the Rio Grande/Río Bravo and lengths of barbed wire fence extending across vacant landscapes. Through their fusion or conflation of national and corporate territories, the "new border establishing shots" explore the relationship between nation-states and transnational corporations, and in the process, document changing spatial configurations in the border region.

The Fence and the River in Art and Popular Culture

Throughout this century, the U.S.–Mexico border has taken on various guises in U.S. visual culture. While General Pershing chased Pancho Villa across Northern Mexico, U.S. postcard photographers represented the border as an obelisk-shaped boundary marker or an imaginary line drawn in the sand.[11] Narratives stressing the historical and social continuity of the border region, like Les Blanc's documentary film *Chulas Fronteras* (Beautiful borders) and Aristeo Brito's novel *El diablo en Texas* (The devil in Texas), challenged the obstacle posed by the national boundary through recurrence to tropes like the binational bridge and the ferry boat.[12] And Chicano/a scholars and activists have, in distinct historical periods, imagined communities called Aztlán and the Borderlands, which erased the border in the first instance, and valorized it as a liminal zone in the second.[13] In the contemporary era, generally speaking, the Rio Grande/Río Bravo and the fence are the two primary icons used to establish the location of a narrative in the border region. Their cultural entrenchment as constitutive of "the border" is perhaps most clearly witnessed in the way that they metonymically mark those Mexican workers who traverse them as either *mojados* ("wets") or *alambristas* ("wire-crossers").

For U.S. and Mexican audiences alike, the border fence has great symbolic currency. As one of Néstor García Canclini's *tijuanense* informants told him, "El alambre que separa a México de los Estados Unidos podría ser el principal monumento de la cultura en la frontera" ("The fence that separates Mexico from the United States could be the principal monument of culture on the border").[14] Chicano artist Willie Herrón used chain-link fence as a central element in his graphic design for the *Chicano Art: Resistance and Affirmation (CARA)* catalogue, which was produced in conjunction with the traveling art exhibition of the same name organized by UCLA's Wight Art Gallery. The chain-link leitmotif of the catalogue reclaims what is in most urban neighborhoods a commonplace marker of private property, and converts it into the emblem of a particular cultural experience. But Herrón and the curators made a distinction between international and intranational borders in their conceptual framework for the show.[15] Herrón introduced a section of artwork about civil liberties, for example, with an image of barbed wire, while he used chain-link fence to introduce a section featuring urban Chicano/a art. His iconography was echoed by some of the artists included in the show. Graphic posters by Rupert García (*¡Cesen Deportación!* 1973) and Malaquías Montoya (*Undocumented,* 1981), for example, both emphasized the harshness of barbed wire to protest the plight of undocumented workers (figure 11).[16] The group Asco on the other hand, of which Herrón was a founding member, featured chain-link fence in its 1990 installation at the Wight Art Gallery (included in the *CARA* show through photodocumentation).[17] In the Asco piece reproduced in the *CARA* catalogue, chain-link distances the spectator from a recessed space filled with media images and precariously balanced TV sets.

The national spectrum of Chicano/a art presented in the *CARA* catalogue gives the impression that the barbed wire border is slightly more hostile than the inner-city chain-link fence because the former represents the state, while the latter only represents private property. Barbed wire is an icon of the alienated *indocumentado* and the experience of crossing national borders, while the chain-link fence connotes both marginality within the nation and a communal experience focused around the barrio. A recent example from the art world that affirms this logic is the 1996 controversy involving a sculpture commissioned by the University of New Mexico from Chiricahua Apache artist Bob Haozous. His work about border crossings, entitled "Cultural Crossroads of the Americas," was approved in maquette form by the University, but the final version was rejected because the artist had added razor wire to the top of the piece, a thirty-foot-tall metal billboard structure featuring silhouetted pre-Colombian and modern urban images. According to the artist, the university wanted the piece to reflect all North American borders, including the Canadian one, while he wanted it to be a statement about the U.S.–Mexico border in particular.[18]

Other artists who treat the U.S.–Mexico border in their work do not uphold this distinction between domestic and international border markers, however. Chain-link is evidently the fence of choice for many border artists, although it is rarely used as a primary fencing material on the borderline itself. In fact, in 1987 photographer Peter Goin found that chain-link ran along no more than fifteen miles of the border's almost two-thousand-mile length.[19] It is not surprising that chain-link should be so common in art about the border experience, because as border cities become increasingly urbanized,

11. Malaquías Montoya, *Undocumented,* 1981, silkscreen, 30⅛ × 22 inches. Photograph courtesy of the artist.

12. Peter Goin, "Because of careful ranch management, grasses survive in the Animas Valley on the United States side of the line (to the right). Overgrazing on the Mexican side encourages creosote (greasewood) bushes to replace the grasses. This view looking west from Monument No. 91 illustrates the visual irony." *Tracing the Line: A Photographic Survey of the Mexican-American Border,* limited edition artist book, 1987. Photograph courtesy of the artist.

they have come to share much of the same spatial imagery that was attractive to groups like ASCO in East Los Angeles. When Terry Allen was interviewed about all the chain-link in his installation, for example, he talked about it as an icon of "the new border":

> I remember the first time I went to Juárez, to the border, those fences weren't there . . . on the bridge and whatever . . . and now it's just like this incredible visual . . . all the chain-link fencing . . . You can't look at anything without a grid kind of being in front of you.[20]

Many artists who work with U.S.–Mexico border imagery explore the metaphoric possibilities of chain-link as both barrier and permeable interface, as abstract grid and everyday landscape. Peter Goin's 1987 photoessay, *Tracing the Line: A Photographic Survey of the Mexican/American Border,* scrupulously catalogued the entire length of the border, and exposed many of the fence's vulnerabilities in the process (figures 12–15). Other well-known photographers of the border such as Don Bartletti, Douglas Kent Hall, Jay Dusard, Max Aguilera-Hellweg, Jeff Wall, Susan Meiselas, and Sebastião Salgado have used the fence in their photographic compostions, often to foreground interactions between Mexicans and Anglos (figure 16).[21] The Border Art Workshop/

13. Peter Goin, "Today, no federal, state or local governments have any concerted policy regarding the border fences. The United States section of the International Boundary and Water Commission constructed fences in a cattle control program that began in 1935 and terminated in the 1950s. At that time, funding was withdrawn and responsibility for established fences was either transferred to local ranchers or abandoned. Most of the fence is barbed wire, usually three to five strand. There are sections of chain-link fence but no more than fifteen miles total along the entire border. This photograph shows a 'drive-through,' ¼ mile west of the port-of-entry at Naco, Arizona, and Sonora. Smugglers use this to avoid the *mordida,* literally translated as 'bite' (bribe), but it is monitored by the United States Border Patrol using ground sensors. The view looks into Mexico." *Tracing the Line: A Photographic Survey of the Mexican-American Border,* limited edition artist book, 1987. Photograph courtesy of the artist.

Taller de Arte Fronterizo (BAW/TAF) of San Diego/Tijuana often highlights border conflict and collaboration in installations and performances featuring chain-link. In BAW/TAF installations dating from the mid-1980s, the chain-link fence appeared as a Moebius strip, as an object of contemplation for "disinterested" spectators, and as constituting the very body of the *alambrista* (figures 17–19).[22] The chain-link fence was set ablaze on the cover of BAW/TAF's 1991 catalogue (figure 20), and stood amidst a garbage-strewn wasteland on the cover of Terry Allen's 1992 catalogue for *a simple story (Juarez).*[23]

Together, the fence and the river have played an important role in the way that maps of the North American continent have been drawn in this century. During the U.S. militarization of the border at the time of the Mexican Revolution, the continent

14. Peter Goin, "View of the border line and fence at the port-of-entry at San Ysidro and Tijuana, looking west. The lines of cars are waiting to enter the United States." *Tracing the Line: A Photographic Survey of the Mexican-American Border,* limited edition artist book, 1987. Photograph courtesy of the artist.

of North America was anthropomorphized through visual gags in which Mexico became the lower body joined to the United States as the upper body, while the border-line served as a geographical waistline (see chapter 3).[24] In the NAFTA era, one essayist recast these hierarchical territories as a "Freudian map," in which Canada was the superego, the United States was the ego, and Mexico was the unconscious.[25] Guillermo Gómez-Peña's 1985 poem (revised 1995) entitled "Freefalling toward a Borderless Future" drew a similar map in which the gonads once again fell to Mexico:

> Standing on the map of my political desires
> I toast to a borderless future
> *(I raise my glass of wine toward the moon)*
> with . . .
> our Alaskan hair
> our Canadian head
> our US torso
> our Mexican genitalia
> our Central American cojones
> our Caribbean sperm
> our South American legs . . .[26]

15. Peter Goin, "The westernmost marker, Monument No. 258, rests in Border Field State Park at the Pacific Ocean." *Tracing the Line: A Photographic Survey of the Mexican-American Border,* limited edition artist book, 1987. Photograph courtesy of the artist.

According to Rolando J. Romero, the association of Mexico with the lower body is still very prevalent in contemporary U.S. popular culture, as in the double entendre of Taco Bell's advertising slogan, "Make a run for the border." The command is ambivalent, invoking at once stereotypes of Mexico as filthy and unsafe, while also urging U.S. consumers to liberate their repressed oral and anal erotic drives through sampling Taco Bell's cuisine.[27] Romero illustrates his argument with a lengthy passage from Joseph Wambaugh's police novel, *Lines and Shadows,* in which the border is described as the point where the United States and Mexico meet one another "asshole to asshole." In this passage, *indocumentados* passing from Mexico to the United States through a drainage pipe are referred to as "turds," and the flow of human beings back and forth between the countries is compared to diarrhea.[28]

Such scatological imagery comes up repeatedly when any number of invasions from the south are discussed in U.S. media. The image of Mexico as lower body is in turn associated with Mexico's food and drinking water, and with the much publicized pollution that plagues the Rio Grande/Río Bravo and border *acequias* in recent years.[29] These tropes have also been taken up by some border writers and videographers in order to denounce the underlying political and economic factors that foster disease and poverty in Mexico. Images of shit, death, and organic waste, for example, are recurrent in the work of Luis Alberto Urrea, a San Diego/Tijuana-based journalist and activist, whose two chronicles of life among Tijuana's poorest residents, *Across the Wire* and *By the Lake of Sleeping Children*, have done much to call attention to issues of social justice in the border region.[30] Urrea's compassion for the people about whom he writes is counterbalanced by a hard-boiled, often dryly humorous prose and lack of sentimentality in his depiction of daily life on the border. His frequent asides to the reader and foregrounding of his role as translator to non-Spanish speakers clearly indicate that he writes for a U.S.-based audience that knows little about

16. Don Bartletti, *Uneasy Neighbors*, 1988, selenium print. "Robert Shade, a homeowners' representative, installed barbed wire and security lights on the perimeter of a housing development. Irritated by the presence of migrant workers from a makeshift squatters' camp, he keeps a gun by his door. Encinitas, California, May 2, 1988." Photograph courtesy of the artist.

this world and can be ruffled by descriptions such as this one of a sign in a bathroom at a Tijuana orphanage:

PLEASE DON'T SHIT ON THE FLOOR / PLEASE DON'T WIPE YOUR ASS WITH YOUR FINGERS / PLEASE DON'T WIPE YOUR FINGERS ON THE WALL

Ancient brown fingerprints and smears angle away from this notice, trailing to faint shadow. They look like paintings of comets, of fireworks.[31]

In a more self-conscious and historically oriented manner than Urrea's writing, Debbie Nathan's essay, "Love in the Time of Cholera: Waiting for Free Trade," examines the

17. David Avalos, Eriberto Oribol, and Michael Schnorr, *Border Realities III*, February 1987. Photograph by Michael Schnorr. Photograph courtesy of BAW/TAF.

erotic and repulsive fascination with the Rio Grande/Río Bravo; the author associates the spread of contagion northward with the spread of free trade southward.[32] Nathan, an El Paso–based journalist and activist, intricately weaves vignettes detailing the response to free trade on the part of journalists, health, and business professionals.[33] The framing narrative is about the author's relationship with Perla, a fruit vendor from Juárez who, over the course of her four-year relationship with the author, has developed the propensity to interrupt Nathan and her husband during their moments of love-making. This time Perla seeks Nathan out because her son Chuyito has been sick for days with diarrhea. "Can this be the famous cholera?" Perla asks Nathan.

Throughout the essay, Nathan foregrounds her own relative advantage in the

transactions she makes with Perla—loans that will never be repaid, limes and avoca-
dos bought from Perla to garnish tonight's supper, an old washing machine that finds
a new home in Perla's one-room, cinder-block house built at the foot of a TV anten-
na on a Juárez hillside. Perhaps most important of these transactions in terms of this
essay is the service that Perla performs as Nathan's informant and guide. At one
point, Nathan decides to make the daily crossing with Perla from Juárez to El Paso.
The women change clothes behind bushes before entering the river. Nathan writes,

18. Michael Schnorr, *Fence "Border line boundary,"* January 1987. Photograph by Sudabeh
Balakhani. Photograph courtesy of BAW/TAF.

We all scooted behind thorny bushes and weeds to change, and immediately I
noticed that among the bushes, human and animal urine and feces were everywhere. I hopped around barefoot, trying to avoid them. It was impossible. I felt
nauseous. I wanted to wash but the river was no relief. A rat floated past. We
crossed, discarded our rags, then ran across I-10. I was wild with fear for the
children. We made it, though, then entered a wet sewer tunnel, bent over like
crones, stumbling through the dark. Someone spotted a light and we climbed
up through the hole. Suddenly we were in my neighborhood.[34]

When Nathan's essay was published in January 1993, cholera had arrived on the border, and NAFTA was soon to follow. According to the author, by that time every ace-
quia in Juárez had tested positive for the cholera bacterium.[35] Nathan's essay is an

attempt to show how the transformations that have taken place along the border in recent decades might be registered through an experimental and fragmented writing style.[36] The border-crossing passage, nevertheless, is central to the essay. It enables the author to link the social conditions of Perla's Juárez to those of Nathan's El Paso, and this experience provokes the narrator to think through the relationships of individual actors within a global economic system. For me, Nathan's essay serves as a bridge between the visual strategies taken up by the border artists discussed previously and the didactic impulse of videos about the border produced by grassroots organizations.

19. Sara Jo Berman and Michael Schnorr, *Border Realities II*, February 1986. Installation view: *Aztep*. Photograph by Philip Brookman. Photograph courtesy of BAW/TAF.

Spin-offs of the Fence and the River: Videos of the NAFTA Era

Benedict Anderson proposes that the representation of a world in which spatially dispersed events occur simultaneously and yet are causally related to one another is concomitant with the consolidation of national literatures. He bases this idea upon his theorization of literate citizens as individuals bound to a given geographical unit through their mutual relationship of horizontal fraternal comradeship.[37] Nathan ironically appeals to a conceptual framework similar to that of Anderson's nation in her essay, but she does so in order to imagine a very different community: her border is at once an international and a local space, and her relationship with Perla is not based on the solidarity of male citizens but rather on the uneven economic relations of female neighbors. The spatial and social contiguity of border metropolises like El Paso/Juárez makes them a logical place from which to imagine such cross-border alliances and to question nationalist projects.

In the last decade, however, the impulse to organize across borders has been emanating from other parts of North America as well, spurred on by resistance to the 1989 U.S.–Canada Free Trade Agreement (USCFTA) and, more recently, to NAFTA. Cathryn Thorup of the Center for U.S.–Mexican Studies has described the 1990s as a new era of U.S.–Mexico relations in which

20. Michael Schnorr, *Burning Fence,* 1991, wood, cloth and gasoline, 8 × 26 feet. Photograph by Lars Gustafsson. Photograph courtesy of BAW/TAF.

> it is possible that conflict may become more class-, issue-, and interest-based [rather] than bilateral in nature. Instead of "U.S." interests facing off against "Mexican" interests on a given issue, a constellation of U.S. and Mexican interest groups will confront an opposing constellation of U.S. and Mexican interest groups.[38]

As the decade draws to an end, Thorup's prediction for increasing transnational organization describes the path taken by many nongovernmental organizations, labor, ethnic, and single-issue movements in the United States and Mexico. Transnationalism, however, has not completely superseded the bilateral model of conflict and resolution.

International organization on the part of progressive and grassroots organizations is a necessary response to transnational capital's flight to Mexico and other low-wage havens in the wake of the world financial crisis of the 1970s. This flight witnessed businesses recycling strategies that were already quite familiar on a domestic level, such as outsourcing, heightened division of skilled and unskilled labor, and tiered wage scales. The old technique of whipsawing—that is, pitting the laborers of one plant against those of another in order to force wage cuts[39]—has crossed national borders, so that capital easily mobilizes racist and nationalist rhetoric to turn labor forces against one another, rather than against their employers. In order to resist these developments, activists themselves face the challenge of building geographically dispersed networks.

Both labor and management increasingly use video as an organizing tool in these struggles because of its relatively low cost and accessibility, and its ability to reach illiterate audiences across linguistic boundaries. In its most promising manifestations the turn toward video has permitted workers on both sides of the U.S.–Mexico border to become producers of their own narratives and to forge ties with workers in other locations.[40] Throughout the continent, over forty documentary videos (and some films) about NAFTA and border issues have been produced in the last twenty years, and many more continue to be made (see the appendix). Their producers are independent documentarists, educators, labor unions, and religious, environmental, and women's groups, many of whom are affiliated with trinational coalitions.

As with border art, this body of videos may be seen as symptomatic of a growing interest in the border region and NAFTA rather than as evidence of a unified movement. Although the works often share common visual and rhetorical strategies, significant differences exist among them in terms of production, distribution, and consumption. The videos range in production values from slick, high-budget documentaries that have aired on public television to short subjects intended for church and union-hall viewing. Their scope too, varies from those like *The Global Assembly Line,* which present a systematic analysis of transformations in the global economy,[41] to shorts such as *What's the Cost of Your Blouse?,* an eighteen-minute video narrated entirely through still photographs, that recounts three local struggles among workers in San Francisco, El Paso, and Nogales, Sonora.[42]

It is important to distinguish among the political histories of these videos, including their sources of funding and the activities and orientation of their creators, a subject that goes beyond the scope of this chapter. Briefly, some of the videos document "solidarity visits" to Mexico by U.S. and Canadian delegations, while others result from long-term activist projects in the border region. This distinction loosely corresponds to historical markers, also. While the videos produced prior to NAFTA's passage tend to refer to the border in the context of binational politics, more recent productions often chronicle campaigns by border activist groups regarding specific issues such as labor, the environment, and immigration. My comments focus primarily on the pre-NAFTA videos. The year 1994 marks an important watershed for these productions because it was an election year in Mexico. The videos produced prior to this date support a continental political program that favors the Partido de la Revolución Democrática (PRD), liberal U.S. Democrats, and the Canadian Liberal Party, and opposes Salinas de Gortari, Reagan, Bush, Clinton, and Mulroney. The 1994 PRD presidential candidate Cuauhtémoc Cárdenas (currently Regente of Mexico City) in particular emerges as a potential savior of Mexico from total colonization by the United States. The conclusion of Dermot and Carla Begley's *Mexico: For Sale* presents an extreme example of this position. The closing sequence features a medium close-up of Cárdenas in slow motion as he makes his way through a crowd of followers, and then cuts to a close-up of Emiliano Zapata's face as the last lines of the "Corrido de Libre Comercio" drift by: "Ándale prietita, hay que zapatear / Que si no hay comercio siempre en México es igual" ("Go on little dark girl, you have to dance / If there's no trade, it's still the same in Mexico").[43]

Unfortunately, many of the videos find it difficult to escape the restrictive binary logic of mainstream NAFTA debates outlined in the previous chapter, in which free trade and protectionism were posed as the only two alternatives for citizens in all three countries. Instead they combine populist elements of both of these options in rather contradictory fashions. This ambiguous political stance is particularly true of the Canadian productions and certain U.S. productions embraced by the mainstream labor movement. The videos marshal international solidarity across borders in the interest of establishing a mutually beneficial nationalism that would ultimately leave borders firmly in place and pressure runaway shops located on the border to come "home." Bruce Campbell, a former research analyst for the Canadian Labor Congress, summarizes this sort of "friendly protectionism" when he argues that

> a different arrangement [from NAFTA] would have to attach *primacy to the rights of national development over the rights of transnational corporations.* It would have to foster upward convergence of social and environmental standards instead of a . . . dynamic which pits worker against worker, community against community [emphasis mine].[44]

All of these videos base their forecasts about NAFTA in part upon an interpretation of the U.S.–Mexico border region. One filmmaker, determined to make an objective documentary about NAFTA, told me that it was much easier for him to find articulate anti-NAFTA spokespersons for his film than pro-NAFTA ones, because the anti-NAFTA side could draw upon thirty years of documentation about the Border Industrialization Program to back up its arguments.[45] Many of the videos dramatize delegations from the United States and Canada making "fact-finding" trips to border maquiladoras and *colonias* in order to better understand economic transformations in their own regions (figure 21). No matter what local struggles these videos address, they share a common tendency to portray the U.S.–Mexico border as a prototype for the future economic development of the continent.

Primitivo Rodríguez of the American Friends Service Committee outlines this perspective succinctly in the documentary *Leaving Home*: "What we witness at the border is what we will see more and more all over the place, so the border is in a sense one of the greatest, nearest laboratories of what the future might provide."[46] Although Rodríguez makes his comment within the context of border environmental activism, his words echo those of people in academic disciplines such as cultural studies who, like Néstor García Canclini, have found in the border region "uno de los mayores laboratorios de la posmodernidad" ("one of the greatest laboratories of postmodernity").[47] The laboratory metaphor signals a certain intellectual frame of reference belonging to many academic think tanks that have mushroomed in the border region in the last thirty years with emphases on quantitative social scientific

21. Waterfill Colonia, Ciudad Juárez, Chihuahua, Mexico, 1994. A group from a Border Justice conference visits *colonia* residents. The conference was held in nearby Sunland Park, New Mexico and was sponsored by the Southwest Network of Environmental and Economic Justice and by the National Council of Churches. Photograph by Jeffry D. Scott. Copyright Jeffry D. Scott/Impact Visuals.

research and public policy formulation. San Diego–based artist David Avalos noted with some irony in his essay contributed to the *La Frontera* catalogue that it took the foundation of two high-profile research institutions, the University of California's Center for U.S.–Mexican Studies in San Diego and the Tijuana-based Colegio de la Frontera Norte, to bring border issues to the attention of a wider public.[48]

By appropriating the border-as-laboratory image, the videos replicate the observer/ observed dynamic of much traditional documentary cinema, in which the testimony of local witnesses is mediated through "expert" talking heads, and both of these in turn are subsumed by a voice-over narrator's authoritative commentary. Often in their ambitious attempt to establish a "North American" oppositional language about labor and environmental abuses, the videos portray the border region as the worst-case scenario. Humanitarian arguments about fair trade and "what's best for Mexicans" are intercut with imagery that depicts the Mexican side of the border as abject. At times, the voyeurism of U.S. and Canadian observers in these narratives panders to sensationalism, as in Repeal the Deal Productions' *We Can Say No!* in which a delegate from Canada recounts through melodramatic voice-over that on a "fact-finding" trip to the border,

> we saw a lagoon of black, bubbling toxic waste created from open dumping by a group of corporations in an industrial park. We followed it to where it met up with an open ditch full of untreated raw sewage and to where this toxic soup ran into what was a small river, past squatters' camps, where children covered in open sores drank Pepsi Cola out of baby bottles.[49]

Rarely is a native of the upper or middle class (save Salinas) seen in these videos; Mexico is most often personified in stock shots of the "poor but dignified people."

As in the work of the artists discussed previously, the videos foreground the river and the fence to distinguish Mexican territory from that of the United States, along with a host of clichéd auxiliary signifiers such as national flags, musical motifs, cowboy hats versus sombreros, and so on. But the videos also introduce two second-tier icons related to the fence and the river, namely, the corporate fence and *aguas negras* (waste water or sewage). The international fence and the Rio Grande/Río Bravo demarcate national space, while the latter two signifiers divide *colonias* from maquiladoras on the Mexican sides of border cities. In many of these videos, the distinction between national and corporate boundary lines collapses altogether, or the importance of national borders becomes secondary to the boundaries of factories and industrial parks. In *Leaving Home,* for example, a highly compressed image superimposes the names of *Fortune* 500 companies doing business in Mexico against a background of chain-link fence, through which one can see one of the international bridges connecting Mexico and the United States.

The chain-link fence is also a focal point where ambivalence about continental solidarity becomes manifest. In the case of the NAFTA videos, corporate fences come to figure prominently in the narratives for very obvious practical reasons. Camera crews—especially anti-NAFTA ones—are not generally permitted to film inside maquiladoras, so the videographers shoot the outside of the factory through the fence, or they interview workers from a particular plant against the fence in front of their place of employment.[50] At any rate, shooting the corporate compounds of such familiar names as Zenith, Ford, and Green Giant as though they were fortresses or citadels puts U.S. spectators in the rather ironic position of constantly gazing at a U.S.-identified space from which they are barred access, while being situated in a space coded by the video as being "Mexican." This dynamic is particularly evident in a video entitled *Stepan Chemical: The Poisoning of a Mexican Community*, distributed by the San Antonio–based Coalition for Justice in the Maquiladoras, and produced by Ed Feigen of the AFL-CIO.[51] (This is the same video that Ross Perot brandished before Al Gore in order to shame the "environmentalist" vice president in the November 1993 NAFTA debate.) *Stepan Chemical* is an exposé about groundwater contamination in a Matamoros *colonia* called Privada Uniones by a manufacturing plant of the U.S.–owned Stepan Chemical Company. The plant literally borders the homes of Privada Uniones residents, and has been blamed for an epidemic of health problems including anencephaly, a birth defect which causes babies to be born without brains.[52] The camera work illustrates the proximity of the two spaces constantly, through rack focus, high-angle pans taken from rooftops that sweep from factory to *colonia,* and hidden camera footage of illegal toxic waste dumping by Stepan, shot through chain-link fence from the backyards of Privada Uniones homes. About halfway through the video, the camera cuts to a high-contrast still of the Stepan fence with the menacing subtitle, "El Lado Oscuro de la Frontera" ("The Dark Side of the Border"). Playing with a language familiar to U.S. audiences, where the border is often portrayed as seamy and lawless, the Stepan Chemical video suggests that the dark side of the border is to be found within the plant's boundaries and back in Chicago, where Stepan Chemical portrays itself as a company with a conscience, and the Stepan family is active in Democratic Party politics and philanthropic causes.

The videos do not always portray corporate citadels as impregnable. Cinefocus Canada's video *NAFTA: Playing with a Volatile Substance* and the American Labor Education Center's *$4 a Day? No Way!* both feature footage of plant occupations, in which workers are shown dancing, cheering, and decorating the fences that surround their factories.[53] The latter video is about a movement on the part of Mexican workers at Ford's Cuautitlán plant to disaffiliate from the *oficialista* Confederación de Trabajadores Mexicanos (CTM) and to elect their own union representatives. When CTM-hired thugs dressed in Ford uniforms showed up at the plant on January 8, 1990, they shot ten Ford workers, killing one, Cleto Nigmo. The video's theme of "extending hands across borders" refers to the trinational organizing efforts in the automotive industry undertaken by progressive elements within the U.S., Canadian, and Mexican labor movements in the wake of Nigmo's murder.

As with the fence imagery, the videos demonstrate considerable compression between images of the Rio Grande/Río Bravo and those of the *aguas negras,* or raw sewage flowing from border industries and *colonias* (figure 22). Along certain stretches of the border, as in Ciudad Juárez, a concrete waste water canal runs parallel to the river channel itself. Almost all of the NAFTA videos feature a segment on environmental degradation of the border region, and others make environmental issues their focal point. One of these, entitled *Dirty Business: Food Exports to the United States,* is quite well-known and received an award at the 1991 National Educational Film and Video Festival.[54]

The framing narrative of the documentary depicts a middle-class couple in a U.S. supermarket selecting some broccoli. The narrator's voice-over introduction questions whether U.S. consumers really know where their food comes from. Then the film cuts to a shot of child laborers on the back of a cabbage truck in Irapuato, Guanajuato, in southern Mexico, where Birdseye, Green Giant, and other food companies have relocated much of their frozen vegetable empires, in order to take advantage of the long growing season and cheap wages. By the documentary's close, we

22. Ciudad Juárez, Chihuahua, Mexico, 1991. A factory worker leaves his house for work. Note the proximity of the factories to the houses. Photograph by Jim Saah. Copyright Jim Saah/Impact Visuals.

learn that these companies use *aguas negras* to irrigate their crops, along with a great deal of information about child labor, diarrhea and parasites, slaughterhouse run-off, and other problems endemic to Irapuato.

Dirty Business subtly concludes twice: first, with a voice-over statement addressed to "everyone" and second, with another addressed to paranoid U.S. consumers. The narrator states that "protections for children and the environment, decent wages and living conditions, and safe, clean food should be basic rights for everyone," as the film returns the viewer to the supermarket of the opening sequence and continues, "As multinational companies continue exporting from this polluted environment, consumers may well wonder about the quality, safety, and social costs of food production in Mexico."

Dirty Business stems from the context of nearly a decade of labor struggles taking place in Watsonville, California, the "frozen food capital of the United States," around the issues of wage cuts and job relocation on the part of the big food processors. In contrast to other NAFTA videos that concentrate on job loss among Anglo and African-American workers in the U.S. manufacturing sector, the Watsonville workers are primarily Mexicans and Chicanos/as with very close ties to Mexican communities in the United States and Mexico. The video is the result of a solidarity visit to Irapuato on the part of Watsonville's frozen food and canning workers, who found it difficult at the time to forge an extensive network because their Mexican counterparts had no union.[55] *Dirty Business* missed a potentially interesting angle in declining to explore the equivocal position that Chicanos/as occupied throughout the NAFTA debates: pitted against Mexicans for relatively low-wage and labor-intensive jobs, on the one hand, and promoted as a vital link in cross-border organizing efforts, on the other.[56]

The narrative of *Dirty Business* never reflects upon its own production history, and perhaps this is one reason why organized labor found it easy to endorse the video in its efforts to lobby Congress for its "Buy American" protectionist agenda. In early November 1993, right before the NAFTA vote, I was residing in Milwaukee, and my Congressman, Jerry Kleczka, sent a newsletter to me featuring a still photograph and a case study lifted straight from the video. "I just can't seem to get the picture you see on this page out of my mind," he wrote. "This is the Jolly Green Giant—or Gigante Verde—a symbol of the forces at work luring American companies south of the border."[57] In this broader U.S. context, the three-way metonymical association that the video draws among Mexican labor, Mexican products, and *aguas negras* becomes very striking, as it once again invokes scatological images of Mexico culled from popular stereotypes. Ross Perot, who as I have noted was also influenced by an anti-NAFTA video, made this association in his inimitable way during the NAFTA debate:

> When you look . . . at the man who works for Zenith in Mexico and you compare him to his counterpart who works for Zenith in the United States, this poor man makes $8.50 a day. You know what his dream is? To someday have an outhouse. Do you know what his big dream is? To someday have running water.[58]

Border Traffic: People, Goods, Ideas

During the 1992 U.S. election campaigns, fear of Mexican immigration to the United States was invoked by both Democrats and Republicans, who resorted to coded (and at times explicit) racism in order both to justify *and* to denounce NAFTA. In the media coverage of NAFTA prior to the Congressional vote in November 1993, free-trade proponents argued that exporting low-wage jobs to Mexico would keep Mexicans from "stealing" U.S. jobs, while protectionists simply wanted to dig trenches and build walls to keep Mexicans out.[59] As I have argued in the case of *Dirty Business,* however, fear of immigrants is only one example of a larger phenomenon, for there is considerable anxiety in the United States about *anything* identified as Mexican crossing the border.

In her essay "Passports," Susan Buck-Morss traces this ambivalence about borders and migrants to medieval European anxieties about the plague, which through the centuries became mapped onto modern industrial demands for cheap migrant labor. The precursor to the visa, according to Buck-Morss, was the *pestpass,* which permitted healthy people to enter communities during epidemics. Passports have their origin in the same era, when they were developed as a means of controlling military desertion. Buck-Morss writes,

> In the application of this ideology [associating aliens with contamination] to control migrant labor, there emerges most clearly the structural contradiction which is inherent in the modern age: Throughout the process of industrialization, capital has needed a highly mobile labor force, and the more docile and submissive the better. Increasingly, as labor has organized to resist exploitation, an absolutely crucial source of supply has been foreign migrants whose precarious status as non-citizens has made them willing to accept whatever the conditions or wages they are given.[60]

Buck-Morss goes on to argue that passports really took on their present form after World War I, as fear of communist revolution within industrialized nations that had ethnically and racially diverse labor forces, like the United States, arose among capitalist classes. One strategy of President Wilson and the League of Nations was to make Bolshevism, an international movement, seem like a national movement through the creation of formal border apparatuses. Buck-Morss explains that this transformation was achieved through a dissimulation of sorts:

> By creating a place of passport control and a practice of passing through it, it gave the appearance that state boundaries were substantive, that they really existed—that a particular state apparatus "owned" a part of the world, in the same way that a private citizen his home, a capitalist his business, a farmer his field, a person his or her own body—except that the state owned all of these first.[61]

The invention of borders as we now know them paved the way for the deportation and persecution of workers in the United States who expressed "foreign" ideas, such as communism and anarchism. In Buck-Morss's words, "Class warfare was recast as international warfare. This was the legacy of Versailles."[62] It bears remembering that another backdrop of the Peace Conference in Versailles, from the North American perspective, was the Mexican Revolution, which not only threatened extensive U.S. and European investments in Mexico, but also marked the first large-scale exodus of poor Mexican immigrants to the United States. During this period, Mexicans joined Chinese as "undesirable aliens" entering the United States from Mexico, and precursors to the Border Patrol were established as federal institutions separate from the

Immigration Service (now the Immigration and Naturalization Service). A 1919 anec-
dote from the biography of Jeff Milton, one of the Border Patrol's early heroic figures, illustrates the extent to which the origin and mission of today's Border Patrol
arose from an interpretation of borders as both physical and ideological barriers.
While serving as a Mounted Chinese Inspector for the Immigration Service in the
Arizona/Sonora desert, Milton was told to report immediately to Ellis Island where
he was charged with guarding Emma Goldman, Alexander Berkman, and "247 more
alien radicals who were so sure that Revolutionary Russia was the promised land."
He eventually escorted them by boat to Hangö, Finland, before returning to duty in
Arizona.[63]

Citing empirical evidence, economist Paul Krugman challenges the notion that
the state and private property can be conflated through an analogical model. He
begins his book about the fashion of pseudo-economic theory in the era of free trade,
Pop Internationalism, with a criticism of the Clinton administration's rhetoric of
"competitiveness" among nations. Such a claim, argues Krugman, rests upon a facile
assumption that both nations and corporations play a zero-sum game. Krugman
counters, "The bottom line for a corporation is literally its bottom line: if a corporation cannot afford to pay its workers, suppliers, and bondholders, it will go out of
business." He continues, "Countries, on the other hand, do not go out of business.
They may be happy or unhappy with their economic performance, but they have no
well-defined bottom line."[64] The willingness of many prominent politicians, advisers,
academics, and voters to believe such rhetoric, nevertheless, suggests that the state
puts on a rather convincing show of masquerading as a corporation. If borders are
one example of the state's attempt to dissimulate private property, then one could
view the NAFTA-era border establishing shots as exposing a type of capitalist spatial
organization that has been fundamental to the existence of the border apparatus in
the modern era. The NAFTA videos foreground the latent duality of borders, which
would cast them at once as the communal property of the body politic and as the do-
main of a state that regulates ("owns") the movement of its citizens. Instead of showing a brief establishing shot of a single border, the videos create a spatial patchwork
of fences and rivers traversing the border region and dividing "foreign" from "local,"
and "workers" from "factories."[65] The spatial dispersal of national boundaries and
their diminished presence vis-à-vis transnational capital along the U.S.–Mexico border does not indicate that the nation-state is defunct, as those who have noted the
implementation of immigration blockades along the border will attest. But it may
mean that nation-states will work in tandem with capital to enforce a division of
labor even among different borders.

While the U.S.–Mexico border became increasingly industrialized in the early
1990s, the Mexico-Guatemala border was apparently selected as the avant-"rear-
garde" of U.S. immigration control. The Mexican government reported that in 1993
it deported a record number of Central Americans (deportations financed in part by

U.S. funds), while the U.S. Immigration and Naturalization Service sent its own agents to train the Guatemalan police. In the words of a priest who aids refugees on the Mexico-Guatemala border: "Tecún Umán [Guatemalan border city] has been converted into a hell, where everything you can imagine is permitted. . . . There is prostitution, alcoholism, drug addiction, money laundering . . ."[66] Another priest states, "There are more [human rights] violations here in one day than there are in a year [on the U.S.–Mexico border]."[67] The "old border" establishing shots of Terry Allen's sets have not disappeared; they have simply become the "new border" establishing shots farther south.

Chapter 3

U.S.–Mexico Border Conflict in U.S. Popular Culture: Recodifications of the Revolution and the Porfiriato

Hollywood's Mexico consists of the U.S.–Mexican border as a specific region and the rest of Mexico as an undifferentiated mass.

—Carlos E. Cortés[1]

The Mexican Revolution of 1910–1920 was concomitant with the rise of certain forms of visual mass media in the United States, such as feature-length films, newsreels, and picture postcards. Within such media coverage of the Revolution, images of the border figured prominently. Many key battles were fought on the Mexican sides of border twin cities, because they were strategically valuable points of entry for arms from the United States as well as collection sites for customs duties.[2] The images of the U.S.–Mexico border of this era mark the emergence of an allegorical way of seeing the region that, I will argue, continues to be invoked to this day. According to this allegorical model, the border is a synecdoche of the nations it divides. That is, developments on the border are perceived to be symptomatic of the overall status of U.S.–Mexico relations, and the importance of border events is presented from the point of view of national actors rather than local inhabitants. This process of marking the border as an internationally strategic site also involved representing it as a militarized zone, rather than merely as a haven for individual deviants, as it had been portrayed in the Western genre.

Turning to this transitional period in Mexican history is also useful for periodizing the historical transformations of border images. In this chapter, I will consider the argument voiced by some Mexican intellectuals that the last three decades represent a "return of the Porfiriato," that is, the three-decade-long dictatorship of Porfirio Díaz, which was toppled by the Mexican Revolution of 1910–1920. The comparison of the two historical periods implies that the futuristic "new border" of the post-1965 era is a resurgence of the "old border" of the pre-Revolutionary era. Or, as Luis Alberto Urrea so aptly puts it in *By the Lake of Sleeping Children,* "It is still 1896 in Tijuana. And it is also 2025."[3] I will argue that in many ways this dual temporality has been acknowledged in U.S. mass media by the recycling and recoding of visual images from the Revolutionary era rather than from the Porfiriato proper.

In analyzing the way that border affairs became subsumed under national and global levels, it must be remembered that the U.S.–Mexico border at the time of the Mexican Revolution was relatively new, having only been drawn in 1848 and 1853. Historians Linda B. Hall and Don M. Coerver have described the Revolutionary period along the border from a regional perspective:

> At the heart of problems along the border was the "absence of an authentic concept of a boundary between the two nations." While diplomacy and military activity had gone a long way toward defining the boundary, much of the border area constituted a geographical, cultural, and economic unit. The Rio Grande was the only major geographical feature that could be used to establish international limits, and even it did not constitute a major physical barrier. In addition, periodic changes in the channel of the river produced a series of diplomatic squabbles lasting more than a century.[4]

For U.S. citizens in regions removed from the conflict, mass media coverage of the Mexican Revolution provided the first photographic images, not only of Mexico and Mexicans but also of newly acquired U.S. territory. When Villa suddenly became the villain, the attention of U.S. media producers turned toward manufacturing differences in a region which was, as Hall and Coerver argue, historically constituted as "a geographical, cultural, and economic unit." An arsenal of well-worn binary oppositions was called into play to distinguish the U.S. from the Mexican side of the border, above all Anglo/Mexican, masculine/feminine, civilization/barbarism, and master/servant. In this respect, it was not just Pershing and Villa, but also the border, as a marker of difference, that became an overnight celebrity.

The Columbus Raid and Its Portrayal in Film and Photography

SEE *your flag across the border to punish those who have insulted it.*
—Advertisement for a 1916 U.S.-produced newsreel[5]

Pancho Villa's raid on Columbus, New Mexico, in 1916 and the ensuing U.S. Punitive Expedition in Mexico, led by General John J. Pershing, have not been the subject of many contemporary portrayals of the Revolution in U.S. popular media. Perhaps this is due to sensitivity over the fact that the United States did not succeed in capturing Villa. As recently as 1959 Hollywood produced a movie about the Punitive Expedition which had Pershing victorious over Villa.[6] Several recent treatments of these events do challenge the way that the raid and the expedition have been portrayed in the past, but they do not amount to a revisionist trend. Although the more recent texts continue to disavow the fact that the United States "lost" to Villa, they portray the U.S. army rather than Villa as the villain. In addition, they quite literally return to earlier representations of the U.S.–Mexico border through devices such as collage and film clips. Before discussing these newer treatments of the Columbus Raid and the Punitive Expedition, I will provide some historical background regarding the raid and coverage of it by mass media.

Prior to the Columbus Raid, Pancho Villa was an ally of the United States and a popular figure in U.S. film and picture postcards. The charismatic general even signed an exclusive film contract with Mutual Film Corporation for $25,000, which allowed the company to film him in battle.[7] But the United States shifted its backing several times during the course of the Revolution, depending upon which faction appeared best to protect its interests in Mexico. After the split between former Constitutionalist allies Villa and Venustiano Carranza, the United States recognized Carranza as Mexico's leader. On March 9, 1916, having grown increasingly frustrated at Wilson's waning support, Villista forces raided the small border town of Columbus, New Mexico, killing seventeen U.S. citizens. That, at least is the most widely accepted theory as to why the raid occurred. Local gossip had it that the raid was in retaliation for an arms deal with a Columbus merchant that had gone sour. Others suggested that it was orchestrated by the U.S. government, which sought a pretext for invading Mexico. Still others saw it as evidence of a German conspiracy to focus U.S. attention on Mexican affairs rather than on European ones. At any rate, the incident immediately turned U.S. sentiment against the revolutionaries and prompted the United States to mount a large-scale military intervention in northern Mexico. U.S. Army regulars under Pershing's command totaled 10,000.[8] After two more Villista raids occurred in May, Wilson posted the national guards of Texas, New Mexico, and Arizona on the U.S.–Mexico border. By June, he had called out all of the remaining states' guard units, until some two hundred thousand guardsmen and regulars were stationed along the border from Texas to California.[9] Forty thousand troops camped in the El Paso area alone.[10]

General Pershing's Punitive Expedition may have served the manifest purpose of capturing Villa, or as some historians have argued, of forcing Carranza to take a more aggressive stand against the revolutionaries.[11] But in terms of mass media and popular culture, the Punitive Expedition had a historical role that has outlived the campaign itself. The photographs, newsreels, and feature films that were churned out almost instantly after the Columbus Raid, served to consolidate the image of the geographical limits of U.S. territory in the minds of its citizenry. Benedict Anderson has argued that a key component in defining a given nation is a shared image of its physical limits, "because even the largest of [nations], encompassing perhaps a billion living human beings, has finite, if elastic boundaries, beyond which lie other nations."[12] The correlation between national territory and citizenship is in turn reinforced through the anthropomorphosis of national borders by the presence of soldiers' bodies. The motifs which Anderson has identified as central to nationalist discourses, such as personal sacrifice and mortality, were mobilized in popular culture during the Punitive Expedition around the image of the U.S.–Mexico border (figure 23).[13]

Despite its brevity and small scale, Villa's raid on Columbus profoundly threatened the ideal of the inviolability of U.S. territory. Throughout the Mexican Revolution, borders figured prominently in the United States as symbols of conflict and conflict resolution. El Paso/Juárez was the site of the first meeting between William Taft and Porfirio Díaz in 1909; it was also the place where the treaty was signed in 1911 that provided for the succession of Díaz by interim President Francisco León de la Barra. In 1914, prior to the Punitive Expedition, when the U.S. Marine Corps landed at Veracruz, a two-month-long peace conference was held in the U.S.–Canada border town of Niagara Falls.[14] Finally, El Paso/Juárez was again chosen as the site of negotiations between General Álvaro Obregón, Carranza's Secretary of War, and General Hugh Scott, U.S. Army Chief of Staff, toward the close of the expedition. Beyond these symbolic invocations of the border, however, Villa's raid on Columbus also highlighted the sensitivity of other types of borders, both internal and external to the United States.

One of these other borders was not international but intranational, and had to do with the assimilation of Mexican American and Native American populations from the new U.S. Hispano-majority states. New Mexico had just been granted statehood in 1912 after a sixty-year period during which it held territorial status. Although pro-statehood factions emerged there as early as 1850, they remained checked due to political infighting and periodic apathy. More important, U.S. lawmakers slowed the process from without because of their racist fears of the Catholic Hispano majority in the region.[15] Before statehood would be granted, the loyalty of New Mexico's citizens to the United States had to be "tested," and that opportunity came in 1898 during the Spanish-American War, in which New Mexicans served in great numbers and fought against their region's former colonial ruler.[16]

In propaganda surrounding U.S. involvement in the Mexican Revolution, however, portrayals of Mexican Americans as soldiers and citizens were conspicuously few.[17] (Even the African-American soldiers captured at Carrizal were featured in newsreels and photos that expressed outrage at this treatment of U.S. citizens.) The cultural and spatial contiguity of the Mexican and Mexican American populations on either side of the border was instead replaced by the archetypal confrontation between Anglo and Mexican, in which racial and physical contrasts were hyperbolized. To be sure, anti-Anglo plots like the Plan de San Diego of 1915 rekindled fears among Anglos as to the loyalty of the Mexican American population.[18] In addition, the upheaval of the Revolution sparked the first large wave of Mexican migration to the United States, which included not only wealthy *porfiristas* but also the rural poor.[19] Members of the latter group were placed in "refugee camps" in U.S. border cities,

23. Cal Osbon, "U.S. and Mexico State Line," 1915. Photograph courtesy of the Southwest Collection, El Paso Public Library.

where they became a favorite subject of postcard and newspaper photographers. The photos of the refugees were sympathetic, but not intimate, portraits of women and children, shot through the barbed wire fence of the camps. Though this type of framing device is common in contemporary U.S. representations of the border (see chapter 2), here it indicates an anxiety about containing the Mexican population within the United States, since the actual borderline was not demarcated by a fence in many photos of the period (figure 24).

A second border issue triggered by the Columbus Raid involved the threat of an overseas invasion of the United States via Mexico, stemming from the tensions caused by World War I in Europe. When the Zimmerman Telegram was decoded and disclosed to the U.S. public in February 1917, some people saw in the Columbus Raid a German plot to destabilize the United States, one in which Villa was acting as a proxy on behalf of Mexico in exchange for the prize of having its former territories returned. Recent historical investigation has turned up evidence to suggest that German operatives in the United States and Mexico were funneling arms to Villa's forces at the time of the raid, although no evidence confirming Germans as architects of the raid has been found.[20]

The phenomenon of modern technology linking the frontier to the metropolis, often mentioned by historians of the Mexican Revolution, was not exclusive to northern Mexico. For the United States, too, the Punitive Expedition ushered modernization into the southwestern states on at least two distinct levels.[21] First, it marked the birth of a particular form of military-industrial organization, and second, the events of U.S. intervention were recorded and distributed by means of relatively new forms of visual technology.

With respect to the former level, the Punitive Expedition is remembered as the swan song of the U.S. Cavalry and the debut of aerial reconnaissance. U.S. historians downplay the fact that Villa was never captured by citing the value of the expedition as a staging exercise for the sophisticated weapons technology which was to play a major role in World War I. "War preparedness" was the era's doublespeak for the complete overhaul of the U.S. military in collaboration with private-sector weapons contractors. Much of the new technology was dysfunctional. Motorcycle gunners were a short-lived experiment, and armored trucks floundered in desert rainstorms. Among other inventions introduced were antiaircraft tanks, trenches and barbed wire, dirigibles, weather balloons (used to gauge artillery coordinates), radio sets, and motorized ambulances. This, too, was the era when a separate division of U.S. military intelligence was founded.[22] Women became institutionally incorporated into the military, not as soldiers or nurses, but as prostitutes. The U.S. movie clichés in which Anglos express surprise at the fact that women accompanied Mexican soldiers into battle are not entirely accurate, since U.S. soldiers stationed in El Paso, Columbus, Colonia Dublán, and other border sites had access to "the remount station" at their camps. This brainchild of General Pershing was staffed in El Paso by an El Paso madam and

24. Unidentified photographer, "Detained at the Refugee Camp." Photograph courtesy of the Southwest Collection, El Paso Public Library.

Juárez prostitutes; in Columbus, military brothels were racially segregated for both prostitutes and soldiers. Before patronizing the establishment, soldiers had to submit to physical examinations by army doctors who checked for venereal disease.[23]

In terms of visual technology, the Punitive Expedition occurred at a time when film was on the verge of becoming the dominant form of visual entertainment throughout the United States.[24] The border was a common setting in feature films almost from the beginning of commercial cinema. Westerns set in "border towns" were a popular subgenre in the early teens and continued to be produced after the Revolution. These did not specifically explore the border as a geographical region; rather, they exploited the narrative possibilities of a dual legal system. They depicted U.S. border towns as zones of (relative) lawlessness, while the "other side" was simply coded as the absence of law altogether. Related to the border Westerns were the so-called greaser films, in which *mexicanos* were vilified in opposition to heroic Anglos. Carlos E. Cortés attributes this racist film cycle to residual prejudice toward Mexicans stemming from the U.S.–Mexican war of the mid-nineteenth century and to the rise of popular fiction about the Western United States in which Indians and *mexicanos* were portrayed interchangeably as the enemies of cowboys.[25]

The possibility of U.S. intervention in Mexico ushered in a new type of border film that not only was specifically concerned with the border per se but also linked it to issues of national defense. In 1916 alone, seven feature films were released that explicitly dealt with military mobilization on the border.[26] One typical plot described the journey of a young national guardsman from the East Coast to the border, where his bravery in a skirmish with Mexicans earned him the love of the woman he desired.[27] Skirmishes between small groups or individual Mexicans and U.S. citizens were manufactured by these films, even though very little military combat was actually taking place in the region.

The newsreel format implicitly connected U.S. military presence on the border with international conflicts, particularly to events going on in Europe. William Randolph Hearst, who himself had extensive investments in Mexico, was behind much of the jingoistic newsreel coverage of the Revolution. In 1914, the year of the U.S. occupation of Veracruz, he started the *Hearst-Selig News Pictorial* series, and later backed several other newsreel series, including *Hearst-Vitagraph, Hearst-International,* and *Hearst-Metrotone.*[28] He also produced fictional films that linked border conflict to global imperialist rivalries. His 1916–17 serial, *Patria,* for example,

> portrayed a Mexican-Japanese alliance to subvert the United States, with Mexican and Japanese saboteurs teaming up in an attempt to wreak havoc by blowing up bridges and munitions factories: fortunately, their evil is equaled by their incompetence, and the American heroes thwart their efforts at every turn.[29]

Universal's 1916 serial, *Liberty,* went so far as to assert that Pershing had already beaten Villa in Mexico.[30] Just one year later, the Punitive Expedition having ended, such movies disappeared, although in 1918 a small flurry of movies began that attempted, retroactively, to link events on the border back to Europe, World War I, and German-Mexican conspiracies.[31]

In contrast to film, picture postcards, which had their heyday in the preceding decade, were on the decline in the early teens. But postcards experienced a brief resurgence in popularity in the United States around the time of the Mexican Revolution. The cards satisfied the public's hunger for images of the war, especially for those who did not have access to movie theaters, which had only thoroughly saturated urban areas by this time. In 1913 alone, the U.S. Post Office reported that it handled 968 million postcards. The postcard boom hit the United States after 1907, when postal service regulations first allowed "divided back" postcards, so that people could write messages on cards without obscuring the picture on the front.[32] Postcards were relatively easy to produce; photographs could be sent to Eastman Kodak to be converted into postcards, or they could be made at most photographers' studios. By 1910, just in time for the Revolution, Eastman Kodak had developed portable cameras especially designed to produce postcards, and other companies followed suit. This enabled entrepreneurs and studio photographers, like El Paso's prolific Walter H. Horne and Otis A. Aultman, to become mobile and to get new images on the market almost immediately after any noteworthy local event had occurred.[33] It also shifted the business of postcard production away from being a cottage industry, in which images were custom-made in studios for individual consumers, to being an industry of mass production with its own "best-sellers" and distribution network.[34]

The postcard industry encouraged regionalism; cities and states were soon producing images of their own distinction through shots of monuments, landscapes, and the like. But the very fact that the postcard was a vehicle of long-distance communication made regional variety itself a binder of U.S. national identity across time and space. In comparison to the Mexican postcards, the U.S. postcards of the Revolution often featured subjects specific in their appeal to a target audience—for example, the hometown or friends and family of a particular group of soldiers. Horne and other border photographers would take individual or group portraits of U.S. soldiers and try to sell them to the same men who had posed for them.[35] But one did not need to know the identity of U.S. soldiers depicted in a picture postcard to know that they were to be viewed as individuals; the details of rank, unit, and location were recorded in their uniforms or in the caption. The emphasis on individuality generally did not carry over into U.S. postcards' portrayal of Mexicans, with the exception of well-known Mexican leaders. According to Paul J. Vanderwood and Frank N. Samponaro, whose book *Border Fury* is an excellent survey of the postcards of this era, the favorite subjects of U.S. postcard producers included dead or maimed Mexicans, burials, lynchings, and executions.[36] Often these were editorialized with captions featuring racial epithets.

Local and Global on the Same Picture Plane

The picture postcards generated around the time of the Punitive Expedition exploited the U.S.–Mexico borderline as a sight gag. In this medium the boundary was primarily designated by three signs: the Rio Grande/Río Bravo, the obelisk-shaped border marker, or a line drawn directly on the photo negative or print by the photographer (figure 25).[37] Many of those who sent postcards drew their own borderline in ink on the photograph, despite the presence of an obelisk, to highlight U.S. and Mexican territory further for the benefit of distant correspondents (figure 26).[38] The fact that photographers

25. Cal Osbon, "Trenches on the Border at Douglas, Arizona," 1915. Photograph courtesy of the Southwest Collection, El Paso Public Library.

and correspondents felt obliged to impose the border by lines and labels attests to how indistinguishable from one another the national territories actually appeared, and to the fact that national differentiation was a process of training spectators by means of symbolic codes. These photos' sense of humor rests in the fact that they assert difference in the foreground through the inclusion of bodies, props, or captions against a background that appears to be contiguous—such as the Sonoran Desert or the main street of Nogales. In the foreground, one sees clearly an appeal to binarisms. People and objects are portrayed in oppositional or complementary relationships to one another, but the landscape and spatial proximity that metonymically unites the subjects is suppressed by the prominence accorded to the borderline itself.

It was common practice in the cards to position national "types" on either side of the borderline. Usually, the U.S. side of the equation was the dominant one, either through the insinuation of a property relation with the Mexican side or through greater physical size. A popular theme produced by many photographers was a shot of a farmer or soldier standing on the U.S. side of the border and holding the reins of a burro that stood on the Mexican side; the caption read: "A U.S. farmer (or soldier) with his ass in Mexico." Another photograph positioned a U.S. soldier and an ascribed Mexican "prostitute" on the borderline.[39] Both cards imputed a sexual valence

26. Unidentified photographer, "International Line at Nogales." Photograph courtesy of the Southwest Collection, El Paso Public Library.

to binational relations, which cast Mexico as "feminine" or "passive" in opposition to the "masculine" United States. In the cards described above, the "ass" or "piece of ass" is not part of the U.S. or Anglo body, as the written text of the first card implies. The lower body has rather been displaced visually and spatially onto Mexico, through the images of the burro and the woman. These hierarchical relations suggest that Mexico, as embodied in its people, products, flora, and fauna, could be bought, tamed, or dominated by the United States. Earlier in the decade, Pancho Villa's masculinity was a selling point for U.S. audiences; that masculinity was now systematically being transferred back to the U.S. side.

One postcard by Cal Osbon, an Arizona-based photographer (and the most interesting of this era in my opinion), stands out because it managed to condense several popular themes of the day into one image (figure 27). Osbon's work wavered between the humorous and the macabre.[40] This sample of his humorous side is a variation of the gag about the soldier with his ass in Mexico. In it, the border marker dominates the frame and bisects the space occupied by the photo's three human subjects, a "Mexican" man, an "Anglo" man, and a young ("Anglo"?) boy. The shot is taken looking westward, with Mexico on the left (south) and the United States on the right (north). Following the placement of text from left to right, which gives President Wilson "the last word," as it were, the organization of space suggests the

27. Cal Osbon, "Long Distance Telephone to President Wilson," 1916. Photograph courtesy of the Southwest Collection, El Paso Public Library.

photographer's U.S. bias. Osbon has also sketched a foreshortened borderline extending outward from the obelisk, in order to separate "Old Mexico" from the "U.S. Side." In keeping with the zealous labeling characteristic of this genre, he has redundantly marked each country's territory several times.

In spite of the dichotomies displayed in the photograph's formal composition, if one imagines the context of the profilmic event in the Osbon photo, as well as in the previous two photos I have mentioned, the proximity of its subjects undermines the notion of the border as a barrier. The obelisk's dominance over the frame seems frivolous, since the subjects could move or touch one another effortlessly. It is the text in the Osbon photo that adds emphasis to the borderline's divisive power. Each side depicts the hypothetical transcript of two long-distance phone calls between Washington, D.C., and Mexico:

> [from Mexico:] Carranza long distance/ telephone to Pres. Wilson/ via/ Douglas Ariz/ July 20 1916/ for him to withdraw/ his soldiers from Mexico/ Carranza [from the US:]Message ret/ July 21 1916/ Message back July 21 1916/ to Carranza when you rest orf [restore] peace/ in old Mexico/ [A]Long the border/ I will with/ draw my men/ Wilson is/ from Missouria [*sic*]/ show him first

The reference to an invisible mass communications network traversing the border suggests how the region and its conflicts were becoming reined in by the respective national "centers" to serve as a conduit and an indicator of international relations. Osbon crudely followed the perspective lines of the image with his text (perhaps to take advantage of dark/light contrast), locating the writing on the picture plane rather than on the print plane. It is as though Wilson and Carranza were literally marking national territory with their words.

Mexico as a Stage: The Actors and the Spectators

> *It means war, boy—honest-to-goodness war! And you're to have yourself a front-row seat!*
> —The War Train[41]

Another significant category of postcards from this era, curiously, did not focus on the Revolution's participants, but rather on its witnesses. These photos portrayed U.S. spectators watching Mexican revolutionary battles and executions. Together with postcards depicting U.S. military maneuvers and camps, this group is unusual in its portrayal of U.S. citizens as a collective rather than as individuals. Throughout the Revolution, large numbers of U.S. citizens turned out on the U.S. sides of border cities such as Tijuana, Ciudad Juárez, and Nogales to watch battles taking place in Mexico. Their vantage points were train cars, riverbanks, and bluffs, which did not always provide protection from stray bullets (figure 28). In the 1911 battle of Juárez, for example, four U.S. spectators were killed, and nine were wounded.[42] This did not stop hundreds of people from flocking to battle zones anyway, and behaving as though they were watching a play or a movie rather than a war. Vanderwood and Samponaro's description of the spectators depicted in one postcard of the El Paso/ Juárez border emphasizes the extent to which Revolution-watching was a middle- and upper-class leisure activity (figures 29–30):

> [L]adies in long white dresses, their fancy parasols and huge bonnets shielding them against a hot sun, saunter along a river bank which slopes toward the Rio Grande. Nicely dressed children wander through the scene. Most of the menfolk in bowler hats and dark three-piece suits (although many have shed jacket and vest because of the heat), line the river bank; some women are with them.[43]

In Tijuana, where members of the International Workers of the World had joined the Revolution, spectators were encouraged to attend the war by the soldiers themselves, who charged twenty-five cents for the opportunity to view the impending battle. El Paso's Hotel Paso del Norte offered its clients luxurious rooftop views of the battles, complete with patio umbrellas and bar service.[44] Local legend has it that in El Paso's Sunset Heights neighborhood, where many *porfiristas* relocated during the Revolution, many of the elegant houses were constructed so as to provide good views of revolutionary activity in Juárez.[45]

In fact, theatrical metaphors common to both visual entertainment and military strategy—such as *stage, theater,* and *shooting*—were ironically coterminous when it

28. F. C. Hecox, "American Sightseers near Madero's Camp." Photograph courtesy of the Southwest Collection, El Paso Public Library.

came to some border battles. But this simultaneity did not necessarily find unity in the sense of a complicity between spectator and actor; rather there was a division along national lines as to whether the Revolution was perceived principally as entertainment or as a historical-political event. Oscar J. Martínez's description of the second battle of Juárez is a good example of how the former interpretation overshadowed the latter from the point of view of U.S. citizens:

> After the epic 1911 battle, El Pasoans swarmed to Juárez in search of souvenirs and to witness Villa's parading of the *federales* (federal troops) in their underclothes. Expecting a reenactment of such drama in the second Battle of Juárez in 1912, El Pasoans expressed disappointment when Pascual Orozco took the Mexican city in a bloodless coup, labeling the event a "big flop."[46]

In the case of the Revolution, historical events were occurring at the same time as representations of them were marketed and consumed. For U.S. audiences of the Revolution, both those who witnessed it in person and those who witnessed it from afar through visual media, the historical impact of revolutionary activity became neutralized, as the entire event was converted into a spectacle for their benefit. In other words, from the U.S. point of view, the Revolution was a drama, and its soldiers were actors. This motif is quite common in the years 1911–1915, prior to the Punitive Expedition, when most of the major border battles were fought, but the Punitive Expedition was also made theatrical in retrospect through characterizations of it as a "rehearsal" for World War I.[47]

29. Unidentified photographer, "Americans and Insurrectos at Rio Grande." Photograph courtesy of the Southwest Collection, El Paso Public Library.

The crowd shots may have served the documentary impulse of many early photographs in that they recorded the presence of U.S. citizens on the border as witnesses to the Revolution. But, as I have argued, they also provided a point of spectatorial identification for U.S. consumers geographically removed from the conflict; therefore, they may be considered in supplementary relation to the photographs depicting the hypothetical objects of the spectators' gaze. The photos of U.S. audiences find their "reverse shots" in the photos of the Mexican Revolution's soldiers and leaders that dominated U.S. postcard production. In this respect, the border becomes just as important a formal structuring device in the crowd photos as it is in the Osbon photo discussed previously. But, while the borderline is hyperbolized in the proscenium space of the Osbon photo, it is either absent or de-emphasized in the shots that depict an audience. Some of the crowd shots are taken from the Mexican side looking north at the spectators, while others are taken from behind the crowd, so that one also sees in the distance military activity taking place in Mexico. When an audience is depicted, the photographers use the border as an "invisible" line that regulates rules of alternation between seer and seen, and their location in a synthetic space.

This pattern of alternation is evident in Walter H. Horne's most financially successful suite of postcards, which relays a sequence of discrete events through reaction shots of an Anglo and Mexican crowd. This 1916 three-card suite was known as the "triple execution series"; it depicted, one by one, the death by Carrancista firing

30. Alexander, "Americans in El Paso watching Mexican Insurrectos from across the Rio Grande." Photograph courtesy of the Southwest Collection, El Paso Public Library.

squad of three suspected munitions thieves in Ciudad Juárez (figures 31–32). Horne took a number of photos on that day besides those of the three executions, and one can reconstruct a narrative sequence from the captions. In addition to a general crowd shot that bears the caption, "Crowd in Juárez, Mex. on the way to an execution," Horne included onlookers at the extreme right in each of the execution pictures. A post-execution shot presents a view of the three dead from a closer vantage point, but still Horne included the crowd in the background staring at the corpses. The last shot of the series is taken from closest range, and it portrays the doctor examining the bodies to verify their death, as spectators look on.[48]

In the crowd photographs, the border acts in its familiar role as the arbiter of national, class, and ethnic difference. In addition, it is a 180-degree line that exploits "off-screen" space, much as film editing does—that is, by using absence and alternation as a means of constructing subjectivity and a privileged point of view.[49] Here, I use "point of view" in a broader sense than simply to refer to the character whose consciousness superintends the photo or film image. "Point of view" refers to the cultural codes conveyed through humor, captions, iconography, and framing that assert the dominance of the United States vis-à-vis Mexico, and that manifest this difference through the depiction of middle-class Anglo citizens as "model spectators."[50] Given that the Mexicans whose images circulated in U.S. postcards of the period were often maimed or dead, one can assume that the dynamic of looking set up by U.S. media effectively ensured that a Mexican "point of view" remained unrepresented.

31. Walter H. Horne, "Triple Execution in Mexico #2." Photograph courtesy of the Southwest Collection, El Paso Public Library.

Recent Treatments of the Columbus Raid

> I'm not sick exactly. I just don't think this is my revolution. I'm a gringo.
> —*Young Indiana Jones*

Scholars of both Mexican and U.S. cinema have argued that the Mexican Revolution has proven to be an extremely elastic vehicle for representing any number of political positions. Thus, treatments of the Revolution in film and literature are not always "revolutionary"; in fact, they have often been quite the opposite. The U.S. cinema, for example, has tended to reduce the numerous regional tendencies of the Revolution into two opposing camps, which makes it quite easy to distinguish the "good side" from the "bad side." Carlos E. Cortés has pointed out that revolutionaries in the United States have either been portrayed negatively, as *bandidos,* or favorably, but in subordinate relations to Anglo mercenaries, depending upon the status of U.S.–Mexico relations in a given historical period.[51] In her work on the figure of Pancho Villa in the U.S. and Mexican cinemas, Deborah Mistron concurs that U.S.

32. Walter H. Horne, "Identifying Soldiers." Photograph courtesy of the Southwest Collection, El Paso Public Library.

movie revolutionaries are either Robin Hoods or bandits. She goes on to argue that the conventions of the Western in literature and cinema, a genre which preceded Villa, required that certain contradictory historical aspects of his character be repressed for U.S. audiences. One of the ideological projects of the Western, according to Mistron, was to distinguish between the proper and improper uses of violence, and to justify the former in the interests of democracy and social welfare. Within the dichotomies laid out by the Western, Mistron concludes, Villa could either be "the lawgiver" or "the gunfighter," "the tyrant" or "the patriot," but never both at the same time.[52]

Recent fictional accounts of the Columbus Raid and the Punitive Expedition from a U.S. perspective also conform to the Manichaean tradition of representing

Villa outlined above. Their distinction lies not in the fact that they break established paradigms, but that they manage to portray Villa and his gringo mercenaries as admirable characters, while *simultaneously* presenting a critical interpretation of U.S. intervention in Mexico. In this section I will discuss two such texts, George Lucas's television production, *The Young Indiana Jones Chronicles* (1992), and Brown Meggs's historical novel, *The War Train* (1981).[53] Both accounts feature a similar type of protagonist. Cassius of Meggs's novel and Indy of the TV show are civilians who, in order to redress a personal offense, become "soldiers" and join the fight against the Mexicans. Cassius literally must enlist in the U.S. Army in order to search for his lost friend in the desert. Indy, on the other hand, is at first threatened with death by Mexican revolutionaries for attempting to retrieve a woman's dress stolen by one of them during the Columbus Raid; soon after that, he himself becomes a revolutionary, only to realize finally that his real sympathies are with the Allied troops fighting in Europe.

While both protagonists may feel ambivalent about Villa, they share a decided dislike for Pershing's forces. *The War Train* portrays U.S. soldiers as conniving, brutish, and barbaric in contrast to the saintly hero. In *Young Indiana Jones,* historical personalities such as Pershing and Patton appear as bloodthirsty jingoists, and on one occasion Indy himself is threatened by their violence. Such antagonism between the military and civilian sectors does have some historical basis dating from the expedition. During that era, the military had not yet established its own corps of transportation and technical workers, so it often hired workers from companies that had military contracts. The vast disparity in wage scales and privileges between enlisted men and civilians led to competition and hostility between the two groups.[54]

The War Train's hero, Cassius McGill, is a young train conductor who is charged with the job of carrying troops from the plains states to the border immediately following Villa's Columbus Raid. Most of Meggs's novel recounts the events that take place en route to the climactic arrival at the border. Based upon oral histories taken from the author's grandfather, who actually did work for the Pullman Company during the Punitive Expedition, the novel is painstakingly researched and employs the collage technique of juxtaposing text with signage, advertisements, and newspaper articles from the period.[55] Cassius's one "border crossing" toward the conclusion of the novel, from El Paso to Ciudad Juárez, is for the purpose of viewing an execution—in fact, the same "triple execution" of Horne's postcard suite. Meggs probably based his description of the event upon studies of Horne's postcards or of Vanderwood and Samponaro's book. The novel's second climax is also spectacular, but it is set in U.S. territory and is described in a manner markedly different from the first.

As with several of the postcards I have discussed (e.g., figure 23), Meggs's novel does not locate "national difference" in the landscape of the border region, but rather in the presence of two opposing military forces. The narration of Cassius's carriage ride across the border with Al (Damon) Runyon intercuts authentic spatial markers (e.g., Mesa Avenue, the International Bridge, Avenida Ferrocarril) with Runyon's war stories and a description of the Mexican army. When the spectators finally arrive at the execution site, Meggs presents detailed descriptions of Horne's camera, the postcard industry, and U.S. celebrities in attendance:

> While Mr. Horne saw to the focus of his camera, his assistants went through the crowd offering postcards made from pictures the photographer had taken several days before. They cost one penny apiece plus another penny for postage. All three poses showed piles of Mexican corpses burnt in the desert. . . .
>
> The crowd was becoming impatient. It was half Mex and half white people, who, like Mr. Webster's party, had come across from El Paso to see the fun. Many correspondents were present besides Mr. Runyon. He was pleased to introduce his friends Floyd Gibbons of the *Chicago Tribune,* Bob Dunn of the *New York Tribune,* Frank Elser of the *New York Times,* and Dan Piggott of *Harper's Weekly.* The reporters were champing at the bit, wanting to get south with Pershing. But Pershing was in no hurry to have these fellows looking over his shoulder, Mr. Runyon said, and so had delayed their means of transport . . .
>
> When Mr. Horne was ready, he nodded to the Carranzista [*sic*] general in charge.[56]

The ascendance of "audience" over "actors" is clear in the above passage; Meggs even promotes the postcard photographer to "director" of the sequence, since it is he and not the general who dictates when the executions are to begin. Descriptions of those about to be executed, the Mexican spectators, and the Carrancistas, on the other hand, are downplayed.

The novel's second climax is curious in its contrasting manner of presenting violent death as a spectacle. The entire driving force of the plot to this point has been building up to some sort of U.S.–Mexico confrontation: Will there be a battle? Will Pershing succeed in capturing Villa? But the book, like the movies produced in the teens, concludes with a skirmish instead of military conflict. Cassius goes off in search of a missing friend to Hachita, New Mexico, where he petitions the commanding officer of U.S. troops there to allow him to search the area. The officer assents, with the proviso that Cassius temporarily enlist in the Army. Newly christened "Private McGill," Cassius manages to overcome the intranational antagonism between soldier and civilian in the face of the greater Mexican threat. In this last adventure, occurring just within U.S. territory, Cassius does find his friend, but too late:

> He had been roped to the tall cactus and his clothes cut off. The skin on his chest hung down in neat strips. The soles of his feet had been sliced free and replaced with slippers of cactus. His private parts were severed and stuffed into his mouth. He wore an awful grin in death.[57]

The spectacle of a dead, mutilated body, so typical of the U.S. postcards of Mexican and Chinese victims of the Revolution, is converted into a tableau from a passion play when the victim is a U.S. citizen. Christ imagery is punctuated in this passage by Irish Catholic Cassius's fervent exclamations to Jesus and the Virgin Mary at the sight. And who are the perpetrators of this deed? Not Mexicans at all, it turns out, but a band of Yaqui Indians that suddenly appears out of nowhere to attack the reconnaissance party. (Yaquis had theretofore been mentioned only once in the novel, when Cassius saw one on the street in El Paso.) Cassius is wounded in the shoulder during the ensuing melee but manages single-handedly to shoot three Yaquis, while his fellow soldiers take down the rest.[58]

Both climactic spectacles in the novel feature the border as a theatrical space: in the one, Mexicans attack other Mexicans to the delight of U.S. spectators; in the other, Native Americans within the United States stage a gruesome spectacle for U.S. citizens. Native Americans and Mexicans in this case cannot be viewed as interchangeable "menaces" as they were in the "greaser" films earlier in this century. Here the abrupt appearance of the Yaquis derails us from acknowledging the outcome of the Punitive Expedition, by diverting that question to one of the intranational anxieties activated by Villa's Columbus Raid.

The War Train is a good example of how border conflict resolution is deflected into the domestic arena and the issue of newly acquired populations in the U.S. Southwest. *The Young Indiana Jones Chronicles,* on the other hand, opts for a deflection of border military conflict into the international arena of U.S. rivalries with other imperialist powers. The series is a television spin-off from the popular Indiana Jones movies starring Harrison Ford as a mild-mannered college professor who leads a double life as a world adventurer. The TV series is based on the hero's childhood and adolescent experiences, which are supposed to have occurred from the turn of the century into the late teens. One of the premises of the Young Indiana Jones episodes is that Indy's adventures come about through his identification with people from a race, culture, class, or nationality other than his own. His adventure with a given group causes him to realize near the story's conclusion that his identification was based upon a misrecognition, which in turn will propel him to identify as a member of another group in the following episode. In various episodes of the series, for example, Indy has been a French spy in Kerensky's Russia, a jazz musician with Sidney Bechet in Chicago, and an insurgent/observer in the Irish Easter Rebellion.

Indy's participation in other cultures suggests that human adaptability transcends cultural, linguistic, and class boundaries. But because Indy's adventures are cursory "visits," often the moment in which he understands others is also the same moment in which he desires to separate himself from them. This dual movement is particularly strong in the episode that deals with the Columbus Raid: it presents the revolutionaries as knowable and understandable from the perspective of a gringo witness, while at the same time it stresses Mexican sovereignty and U.S. nonintervention in Mexican affairs.

The liberal outlook of the series is a counterpoint to its intense nostalgia—a longing not so much for the eras it represents but for other movies depicting those eras. The credit sequence, for example, consists of scratched, grainy, black-and-white images from the episodes, simulating silent newsreel footage. The settings, historical frame, and general premise of the series recall Hollywood action-adventure films from the 1920s through the 1940s, while individual episodes often quote genres such as the Western, the horror movie, the spy thriller, and so on. The two-hour episode I will discuss consists of two parts; the first, set in Egypt, features Indy as a young boy, and the second, set in Mexico, features him as a teenager. The first part could be re-titled "Young Lawrence of Arabia," since it has Indy team up for an adventure with a Peter O'Toole look-alike, who is supposed to be T. E. Lawrence before the Bedouin campaigns. The most obvious intertext for the Mexican half of the episode is the 1985 film *The Old Gringo,* itself a pastiche of other Anglo mercenary movies such as *Viva Villa!* The *Young Indiana Jones* episode not only uses some of the same stock footage that appears in *The Old Gringo,* it also lifts entire narrative sequences from that movie, such as the "false execution" scene, the "revolutionary train storming the ha-cienda" scene, the use of Hearst as an absent character, and Pancho Villa's speech about "why we are fighting."[59]

As in the case of *The War Train, Young Indiana Jones* also recycles older visual propaganda from the Punitive Expedition, and reconfigures it in a way that is critical of U.S. intervention in Mexico. Seeing these images prompts Indy's realization that he is not Mexican, that the Revolution is not his war. (On the other hand, the images do not persuade him to fight with Pershing.) In one key scene, the revolutionaries decide to issue a symbolic blow to the gringos by attacking the Mexican hacienda of William Randolph Hearst. Already Indy begins to feel ill-at-ease when he sees his comrades ransacking private property. But the feeling really hits him later that night as he and the soldiers screen movies in Hearst's private theater. The soldiers watch the images, while Indy translates the intertitles into Spanish. Alternating between shots of the screen and of the Mexican audience, this sequence portrays the Mexicans as "premodern" spectators, who are overly invested in the reality of the image, much in the same way that early French cinema-goers are said to have fled at the projected image of an oncoming steam locomotive. A melodrama provokes them to sigh and sob at the sight of a soldier bidding farewell to his lover.[60] The next selection is an *International* newsreel from March 1916. Indy translates the intertitle about the German invasion of Verdun correctly, but invents phony dialogue to correspond to images of the Punitive Expedition, because he does not want to rile the soldiers.[61] The Mexicans disregard his lies and actually begin shooting their pistols at Pershing's screen image.

In this scene with the newsreel, mass media is the great reinforcer of national identity. Through the images of war-torn Verdun, Indy's fellow mercenary, Remy, is shamed into rediscovering his Belgian patriotism. Indy realizes that his own sympa-thies lie more with Hearst, another U.S. civilian, than with the revolutionaries.[62] The Mexicans, however, read the images of Pershing correctly, despite Indy's attempts to detour their interpretation; they quite literally understand that their position is on the other side of the 180-degree line, as the objects of Pershing's quest. One may compare these Mexican spectators, who are incapable of maintaining a critical distance from the visual image, to the cool Anglo spectators situated along the Rio Grande in the postcards discussed previously. The Mexicans perceive the representation as the "real thing," whereas the Anglos perceive the "real thing" as a representation.[63]

Indy's final disillusion with the Mexican Revolution comes through an encounter that he has with an elderly campesino whose chickens are being expropriated to feed the Villista troops. Indy defends the action by explaining to him, "Pero luchamos por Ud.!" ("But we're fighting for you!"), which earns him an irate and impromptu history lesson from the old man, illustrating the futility of all revolutions:

> Escucha, hace muchos años cabalgué con Juárez en contra del Emperador Maximiliano. En esa época perdí muchas gallinas. Pero yo creí que valía la pena ser libre. Cuando Don Porfirio subió al Presidente lo apoyé pero se llevó las gallinas. Vino Huerta y se llevó las gallinas. Le tocó el turno a Carranza, y también se llevó las gallinas. Ahora viene Pancho Villa para liberarme y lo primero que hizo fue robarme las gallinas. . . . ¿Qué diferencia hay entre uno y otro? Mis gallinas no lo saben. En el mundo entero las revoluciones vienen y van. Los presidentes suben y caen. Todos roban tus gallinas. Lo único que cambia es el nombre de quién se llevó la gallina.

> (Listen, many years ago I rode with Juárez against Emperor Maximiliano. In that time, I lost a lot of chickens. But I thought it was worth it to be free. When Don Porfirio rose to the presidency, I supported him but he took my chickens. Huerta came and he took my chickens. It was Carranza's turn, and he too, took my chickens. Now Pancho Villa comes to liberate me and the first thing he did was steal my chickens. . . . What difference is there between one and the other? My chickens don't know. In the whole world revolutions come and go. Presidents rise and fall. The only thing that changes is the name of the person who took the chicken.)

The encounter reproduces the teacher/pupil framing narrative of the series in which an elderly Indiana Jones recounts his adventures to two skeptical young boys in a museum, as a "painless" way to learn history. During the flashbacks Young Indy is continuously apprenticing himself to older male mentor figures. Immediately after this scene, Indy will read a letter from his old friend, T. E. Lawrence, in which the latter describes his impending departure for Arabia: "I must take part in this war. I believe something honorable can be achieved here." The Mexicans are destined, Indy realizes, to live through countless cycles of revolutions and dictators; meanwhile the "honorable" war is being fought elsewhere. Indy's decision to head off to the "honorable" war in Europe implies that the "dishonorable" war is this entire "war game" being staged in Mexico, which Anglos and Mexicans alike have been using to amuse themselves. Trivializing the Mexican Revolution, in other words, also involves trivializing U.S. intervention or presence in Mexico.

Making Mexican politics and U.S. intervention in Mexico seem relatively innocuous may have been a convenient cover-up for a less-than-successful military exploit. Today, a similar rhetoric is being invoked once again in order to downplay the vast extent to which the border has become militarized. Terms like *paramilitary* and *low-intensity struggle,* frequently used by law-enforcement authorities to describe U.S. participation in border affairs (and in Latin America in general), do not give the impression that such operations are intensive in scale or harmful in their effects.

Although the U.S.–Mexico border region is no longer the site of a full-scale military effort by the U.S. armed forces, militarization of the border by sectors of the armed forces in conjunction with the Border Patrol and local law-enforcement authorities has increased greatly in recent decades, especially under the auspices of the Reagan-Bush-Clinton era's War on Drugs. Often, the same technology and personnel involved in drug interdiction are deployed in arresting and deporting immigrant laborers.[64] These practices are contemporaneous with a stepped-up presentation of the U.S.–Mexico border region as a "staging area" for "war games."

Tragic incidents involving armed forces stationed on the border for such purposes are becoming increasingly common. In 1989, for example, a small group of Marines shot a flare to assist in apprehending some smugglers and inadvertently ignited a three-hundred-acre forest fire.[65] The Marine who shot and killed eighteen-year-old high school student Esequiel Hernández in May 1997 while the latter was tending his family's goat herd in Redfield, Texas, was part of a combined military and Border Patrol drug interdiction force (Joint Task Force-6) operating throughout the border region. In August 1991, two hundred Marines from Camp LeJeune, North Carolina, were spotted in an encampment near Naco, Arizona, where they engaged in practice exercises for a "wartime mission" that involved wearing green facepaint and camouflage and crawling through grass along the border.[66]

This last scene in particular resembles a description from a recent controversial book by former U.S. Secretary of Defense Caspar W. Weinberger, entitled *The Next War,* in which detachments of Marines from Camp LeJeune play an important role. Less a work of speculative fiction than one would hope, *The Next War* is an evaluation of "threats" facing the United States in the twenty-first century, based upon the Pentagon's computer-generated war games. One scenario has U.S. tanks pouring over the border at Brownsville and McAllen, Texas, assisted by sixty thousand U.S. ground troops, amphibious landings, and air assaults. Two of the three factors that provoke this war in Weinberger's book are already reality, and the last is within the range of possibility: massive immigration of Mexicans to the United States, the infiltration of the Mexican government by drug cartels, and the election of a left populist (i.e., anti–free trade) president in Mexico.[67]

Border vigilante and nativist groups, such as Light Up the Border, Citizens Materiél Assistance, and the WARBOYS, have also resorted to strategies of theatricality in publicizing their cause. Light Up the Border, an anti-immigration movement initiated by the widow of a slain Border Patrol officer, was a group of San Diego residents who met periodically in the early 1990s and shined their headlights into canyons and ravines along the border in order to illuminate any Mexicans who might be trying to cross.[68] (Now gigantic floodlights have been installed in those areas.) Though they claimed to be assisting Border Patrol agents with their duties, they also maintained that their activities were symbolic, and on one occasion the former mayor of San Diego defended them by saying that it was "performance art."[69] In another well-known incident that occurred in February 1990, a videotape made by a group of San Diego junior high school youths was aired on the Fox TV show, *The Reporters.* The video depicted the young men, dressed in combat fatigues and armed with BB guns, chasing down Mexican families along the border and forcing them to kneel, hands on their heads, while the youths interrogated them. In a subsequent press conference, the youths stated that this was a game in which they were hunting one another, not Mexicans.[70] These vigilantes portray themselves as bystanders who have been unwittingly drawn into violent scenarios by their proximity to the border. They are the modern-day inheritors of such paramilitary heroes as Indy and Cassius.

The theatricalization of Anglo-Mexican border conflict is promoted in U.S. mass media at the expense of recognizing several local dynamics, which not only are part of today's border social system, but were prominent during the Porfiriato and Revolutionary eras as well. Free trade and protectionist opposition movements, for example, are nothing new to the region. From 1885 to 1905, free trade existed along the border and turned several Mexican border cities into boom towns. During that period, free trade was opposed by representatives of the U.S. business community who felt that it gave an unfair advantage to Mexican merchants. In 1924 Juárez civic leader Ulises Irigóyen tried to reinstate Perímetros Libres (free-trade zones), but this time his plan was met with opposition from Mexicans of the interior who felt that it would deracinate the region.[71] It was not until the 1930s that President Lázaro Cárdenas would introduce free trade on a small scale in the region. In an effort to discourage Prohibition-era vice industries that had flourished in border cities, Cárdenas declared Tijuana and Ensenada to be free-trade zones and permitted free importation of consumer goods in other border cities.[72]

Another aspect of the border social system that is obscured by the focus on Anglo-Mexican conflict is the heterogeneity of the two terms "Anglo" and "Mexican" themselves. Many "Mexicans" on the U.S. side of the border at the time of the Revolution had been longtime residents in the United States and were annexed along with their land by the Treaty of Guadalupe-Hidalgo more than a half-century before the Revolution. The great waves of migration that began during the Revolution continue to this day (this subject is discussed further in chapter 4). The combined processes of migration and historical settlement have served to create a complex and multilayered social system among people of Mexican origin and English-speaking people on both sides of the border, in which they identify themselves differently depending upon context and according to a vast array of factors, including social class, nationality, language proficiency in English and Spanish, place of birth, education, and employment.[73]

Suppression of these issues—trade, migration, and identity formation—could be summed up as a general denial of the border as a zone of long-term historical contact on the part of mainstream U.S. media. The recent portrayals of the U.S.–Mexico border that I have discussed continue to portray the border as a war zone, not a contact zone, and as space, not place. They show the border as a world where cultural understanding is possible *without* large-scale migration or historical contact, and where national self-determination *and* a North American brotherhood coexist harmoniously.

NAFTA and the "Return of the Porfiriato"

The U.S. fantasy vision of the border during the Mexican Revolution has been constructed largely without the inclusion of a Mexican point of view. In contemporary news and documentary media in the United States, on the other hand, several Mexican intellectuals, Jorge Castañeda and Enrique Krauze among them, are consistently called upon to provide the Mexican perspective on such issues as free trade, immigration, and U.S.–Mexico relations. Despite their diverse intellectual and political orientations, it is interesting to note the frequency with which they, too, describe present-day binational relations through comparisons to a previous era. In this case it is not the Revolution per se to which they recur, but the Porfiriato.[74]

To dub the present era "a return to the Porfiriato" is a shorthand gesture that designates certain basic similarities between the two epochs. One such similarity is that post-NAFTA Mexico represents the return to an openly pro-capitalist, antiprotectionist economic and political program such as the one that existed during the Porfiriato.[75] Díaz and his positivist advisers, *los científicos,* promoted foreign capital investment as a means to achieve Mexico's modernization. In the early 1990s, the PRI found itself in a similar position. It intensified the old rhetoric of modernization— a modernization which has never finished arriving, to paraphrase Néstor García Canclini[76]—and it shifted its tentative position on free trade in the late 1980s to an aggressive promotion of it by the turn of the decade.[77]

Another similarity between the two eras concerns unrest over the level of democratization in Mexico and the PRI's extended control over politics at the national level. Historians have often cited Díaz's fateful remark, made in 1908 to a U.S. journalist named Creelman, that Mexico was ripe for democracy as marking the beginning of the Mexican Revolution, for it prompted Liberal leader Francisco Madero to rise up in rebellion when the promise was not honored.[78] Today, parodic references to Díaz's response to Creelman are also frequently repeated as a means of criticizing the PRI's dominance of the Mexican political system.[79]

References to the Porfiriato in nonfiction U.S. media are probably lost on many U.S. readers who are sorely ignorant of Mexican history. One of the reasons why the Revolution is represented as innocuous time and again in Hollywood movies and TV shows, however, may be because the U.S. investments in Mexico made during the Porfiriato were not ultimately threatened by Carranza and other relatively conservative factions that emerged victorious at the close of the Revolution. Thus in the United States, pre- and post-Revolutionary eras are not so sharply distinguished from one another as they are in the Mexican cinema.[80] In 1911, at the beginning of the Revolution, U.S. investments in Mexico totaled $646 million, a sharp increase over nineteenth-century figures.[81] This period saw the United States vying with Western European interests for control over Mexico's natural resources, particularly in industries related to oil, minerals, and railroads. Although anti–U.S. sentiment in part fueled the Revolution, by the end of the war in 1920, U.S. intervention in Mexico and the polarization of industrialized nations in World War I had successfully jockeyed the United States to the position of dominant foreign power in Latin America. In that year, U.S. investment in Mexico reached an all-time high of more than $1 billion. The truly substantial threat to U.S. investment in Mexico would only come two decades later, when many industries were nationalized under the Cárdenas administration. Today U.S. investment and profits in Mexico are at their highest point since the Revolution, and they continue to rise. The cloak-and-dagger international intrigues of the Revolutionary era have been replaced by NAFTA's genteel "rules of origin" stipulations, which are designed as much to curtail the activities of Japanese and European interests in Mexico as they are to open the Mexican market up to U.S. goods.

During the Porfiriato, free-trade zones along the border were set up in an effort to encourage marginal regional economies, relative to those of the Mexican interior, just as the Border Industrialization Program of 1965 sought to encourage regional development in the modern era. The contemporary texts about the border that I have discussed recycle older formulas as a means to enact repressions similar to those enacted during the Mexican Revolution. These narratives also display an aversion to closure that would resolve the conflict put forth at their beginnings—this despite the fact that with almost ninety years of historical distance, we already know what happened *after* the Porfiriato and what became of the Punitive Expedition. Here is another motive to trivialize Mexican political struggles from the U.S. national perspective: Though the Mexican Revolution ultimately did not prove threatening to U.S. interests, future revolutions might.

Chapter 4

Narratives of Cross-Border Migration during the Revolution's Developmentalist Phase

The First "Return of the Porfiriato"

As caricatured as the border region may seem in the *Young Indiana Jones* episode described in the previous chapter, it has not fared much better in Mexican commercial cinema, where according to one scholar, the border's defining features are gunshots, prostitution, drug traffic, and violence.[1] Many U.S. stereotypes of the border in fact have their own counterparts in Mexican cinema. The scene from *Young Indiana Jones* in which Mexican soldiers fire at the movie screen, for example, is apparently inspired by Martín Luis Guzmán's *El águila y la serpiente (The Eagle and the Serpent),* a classic Mexican account of the Revolution first published in serial form in 1927–28. In one comic vignette from this work, the author describes an evening spent watching newsreels at the 1914 Revolutionary Convention in Aguascalientes. He and his two companions arrived late to a standing-room-only crowd and decided to view the movies from behind the curtain that was serving as a makeshift screen. Guzmán writes,

> Don Venustiano [Carranza], por supuesto, era el personaje que más a menudo volvía a la pantalla. Sus apariciones, más y más frecuentes, habían venido haciéndose, como debía esperarse, más y más ingratas para el público convencionista. De los siseos mezclados con aplausos en las primeras veces en que se le vio, se fue pasando a los siseos francos; luego, al escándalo. Y de ese modo, de etapa en etapa, se alcanzó al fin, al proyectarse la escena en que se veía a Carranza entrando a caballo en la ciudad de México, una especie de batahola de infierno que culminó en dos disparos.
>
> Ambos proyectiles atravesaron el telón, exactamente en el lugar donde se dibujaba el pecho del Primer Jefe, y vinieron a incrustarse en la pared, uno a medio metro por encima de Lucio Blanco, y el otro, más cerca aún entre la cabeza de Domínguez y la mía.

(Don Venustiano [Carranza], naturally was the figure who most frequently returned to the screen. His repeated appearances were becoming more and more
displeasing to the Convention audience, as might have been expected. The hisses
mingled with applause that greeted him on his first appearances were turning
into unalloyed hissing; then into hissing that verged upon hooting; then into
open booing, and finally into an uproar. Stage by stage, it reached its climax in
the scene where Carranza was making his entry on horseback into Mexico City.
At this point it became a kind of hellish din that culminated in two shots.

Both of them perforated the curtain at the height of the First Chief's breast,
and buried themselves in the wall, one half a yard above Lucio Blanco and the
other still closer, passing between Domínguez's head and mine.)[2]

As one can see, Pershing was simply substituted for Carranza as the "bad guy" in the
scene from *Young Indiana Jones.*

Beyond this particular account, the overall presentation of the Revolution as an
entertaining but doomed undertaking became a stock formula in the conservative
Mexican movies of the post-Cárdenas era. The campesino whom Indy encounters at
the conclusion of the *Young Indiana Jones* episode recalls Mexican movies from the
"Golden Age" of the 1940s and 1950s, which often told stories of peasants who left
their villages, seduced by wealth, or fame, or by the Revolution itself, only to realize
at the end that they were better off remaining where they were in the first place.[3]

During the Ávila Camacho and Alemán *sexenios* (1940–52), the Mexican film industry was in the hands of an entrepreneurial class that was quite leery of the socialist
tendencies of the Lázaro Cárdenas administration (1934–40) and of popular struggles
in general.[4] Both Ávila Camacho and Alemán augmented state protection of the film
industry, a sector that had already been given a boost during the World War II years,
when the United States rewarded the political alliances of Mexico over those of
Argentina through relaxing restrictions on the exportation of raw film stock. The development of a strong star and genre system in this era contributed to a large output
of commercially successful movies, directed primarily at middle-class audiences.[5]

This was a watershed period in which the new bourgeoisie brought to power by
the Revolution reached its zenith, thanks to protection from state subsidies and political structures. As Sara Sefchovich explains, there were actually two factions of the
national bourgeoisie during the 1940s and 1950s: the older Porfirian faction, concentrated in the north and closely tied to foreign capital, was associated with traditional
industries such as mining; the newer faction, concentrated in the Valle de México,
tended to specialize in the manufacture of modern consumer goods. As the decade of
the 1950s unfolded, however, the latter faction became reconfigured around its relation to foreign capital. The petite and middle bourgeoisie remained nationalist and
anti-imperialist, while larger firms became hostile to state intervention in the private
sector and invited associations with foreign investors.[6]

Mexican essayist and scholar Daniel Cosío Villegas protested the growing authoritarianism and corruption that he witnessed during this period, which he termed

the Revolution's "developmentalist" phase.[7] In his famous 1947 essay, "La crisis de México" ("Mexico's Crisis"), Cosío declared that "the goals of the Revolution have been exhausted, to such a degree that the term *revolution* itself has lost its meaning."[8] Cosío did not indict Presidents Ávila Camacho or Alemán personally, but rather an entire generation of leaders whose earlier political commitment had given way to moral decay and corruption. He concluded that the only hope for Mexico lay in the "reaffirmation of principles and a purification of men." Otherwise, he warned, "The country will lose much of its national identity, and in no long period of time."[9] Fellow writer José Revueltas agreed with Cosío's pessimistic assessment of the developmentalist phase, but he argued that the root of the crisis lay not in moral weakness, but in class antagonisms. In a written response to Cosío, Revueltas chided him for his lack of historical perspective. The effects of Revueltas's critique were decisive in terms of Cosío's own biography.[10] The following year Cosío began to work on his monumental *Historia moderna de México,* a project that Charles Hale has argued was "the effort of a public figure and an intellectual, who was yet a virtual newcomer to the field of history, to find guidance in the past for a nation in crisis."[11]

In his *Historia* and in subsequent journalistic work, Cosío elaborated his description of post-1940 Mexico as a "neoporfiriato," by which he referred to the era's drive for modernization and its authoritarianism.[12] He continued to write of the "neoporfiriato" through the 1960s, and as I will argue in the case of filmmaker Alejandro Galindo, the epithet became generally adopted by oppositional intellectuals. In chapter 3, I pointed out that contemporary intellectuals such as Jorge Castañeda also described the neoliberal economic policies of the late 1980s and 1990s as a "neoporfiriato." Given the history of the term in Mexico, its current usage indicates not only a similarity among the three eras in question (the neoliberalism of the 1980s–90s, the developmentalism of the 1940s–50s, and the Porfiriato itself), but also an oppositional political tradition on the part of those who employ the term, characterized by anti-imperialism and opposition to the PRI.

The banner of nationalism is an important one for both the PRI and its opposition because, as Charles Hale explains, the ruling party has often reaffirmed its commitment to national sovereignty, even while it has simultaneously pursued economic strategies encouraging foreign investment.[13] Historically, the pendulum has swung toward nationalist and revolutionary rhetoric during periods when it was necessary to conciliate opposing factions internal to the party. Hale points out, for example, that in 1992 President Salinas de Gortari began to advocate "social liberalism," stressing "classic revolutionary concerns such as democracy, social justice, the indigenous population, health, and living standards."[14] These issues were identified with the PRI's domestic welfare program, *Solidaridad.* Salinas defended the goals of "social liberalism" in opposition to a "militant neoliberalism," an economic policy with which he and his administration had been previously identified.[15]

The first return of the Porfiriato in the late 1940s was also a critical period in which orientation toward the United States became pivotal in determining which faction of the national bourgeoisie would gain political hegemony. It was not just U.S. investment in Mexico and trade issues that garnered the attention of Mexican intellectuals and politicians during this period, but also the presence of Mexican workers in the United States, for these were the years of the Bracero Program that ran from 1942–64.

One of several programs in the twentieth century through which the United States has openly recruited immigrant laborers, the Bracero Program was intended to compensate for the labor shortage precipitated by World War II. Many Mexicans did not go through the necessary steps to obtain U.S. work permits in Mexico (which often involved bribes and bureaucracy) and simply crossed the border illegally. The Bracero Program was temporarily suspended from 1953–56 during a recessionary period in the United States. For those four years, General Joseph M. Swing, a veteran of General Pershing's Punitive Expedition, headed Operation Wetback, a program reminiscent of the massive deportations of Mexicans that had occurred during the Repatriation Program of the Depression era. In the mid-1950s Mexican deportees were not given funds to return to their homes in the Mexican interior, and consequently many braceros ended up settling in Mexican border cities.[16]

The Border Industrialization Program of 1965 that paved the way for the maquiladora industry was designed in part to absorb some of the unemployed braceros returning to Mexico from the United States. Ironically the mid-1990s have witnessed the tide turning yet again toward the implementation of a new Bracero Program, amidst contemporary demands to control illegal immigration. In 1995 the National Council of Agricultural Employers began lobbying for the reinstatement of a guest worker program with Mexico. The proposal received support from California Governor Pete Wilson, Proposition 187 coauthor Harold Ezell, and the *Los Angeles Times,* before it was finally axed from Congress's anti-immigration legislation package in March 1996.[17] At this writing a revised, two-year pilot guest-worker bill known as the Temporary Agricultural Worker Act of 1998 was pending in both houses of Congress.[18]

The Bracero Program was a political hot potato, and Mexican filmmakers and writers were not quick to generate stories about it. On the one hand, if they approached the problem from the point of view of mistreatment of Mexican nationals by the United States, they risked provoking an "international incident" with Alemán's ally to the north. On the other, if they criticized Mexico's failure to take care of its own citizens (and there were allegations that the Bracero Program was a convenient "safety valve" for the rural poor displaced by industrial development),[19] they challenged the government's avowed nationalism. In either case, they risked government censorship.

Not surprisingly, the first commercial movie to deal with braceros avoided both of those critiques, and that is why Mexican film historian Emilio García Riera described *Pito Pérez se va de bracero (Pito Pérez Goes Away to Be a Bracero)* as a "totally frustrated" project. Released in 1947 (the same year as Cosío Villegas's essay), the film failed, according to García Riera, "not only due to the manifest incompetence of the director, [Alfonso] Patiño Gómez, but also due to the placement of the main character on the impossible border that divides two cinemas: the one preceding and the one following the Alemán *sexenio*."[20] The movie was a "tragicomedy" without social critique; its "bad guys" were an isolated group of Italian *coyotes* in the border region.[21]

Even those who attempted to make a political statement about the plight of the braceros found strange allies, in that the "stay at home" moral,[22] invoked by conservative Mexican narratives to check a restless underclass, also appealed to leftists who adopted an anti-imperialist and nationalist political position. The figure of the bracero became the focal point of many contradictions: he was at once a traitor to the nation, a victim of U.S. imperialism, and a heroic figure who refused to accept his lot in life. Two of the earliest narratives to deal with braceros in the post–World War II era, Luis Spota's 1948 novel *Murieron a mitad del río (They Died in the Middle of the River)*, and Alejandro Galindo's 1953 movie, *Espaldas mojadas (Wetbacks)*, make an interesting comparison because although their creators come from opposite ends of the political spectrum, the texts are quite similar structurally and thematically.[23] Both works sympathetically portray the injustices suffered by braceros through recourse to a rhetoric of journalistic or documentary exposé. Though both are fictional works, *Murieron a mitad del río* begins with two prefaces stressing the basis of the novel in lived experience; *Espaldas mojadas* begins with traditional documentary voice-over and stock footage of the border region. In addition, both works provoked minor scandals upon their release. The Mexican Consul General in San Antonio pressured the Secretary of Foreign Relations to censor Spota's novel, fearing a U.S. protest. President Alemán laughed off the request, however, and Spota was promptly offered the post of Director de Espectáculos (Director of Spectacles) by Fernando Casas Alemán, who was Regente of Mexico City at the time.[24] Owing to pressure from the U.S. State Department, Galindo's movie was *enlatada* (canned) for two years, a subtle form of government censorship in which controversial movies are withheld from distribution because they allegedly cannot find distributors. During this period a prefatory statement was added to the beginning of the movie in order to downplay its anti–U.S. content.[25] When it was finally released in 1955, *Espaldas mojadas* won four Ariel awards, including "best original story" and "picture of greatest national interest."[26]

Luis Spota's *Murieron a mitad del río*

Luis Spota is perhaps best known as one of Mexico's most popular novelists, but actually he worked in a variety of media, including journalism, film, and TV, and he also held several government posts throughout his career. In his youth, his political orientation seemed to vacillate. Fellow journalist José Revueltas persuaded him to join the Communist Party for a brief period, but his association with Miguel Alemán proved to be decisive in terms of Spota's mature political orientation. In 1945, Alemán asked Spota to join his presidential campaign as a press attaché.[27] Spota was devoted to the future president; he held two government posts under Alemán, and although later he became greatly embittered by the corruption of the administration, according to his biographer and lover, Elda Peralta, he never held the president personally accountable for the failures of the *sexenio*.[28]

It was immediately after the close of the successful electoral campaign, while Spota held a post with the Secretaría de Educación Pública, that he turned his attention to the issue of the braceros. In a preface presumably penned by Spota and signed by the bracero protagonist "J.P." (José Pavlán), the character declares the following to be the first work to speak out on this delicate issue:

> Esta es la primera vez que se hablará, con la crudeza del que no tiene que cuidar un puesto diplomático o consular . . . de un problema que los gobiernos de dos países . . . no desconocen, pero que no han querido, o no han podido, resolver con valor y decisión.

> (This is the first time that anyone will speak, with the bluntness of one who does not have to worry about a diplomatic or consular post . . . of a problem which the governments of two countries . . . do not fail to recognize, but which they have not wanted, or have not been able to resolve with courage and decisiveness.)[29]

Despite the potential embarrassment that *Murieron a mitad del río* presented to the Alemán administration for its reference to the emigration of rural poor and its negative portrayal of the United States, one also wonders whether it was in fact intended to bolster Alemán's commitment to the working class at the outset of his administration. There is only one reference to the president in the novel, which implies that Alemán had proposed a repatriation plan but that it had been met with political opposition. In one scene a character thumbs through an old issue of the Mexican magazine *Todo*, "que hablaba fríamente de repatriación de braceros sugerida por Miguel Alemán" ("that coldly spoke of the repatriation of braceros suggested by Miguel Alemán").[30]

In the preface attributed to "J.P." the character claims to have worked for fifty weeks as a bracero and to have crossed the border twice illegally, while Peralta recalls that Spota spent two to three weeks researching the novel in the Brownsville/Matamoros region.[31] The novel highlights the mistreatment of Mexican braceros by a variety of social groups, including U.S. employers, the Border Patrol, *coyotes* and *pateros*, as well as Mexican authorities in the border region. An admirer of U.S. popular culture and a supporter of U.S. investment in Mexico, Spota minimized his negative portrayals of gringos by writing in a prefatory statement that his descriptions pertained specifically to the problematic state of Texas and were not intended as an indictment of the U.S. government.[32]

The novel charts the adventures of José Pavlán, a native of Mexico City, and his companions Luis, Lupe, and Cocula, as they cross the border in search of work and wealth in the United States. Cocula, negatively portrayed as a whining, narcissistic homosexual, becomes frightened and deserts his companions during the crossing. Cocula reappears at the end of the novel; having bought a fake social security card, he now leads a successful life as a cook in a small Texas town. The other three men find sporadic employment in agriculture and fishing, but are obliged to flee from each situation due to threats of violence and mistreatment at the hands of Chicanos/as and Anglos. While crossing the river after spending the eve of Mexican Independence in Mexico, Lupe is shot to death. Later, Luis is apprehended by the Border Patrol. The novel concludes with a bitter, alienated Paván being deported to Mexico by U.S. authorities.

As Mexico's first World War II–era bracero novel, Spota's work established some conventions that have endured in Mexican popular fiction and movies about illegal border crossing even to the present day.[33] Among these are the motif of beginning and ending the narrative with the crossing itself, crude stereotyping, a preoccupation with laying blame for the plight of the braceros on a particular social group, and a fierce nationalism that turns on gender, racial, and spatial oppositions.

The narrative of *Murieron a mitad del río* is circular, beginning with the trip to the United States and concluding with the return to Mexico. Few descriptions of the characters' lives in Mexico or their reasons for leaving are provided. Spota writes of the border-crossing sequences as if they were symbolic rites of passage, such as from life to death, or from childhood to adulthood. "Van a sufrir. Se harán hombres" ("They are going to suffer. They will become men"), predicts the wife of a friend in Matamoros before the foursome depart for the United States. While on the river-bank, Paván digs a hole in the sand to hide from the Border Patrol, "como un muerto que prepara su propio hoyo" ("like a dead man who prepares his own grave"). Upon his return to Mexico, Paván is described as "spiritually dead," and "amargado, endurecido, frustrado" ("embittered, hardened, frustrated"). If going to the United States is associated with death, then the braceros' nostalgia for Mexico is repeatedly described as a yearning for legitimate birth and parental protection. Benito Fortis, a young bracero, complains to Paván, "Nosotros somos unos infelices, como hijos de nadie, sin documentos de registro civil. Somos puros *güerfanos*" ("We are miserable, like sons of no one, without documents of civil registry. We're pure orphans"). Drawing upon the slang usage of the word *madre* (literally, "mother"), at one point Lupe exclaims, "Prefiero México a esta madre" ("I prefer Mexico to this crap.")[34]

From Paván's first line of the novel, an exasperated "¡Perros texanos!" ("Texan dogs!"), to his last, "¡Gringos, hijos de perra!" ("Gringo sons of bitches!") the narrative of *Murieron a mitad del río* expresses the idea that all struggle to improve one's lot in life is futile.[35] Despite their efforts, the characters end up worse off than they were at the beginning of the story. According to Sefchovich, author of a study focusing on Spota's novelistic series *Las costumbres de poder* (The customs of power), this sense of fatalism combined with sparse, action-oriented prose, is emblematic of a pragmatic and conservative tendency that pervaded Spota's works, and strongly resonates with the paradoxical philosophy of the Alemán *sexenio*: "cambio sin cambios," or "modernización sin ruptura" ("change without changes," "modernization without rupture").[36]

Although the narrative de-emphasizes character development and omniscient interpretation, several important passages of free indirect discourse are attributed to Paván, who functions as an intermediary between the intellectual journalist Spota and the other braceros, most of whom are illiterate campesinos. Paván does not identify himself with his companions because he is light-skinned, urban, independent, ambitious, and educated. In one passage he contrasts himself to a coworker:

> [Benito Fortis] era un muchacho del campo mexicano. No como él [Paván]. De algo le servirían sus tres años de secundaria. Para defenderse, para no sufrir igual que los otros de menos recursos. Podría emplearse en una tienda, cosa que Benito jamás conseguiría. Era blanco, no moreno. Su inglés no resultaba tan escaso como creyó. . . . Además no aspiraba a quedarse en una ranchería texana. Texas era sólo un principio para él; el fin para los otros.

> ([Benito Fortis] was a kid from the Mexican countryside. Not like him [Paván]. His three years of secondary school were good for something. So he could defend himself, so he wouldn't have to suffer the same as those with fewer resources. He could get a job in a store, something that Benito would never be able to do. He was white, not brown. His English didn't turn out to be as scarce as he thought. Besides, he didn't aspire to stay on a Texas ranch. Texas was only the beginning for him; the end for the rest of them.)[37]

Paván's disillusion by the novel's close does not awaken within him a sense of fraternity toward his fellow braceros, for he remains just as alienated from them as he was at the beginning of the story. Rather, his experience emphasizes that in the United States all Mexicans are ill-treated regardless of their social background. Even the Virgin of Guadalupe does not escape victimization: at one point in the novel, a white racist throws her image into a fire, screaming "¡Ella es una greaser!" ("She is a greaser!").[38] The novel's conclusion thus reinforces the idea that Mexican citizens should stay south of the border, where at least those with "resources" will be recognized and compensated.

To be "in the middle of the river," the metaphor of the novel's title, is synonymous with being illegal. Regardless of their physical proximity to the border, the braceros always occupy an indeterminate social space. In the United States, they are constantly under surveillance, and yet their individuality and humanity remain invisible to others; in Mexico they are taunted and victimized by residents of the border cities. Spota describes the border itself as a "barrera de agua" and a "frontera líquida" ("water barrier," "liquid border"); in spite of its fluidity, it is highly militarized by Border Patrol agents who have "shoot-to-kill" orders for all Mexicans trying to cross illegally.

According to the novel, Mexican national identity cannot survive in Mexican border cities, due to their proximity to the United States. The protagonists receive a brief lesson in this regard when they go to Matamoros on the eve of Mexican Independence. Their Chicano boss, Chebo, explains to them, "Toda la frontera, del lado mexicano, es un gran burdel para los gringos . . ." ("The entire border, on the Mexican side, is a great bordello for gringos . . ."). In this episode, the omniscient narrator observes that there really is no difference between the incivility of border Mexicans and Anglos, "Mexicanos and sureños iguales en el alcohol—borrachos que se orinaban en las esquinas o que vomitaban en los zaguanes" ("Mexicans and Southerners alike in alcohol—drunks who urinated on street corners or vomited in the ditches").[39] But perhaps the best exemplars of regional deracination are the Chicano/a characters in the novel, derogatorily described as *pochos* or *mexicanos renegados* ("renounced Mexicans"), and at times shown to be as cruel and greedy as the Anglos. Chebo, the kindly Chicano owner of a fishing fleet in the Gulf, finally redeems himself by moving to Mexico. At first the braceros intend to rob him, but they come to sympathize with him after he is driven from his home by a mob of racist Anglos.

With all of the harsh experiences endured by the braceros in the United States, it is remarkable that references to Mexico are few in the novel, and details about what the men miss the most about their native country remain vague. Among these references are the desire to die on their native soil; a few lines from a song about Querétaro; and the characters' mutual recognition of one another as *raza, paisanos,* and *connacionales.* The characters' nostalgia for the sense of plenitude and state-familial protection that they once enjoyed in Mexico in fact is defined almost exclusively in contradistinction to the United States, where the braceros continually confront violence and lack of recognition.

Cocula, the gay character best adjusted to his new life, serves as an ironic and derogatory comment about what kind of Mexican can "make it" in the United States. The three heterosexual braceros, in contrast, constantly fend off threats of emasculation from white men, who are fearful that they will violate white women. Though desirable to the braceros, white women also pose a threat. Early in the novel, Paván becomes the *mantenido* ("kept man") of Leslie, the sex-hungry wife of an alcoholic rancher. Later he renounces her because she was "too much of a woman," hence "too masculine":

Reconocía ahora que no le había gustado nunca mucho porque era demasiado blanca, demasiado mujer en el sentido de su exigencia para con él, como hombre.

(He recognized now that he had never liked her very much, because she was too white, too much of a woman in the sense of her demands upon him, like a man.)

Elsewhere this castration anxiety is expressed more abstractly, as Paván's inability to earn money or his fear of having others dependent upon him. When he attempts to rob Chebo in the middle of the night, for example, he finds himself unable to grab the cash box with his injured arm and breaks down sobbing at his own "impotence."[40] Toward the novel's conclusion, Paván and Luis are kicked out of their place of employment because Luis has contracted gonorrhea from a prostitute. As Luis grows increasingly frail and requires Paván to care for him, Paván resents his friend and entertains fantasies of abandoning him.

Women are marginal in Spota's narrative in comparison to the relationships of domination and subordination established between Mexican and U.S. males and among the braceros themselves. In the United States, the braceros are deprived of romantic sexual relationships and tend to express their sexual urges in the same language in which they express their desire for U.S. commodities. At one point Paván looks at a Coca-Cola poster and wishes he had both the Coke and the girl pictured in it. The commoditization of women is not carried to the point of being a commentary about the impact of U.S. commercial culture on the bracero. Whereas the novel continually shows its partiality to the Mexican male over the Anglo male, Mexican women do not enter this distinction. One of the most disturbing sequences occurs when Paván, Luis, and their friend Raúl share a campsite with a married couple from Zacatecas. (The woman is the only *mojada* to appear in the novel.) At an agreed-upon moment, Paván and his companions bludgeon the man and gang-rape the woman, knowing that their illegal status affords them some protection from retribution: "Por fortuna, la policía no le hizo el menor caso: eran mexicanos y mexicanos fueron también sus asaltantes" ("Fortunately, the police didn't pay him the least attention: they were Mexicans and so were their assailants").[41] As in the passage quoted previously in which Paván compares himself to another less fortunate bracero, the rape is an incident in the novel where inequalities within the idealized Mexican nation become apparent. But rather than exhibit any self-reflexivity about these issues, the narrative ignores them, opting instead for another critical comment about the double standards of U.S. democracy.

Espaldas mojadas and the Cinematic Neoporfiriato

Among the directors who gained recognition during the "Golden Age" of Mexican cinema, Alejandro Galindo stands out as one who went against the dominant political current of the time. He consistently addressed difficult social issues in movies such as *Campeón sin corona* (Champion without a crown) (1945), *Una familia de tantas* (An ordinary family) (1948), *¡Esquina bajan!* (Corner, getting off!) (1948), and *El juicio de Martín Cortés* (The trial of Martín Cortés) (1973). Carl Mora argues that a major theme of Galindo's work is the Mexican "inferiority crisis," stemming from the repression and deprecation of indigenous culture in Mexican society and from U.S. cultural imperialism.[42] Galindo's movies, the work of a self-described "leftist," are sympathetic in their portrayals of the Mexican working class, and critical of the middle and upper classes. Galindo is also a committed nationalist; in a 1974 interview, he proposed, "Films could make the Mexican sincerely love his country, with an active love," and that the goal of Mexican cinema should be one of "creating a consciousness in our people."[43] Like Spota, Galindo, was the first in his field to undertake a serious analysis of the bracero issue. He wrote and directed *Espaldas mojadas,* in his words, to "convince Mexicans not to go to the United States."[44] Produced and released during the Operation Wetback years, the movie's title evokes the vicissitudes in the relationship between U.S. industry and Mexican labor throughout the run of the Bracero Program.

In several reviews of the movie from cine-club journals collected by Emilio García Riera, *Espaldas mojadas* was praised for its unconventional usage of English and Spanish dialogue, its sympathetic portrayal of the bracero, and its frankly critical portrayal of life for Mexicans in the United States. These journals rebuked the mainstream press and the government for conspiring to ignore or suppress the movie and its message.[45]

The plot of *Espaldas mojadas* is not unlike that of *Murieron a mitad del río,* the major differences being that the movie is set in El Paso/Juárez, and this time the bracero falls in love with a Chicana who saves him from "spiritual death." The lovers redeem one another by crossing to Mexico at the end of the film. As in Spota's novel, the movie begins and ends at the border. The protagonist, Rafael Améndolla Campuzano (David Silva) has fought with the son of a landowner over a woman and now seeks to escape his past by becoming a bracero. To cross the border, Rafael enlists the help of a corrupt Mexican *patero,* working in partnership with a cruel gringo labor contractor named Mr. Sterling (Víctor Parra). Once in the United States, Rafael flees from a series of jobs because he does not have proper documentation. He finally turns to Sterling's railroad crew for employment, but Sterling insults him when Rafael defends a fellow bracero who has been injured. Rafael runs away from the railroad, with Sterling and the cops in hot pursuit. He seeks refuge in a café, where he falls in love with the waitress, María del Consuelo (Martha Valdés). The two make plans to meet one another the following day in Juárez and begin a new life together. When Rafael returns to Juárez for María, he runs into Sterling and challenges him to a fight on his own turf. Before Rafael is about to deal the coup de grâce to Sterling, he is persuaded by onlookers to "see how well Sterling can swim." At the end of the movie, Sterling is shot to death in the middle of the river by U.S. Border Patrol agents who mistake him for a bracero, while Rafael, María, and other braceros look on in horror.

Like his literary counterpart Paván, Rafael is a loner and has skills that distinguish him from other braceros, but this is not evident at the outset of the movie. Rafael is introduced to the viewer through a voice-over documentary sequence that concludes with the camera tracking on Rafael as he walks along a Juárez street. Here he is a generic representative of the Mexican *pueblo.* Two shots later however, framed in the doorway of the Big Jim Café in Juárez while lighting a cigarette, he is converted into a leading man. Rafael's "tough guy" good looks, his fedora and leather jacket, the film noir lighting of his embattled hero's face, and the fact that he occupies the foreground in most group shots all emphasize his individuality.

Rafael's complexion, brought up several times in the movie, also sets him apart from other braceros and presents an interesting problem for the narrative. We have seen that Spota's novel contrasted the subtle system of social identification based upon skin color in Mexico to the fact that "all Mexicans look alike to gringos." *Espaldas mojadas* in contrast must repeatedly account for Rafael's fair skin in encounters with both Chicanos/as and Anglos.[46] In the United States, characters call attention to his features: María first addresses him as "*güerito*" ("blondie"), and a U.S. cop describes him by saying he "looks more like a wop than a Mexican." When Rafael returns to Mexico, on the other hand, he seems to undergo a change of racial identity. He is picked up by Mexican authorities who demand proof of his citizenship. Incredulous that anyone but a Mexican would *try* to enter Mexico illegally, Rafael attempts to convince a customs official of his nationality by offering to take off his shirt and show him his brown skin.[47] The official replies,

> Eso no hace prueba. Hay muchos americanos trigueños, mexicanos nacidos allá, pochos. . . . Hay muchos franceses morenos, españoles, italianos. . . . La mitad del mundo es morena.

> (That's no proof. There are many dark Americans, Mexicans born over there, *pochos*. There are a lot of brown French, Spaniards, Italians. . . . Half the world is brown.)

Being dark is not enough; the only legitimate proof of Rafael's identity lies in his birth certificate (echoing *Murieron a mitad del río*), which prompts a lecture from the customs official about "all the trouble you *mojados* cause the government." Rafael proceeds to mollify his interrogator with an impassioned speech in which he demands the right to work in his own country and breaks down sobbing. Though Rafael's movie-hero past is not typical of most braceros, this scene is the strongest allusion that the film makes to the "push factors" forcing braceros to leave their country.[48]

The theme of cross-border romance also enables the movie to contrast two different national conceptions of race. In the United States, Rafael identifies himself to other Mexicans as *raza*, an inclusive term that is valorized in the movie as it is in Spota's novel. Associated with the Mexican intellectual José Vasconcelos (who coincidentally spent his formative years in the Lower Valley of the U.S.–Mexico border region), the idea of *la raza* is emblematic of the effort to consolidate national identity in post-Revolutionary Mexico, especially through intervention in the educational and cultural sectors. Recurring to both cultural and genetic factors in his arguments, Vasconcelos viewed *la raza* as a synthetic entity encompassing the categories of culture, civilization, people, customs, and language. He distinguished between two currents within the white race, *sajones,* or people of northern European descent, and *latinos,* or those of Iberian descent, and he looked forward to the ascendance of a new cosmic race in Latin America, one that would blend *latino* and indigenous elements.[49]

In contrast to Rafael, María is identified in the movie with U.S. racial divisions during a particular historical moment in which Chicanos/as occupied an equivocal social position, one that rested somewhere between race and ethnicity, between de jure and de facto segregation. In an important scene, which I will discuss shortly, María contrasts her placelessness as a *pocha* to the positive cultural identity of African-Americans, who in her opinion have pride precisely because they are recognized as a group separate from Anglos. It is interesting to note that in this pre-Chicano/a movement film, *la raza* and *la patria* are coterminous; María is excluded from *la raza* until she decides to cross the border and embrace Mexico.

In addition to race and gender differences, *Espaldas mojadas* relies upon the borderline and deictic linguistic markers established in its opening sequence in order to construct national difference. As stated previously, the movie opens with a documentary portion in which a voice-over narrator introduces the viewer to Ciudad Juárez and El Paso. The sequence consists largely of stock footage of the downtown areas of each city, the river, and the international bridge, often taken from aerial perspectives. The narration celebrates the "laborious rhythm" of Juárez, downplaying the city's pre-Cárdenas reputation as a vice capital, and then works in a dig at the U.S. film industry as it turns to consider El Paso:

> Puerto de entrada de ese país que cuarenta años de cine le han hecho aparecer ante el mundo como una nación donde todos los habitantes son felices y donde todo se cuenta por millones.

> (Port of entry of that country, which forty years of cinema have made appear to be a nation where all of the inhabitants are happy and where everything is counted by the million.)

The narration continues to contrast the two cities based upon their respective standards of living and cultural attributes:

> De este lado es México donde todavía se habla el español y se canta a la Virgen con guitarras. Allá del otro lado, los rascacielos, símbolo arquitectónico del país más poderoso del mundo, donde todos los habitantes tienen radio, automóvil y televisión.

> (On this side is Mexico, where Spanish is still spoken and the Virgin is sung to with guitars. Over on the other side, the skyscrapers, architectonic symbol of the most powerful country of the world, where everyone has a radio, car, and television.)

At least from an aerial perspective, the border is clearly portrayed as a cultural trench. The differences are a little less pointed in the soundstage where the rest of the movie was shot. There, the only prop used to distinguish the U.S. from the Mexican side of the river is a Border Patrol watchtower and a rock with English graffiti on it (figure 33).

33. Publicity still from *Espaldas mojadas,* 1953. Linguistic markers and the Border Patrol watchtower distinguish one side of the river from the other. Photograph courtesy of Rogelio Agrasanchez.

The movie's imaginative use of English and Spanish dialogue is another way that it locates the characters on either side of the border. The liminal experience induced by border crossing that I have discussed in Spota's novel is figured in this text through a series of name changes. While Rafael waits to cross in a Juárez bar, a prostitute can spot him as a novice because he still uses his paternal and maternal surnames, according to Mexican custom. His name becomes abbreviated to Ralph Campuzano in the States, just as his vagabond buddy, Luis Villarreal, changes his name to Louie Royalville. Mary, the Chicana, only becomes María del Consuelo after Rafael's acceptance and love offers her the opportunity to "become Mexican."

The diegetic musical soundtrack is one of the privileged domains of Mexican nationalist discourse in *Espaldas mojadas.* In the rough and tumble Big Jim Café in Juárez, the habitués perform ensemble musical numbers to such Revolutionary hymns as "La Adelita" and "Valentina," and other songs with defiant *norteño* lyrics. In the United States, in contrast, the braceros mournfully strum guitars and sing haunting songs of loneliness, exile, and nostalgia for Mexico, such as "La canción mixteca" with its heartbreaking lyrics and melody: "O tierra del sol / Respiro por verte / Ahora tan lejos / Yo vivo sin luz, sin amor" ("Oh land of the sun / I breathe to see you / Now so far away / I live without light, without love"). These songs, as well

34. Publicity still from *Espaldas mojadas*, 1953. Anomie and nostalgia for Mexico characterize the braceros' experience in the United States. Photograph courtesy of Rogelio Agrasanchez.

as "La Adelita" and "Valentina," which are about *soldaderas* leaving their *soldados,* establish two very strong and interrelated thematic currents in the movie: the longing for an idealized Mexico of the past and the duplicity of women.

In *Espaldas mojadas,* betrayal and redemption by women is the primary driving force of the plot: a bad woman makes Rafael cross the border and a good one gives him reason to return again. To be in the United States for the bracero means deprivation of maternal and nurturing love, and only fleeting encounters with prostitutes. Heartsickness causes one bracero on the railroad crew (played by Eulalio González, "El Piporro") to go on a drunken binge and run amok in the desert, shouting petitions to his lost love and the Virgin of Guadalupe (figure 34). Only in Mexico can Rafael envision a happy ending with María.

For María, on the other hand, happiness is a bit more complex. She and the comic tramp, Luis, are interesting characters, because they are skillful code-switchers, and yet their situation is perceived as tragic by Rafael, who eventually convinces both of them to return to Mexico with him. Whereas Rafael is identified by others in terms of his skin color, María is identified by others in terms of her voice, or more specifically, her bilingualism. As the only fully bilingual character in the movie, she is an emblem of what was perceived by critics as experimental and innovative in

Espaldas mojadas at the time of its release. María repeatedly uses her language abilities to avoid fixing her identity in the eyes of her interlocutors. In the United States María pretends that she does not speak English to get rid of the cops; in Mexico she uses the same trick in reverse to get rid of a masher. Her lines exploit the division between intention and enunciation, that is, until she falls in love with Rafael.

The story of Rafael and María's courtship is narrated economically through four scenes: two set on the U.S. side of the border, two on the Mexican side. The couple's first meeting actually occurs just after Rafael has crossed the border. María stands amidst a patriotic throng on the sidewalk watching a Memorial Day parade in El Paso, as a conspicuously dressed Rafael works his way toward her. In a two-shot, María helps Rafael to order a hot dog from a vendor because Rafael does not speak English. This scene sets the stage for many formal motifs that will recur in the movie, and for María's eventual transfer to a place and situation where Rafael instead will have the upper hand. This scene also presents the border as a militarized zone in which the privileged form of human spatial organization is shoulder to shoulder, a variation on the metaphors of horizontal fraternal comradeship and the "long grey line" that Benedict Anderson has argued characterize nationalist imagery.[50] When next they meet in the café, María spies a hunted-looking Rafael through a glass window in an over-the-shoulder-shot from within the café. This precedes the turning point in terms of the power dynamic of their relationship, when María tearfully confesses to Rafael that she is not Mexican, but rather a *pocha*:

> Nuestra desgracia es más grande que la de los negros. Aunque ellos nacieron aquí como nosotros, en cambio no saben de donde vienen. Ni tienen la tentación de una patria. Además ellos se defienden. Hacen grupos. Tienen sus bailes. Entre ellos se casan y se consuelan. A nosotros la raza no nos quiere. Y los bolillos, ya viste . . .

> (Our disgrace is worse than the blacks. Although they were born here like we were, in contrast they don't know where they come from. Nor do they have the temptation of a homeland *[patria]*. Besides, they defend themselves. They form groups. They have their dances. They marry and console one another. As for us, the Mexicans *[raza]* don't want us, and the whites *[bolillos]*, well you've already seen . . .)

After this pivotal scene, the established rhythm of their courtship begins to repeat itself: the shot of Rafael entering María's workplace finds its rhyme later in the movie when a skittish María is filmed through the window of his milieu, the Big Jim Café in Juárez. The last scene of the movie has the two lovers once again standing shoulder to shoulder, now on the Mexican bank of the Rio Grande/Río Bravo (figure 35). María affirms her commitment to Rafael by telling him, "Para una mujer no hay más mundo que el hombre que uno quiere" ("For a woman there is no world other than the man whom one loves"). María finds her place then, under the sign of the three M's: man, Mexico, and monolingualism. Taking Rafael, the world, and Mexico as synonymous in her last line is entirely plausible from the 1950s Mexican perspective.

35. Publicity still from *Espaldas mojadas,* 1953. "For a woman there is no world other than the man whom one loves." Photograph courtesy of Rogelio Agrasanchez.

Jean Franco has argued, for example, that post-Revolutionary Mexican narratives often constructed the subjectivity of male citizens at the expense of silencing female ones, and Roger Bartra has noted the tendency in twentieth-century Mexican intellectual history to treat the nation and the individual male subject as homologous categories of analysis.[51]

In much the same way that the romantic happy ending provides an identity for María that substantially alters her previous characterization in the movie, so too does the ending compel Rafael to undergo a transformation from being a solitary loner to being the member of a community. Rafael's key scene in this regard occurs in the middle of the movie, when he discusses his frustrations as a bracero with his friend Luis. Standing in the middle of the desert, he slowly walks away from Luis and approaches the camera, as in a dramatic soliloquy:

> Y luego en esta tierra tan extraña para mí, se siente uno como cortado de uno, solo. En una rueda de soledad. . . . Tú en el centro, y no tienes ni un ruido, ni una mirada. Nadie te ve, nadie te oye. ¡No existes!

> (In this land that is so strange to me, one feels cut off from others, alone. In a wheel of loneliness. You're in the center, and you don't have a sound, a look. No one sees you, no one hears you. You don't exist!)

This statement sums up the anomie that haunts all of the characters in the movie. Ironically, the very ingredients that made up the quasi-existential *bracero* experience according to both Spota and Galindo—alienation, detachment, isolation from others, and above all, futile attempts at dissimulation and mimicry in order to "fit in"— also describe to the letter essential aspects of the "Mexican" character as outlined by Octavio Paz in his landmark collection of essays, *El laberinto de soledad (The Labyrinth of Solitude),* which appeared in 1950.[52]

That Paz and Galindo share common intellectual concerns is obvious from Galindo's filmography, dominated as it is by themes of Mexican self-denial and *malinchismo.* Galindo in fact chose to conclude his 1985 memoir about the Mexican film industry with two quotes from Paz's *El laberinto,* one about La Malinche, and the following one about the self-imposed exile of the Mexican:

> El mexicano y la mexicanidad se definen como la ruptura y negación y asimismo como búsqueda, como voluntad por trascender ese estado de exilio. En suma, como viva conciencia de la sociedad, histórica y personal. La historia, que no nos podía decir algo sobre la naturaleza de nuestros sentimientos y de nuestros conflictos, sí nos puede mostrar ahora cómo se realizó la ruptura y cuáles han sido nuestras tentativas para trascender la soledad.

> (The Mexican and *mexicanidad* are defined as rupture and negation and at the same time as a quest, as a will to transcend this state of exile. In sum, as the living conscience of society, both historical and personal. History, which could not tell us anything about the nature of our feelings and our conflicts, can show how the rupture occurred and what our attempts have been to transcend solitude.)[53]

Just as Galindo chose to conclude his memoir, entitled *El cine mexicano: Un personal punto de vista (Mexican Cinema: A Personal Point of View),* with a quote from the 1950s, so he decided to end Mexican film history in that decade, in 1953 to be precise—the same year that he made *Espaldas mojadas.* There is only one mention of the movie in the text; it is listed along with three other films from that era that were *enlatadas* due to their political content. The year is otherwise significant in Galindo's view as the end of an era in Mexican film production, after which it became impossible to make a movie about political or social issues. The exile of the bracero from the state that ignores him thus concurs with the exile of the politically committed filmmaker. Galindo finds nothing but bile to describe the "neoporfirista" cinema that followed the early 1950s:

> [E]l cine vive una vida muy similar en género a la que prevalecía en tiempo de Porfirio Díaz, cuando existían las leyes de reforma pero que no se las cumplía.

> ([C]inema leads a life similar in a respect to that which prevailed in the time of Porfirio Díaz, when the laws of reform existed but were not carried out.)[54]

His attack on contemporary Mexican filmmaking is so relentless that Octavio Colmenares seems at pains to counter it with numerous examples about the vitality of post-1950s Mexican cinema in his prologue. One of the interesting points raised by Galindo's periodization of Mexican cinema is that rather than looking inward to the failure of the Revolution to find the roots of the crisis, as Cosío Villegas did in his 1947 essay, Galindo blames McCarthyism for having cast a pall of censorship and authoritarianism over the entire continent. Thus, not only does the U.S.-trained filmmaker identify himself with the bracero in terms of his distance from the Mexican state, he also identifies with him in terms of his unpleasant proximity to the United States.

As a postscript to *Espaldas mojadas,* one of the abysmal post-1953 movies that Galindo neglects to mention in his memoir is his own *Los mojados,* a 1977 production that returns to the themes of his earlier classic.[55] Starring Jorge Rivero as the lone bracero, this movie is an action-packed vehicle with low production values, similar in many ways to the hundreds of immigration movies churned out since the mid-1970s that are aimed at provincial Mexican and U.S. *indocumentado* audiences. Read in light of Galindo's 1985 commentary about the decline of the Mexican film industry, the conclusion of this movie is both painful and cynical. The bracero Juan is really an undercover Mexican agent in partnership with a liberal Mexican journalist who is out to expose the injustices suffered by braceros. Juan falls in love with a Chicana, and takes on the mafia as in the earlier production, but before he makes it back to the river, he is abruptly killed by a sniper. The movie ends with an aerial shot of Juan's car smashed into a tree.

Nationalism and Anti-imperialism

I have proposed that *Murieron a mitad del río* and *Espaldas mojadas* are not just socially conscious narratives about braceros, but that they are also meditations about Mexican identity staged abroad rather than domestically. What is achieved by this change of venue? One obvious response to this question is that the texts' strong nationalism, insistent upon marked distinctions between the United States and Mexico, denies recognition of the border region and its complex social system, just as I argued in chapter 3 with regard to U.S. popular texts about the border. From their nationalist and centralist perspectives, *Espaldas mojadas* and *Murieron a mitad del río* simply view Chicanos/as as bad Mexicans, a stance whose epistemological claim to authenticity has been challenged a great deal in recent decades in favor of more plurivalent or hybrid conceptions of identity (see chapter 5). Historian Oscar Martínez, for example, outlines a social typology of the border region in which he identifies and praises a character type that he calls the "core borderlander." Such people are characterized by "a common international mind-set and a binational form of behavior resulting from an intense involvement in transnational, transethnic, and transcultural processes."[56] Not surprisingly Chicanos/as comprise the greatest numbers of this sector, according to Martínez. Had *Espaldas mojadas* been produced from this perspective, María's capacity to negotiate nations, languages, and linguistic registers would have made her, and not Rafael, the hero of the movie.

A second ramification of staging the Mexican quest for identity in the United States involves the relationship between gender and nation that is so prominent in both the novel and the movie. Both narratives identify the United States with castrating male authority figures: bosses, overseers, police, Border Patrol agents, and swindlers. The gender identification of Mexico, on the other hand, is rather murky: as a remembered entity, the nation is identified with familial security; in the present, however, it is populated by benign but ineffectual male authority figures (e.g., the customs official in *Espaldas mojadas*), as well as corrupt police, *pateros,* and *coyotes.*

According to Paz's essay from *El laberinto,* "Los hijos de La Malinche" ("The Sons of La Malinche"), the foundational romance of Mexico is the troubled family produced from the union of the conquistador Cortés and his indigenous mistress La Malinche. Their illegitimate mestizo offspring (a male Oedipus figure) tends to identify with and rebel against his Spanish colonial father, while he denigrates or represses his indigenous mother. Paz issues a call for Mexicans to recognize and valorize their maternal cultural heritage and thereby to integrate the three building blocks of the Mexican nation.[57] Despite his attempt to ground *mexicanidad* in five centuries of history, Paz's preoccupation with national identity in the 1950s was very much a modern concern, arising from the abrupt social changes brought about by the Revolution and the resultant desire for a stabilizing agent in the form of a strong middle class or a prototypical national type.[58]

The bracero stories I have analyzed reconfigure Paz's familial triad by substituting a host of U.S. patriarchal figures in place of the Spanish colonial father as the source of the bracero's sense of illegitimacy. In this manner they backhandedly acknowledge the threat posed to Mexico by U.S. imperialism. But the transformation of the conquistador-indio-mestizo triad into the U.S.-mexicano-bracero relationship is not stable in these texts. As a term of negotiation between two "opposites," the bracero comes into conflict with the Chicano, who also occupies the middle rung in the strong three-part class hierarchy internal to the United States, consisting of the Anglo boss, the Chicano overseer, and the Mexican worker. This "in-between" position is what draws the lovers together in *Espaldas mojadas*: Rafael and María are both portrayed as middle terms, corresponding to Paz's positioning of the mestizo. The lovers identify with one another because each experiences a profound sense of solitude.

In contrast to Paz's call for integration, however, the stories cannot and do not wish to unify the newer versions of the family romance, for that would involve inclusion of the United States and Anglos into the mythical Mexican social structure or the inclusion of Mexicans into the U.S. social structure: in either case it would pose a threat to Mexican nationalism. Moreover, consideration of the braceros' social "place" within both countries would require that "the economic" and "the national," identified with the United States and Mexico respectively, be considered as interrelated phenomena. The bracero stories do not take an international approach to understanding the "push" and "pull" factors influencing migration, preferring instead to dwell on the "pull" factors: Anglo greed and the "lure of the dollar."

A central preoccupation of both texts is laying blame for the plight of the bracero at the feet of one social group or another. With their somewhat atypical protagonists relative to the era's poor, displaced border crossers, these narratives easily lend themselves to conventional readings as morality tales of sin and redemption. That Anglos are faulted is obvious, but Chicanos, women, and the braceros themselves are also depicted as traitors in these stories. In her analysis of the bracero figure in folklore and elitelore, María Herrera-Sobek found that Mexican narratives about migrants since the Depression era have tended to prefer Chicanos as scapegoats over Anglos.[59] While the stories spread blame profusely on behalf of the braceros, conversely they withhold agency from them. At the conclusion of *Espaldas mojadas,* an anonymous bracero consoles Rafael by telling him that no one was really responsible for Sterling's death but Sterling himself.[60]

A nostalgic pre-Oedipal Mexico thus remains opposed to the U.S. interloper in the bracero narratives. In them, Mexico exists as something remembered or hoped for but not something tenable in the present. The stories' sentimental nationalism, cued by traditional music and references to the land, echoes the idealized provincial past that was promoted during the "Golden Age" of Mexican cinema by such genres as the *comedia ranchera.* Spota's protagonist Luis Paván reflects upon his life on several occasions by imagining his mind as a movie screen upon which images are projected. In another scene from the novel, the narrator describes two braceros reminiscing about Mexico in phrases often reserved for the cinema:

> Parecían una máquina, zumbadora y humana, productora de sueños, reconstructora de pasados que a nadie, sino a ellos mismos, importaban.

> (They seemed like a humming, human machine, producer of dreams, reconstructor of pasts that were important to no one else but themselves.)[61]

For Sefchovich, the reconstruction of the past through narrative forms was important not only to isolated braceros but to an entire social class that rose to power in the 1940s. Writing of Spota's commitment to this class and its "neoporfirista" project, she argues,

> Ese proyecto que parece mirar hacia adelante y en realidad hace precisamente lo contrario y pretende volver el reloj cuarenta años atrás en la historia nacional, para plantear hacia el futuro un esquema histórico que ya fue puesto a prueba y que, a pesar de la insistencia de la derecha por revivirlo, ya fracasó.

> (That project seems to look ahead and in reality does precisely the opposite; it pretends to turn the clock of national history back forty years in order to propose a historical scheme for the future that was already put to the test [during the Porfiriato], and in spite of the right's insistence upon reliving it, already failed.)[62]

The same forty-year period is interpreted differently by *Espaldas mojadas,* despite its similarity to *Murieron a mitad del río.* Recall that in the voice-over narration of *Espaldas mojadas,* the time period was significant because it harked back to an era when U.S. cinema had not yet claimed Mexican audiences. Produced at the end of the "Golden Age," the movie's nostalgia is self-reflexive, populist, and anti-imperialist, but, conveniently, its brand of nationalism was mainstream enough to fit in with the dominant political current of the time. As Emilio García Riera quipped, if the movie were *that* radical, it would have been *enlatada* for much more than two years.[63]

Chapter 5

Mass Media, Site-Specificity, and Representations of the U.S.–Mexico Border

All major metropoli have been fully borderized. In fact, there are no longer visible cultural differences between Manhattan, Montreal, Washington, Los Angeles, or Mexico City. They all look like downtown Tijuana on a Saturday night.
            —Guillermo Gómez-Peña, "The New World (B)order"[1]

Its exact location is problematical; the awkward fact is, Borderland can apparently be found by heading for the ruins of just about any large twentieth-century city. This reporter found it in the rubble of Detroit.
                        —Life on the Border[2]

Today, *the border* and *border crossing* are commonly used critical metaphors among multicultural and postmodernist artists and writers. According to Chon Noriega, however, these terms were first employed in the 1960s and 1970s by Chicano/a and Mexican scholars to refer to the experience of undocumented workers from Mexico crossing to the United States.[3] Indeed, in Chicano/a arts and letters, "Borderlands" has replaced Aztlán as the metaphor of choice in order to designate a communal space.[4] But even though the U.S.–Mexico border retains a shadowy presence in the usage of these terms, the border that is currently in vogue in the United States, both among Chicano/a scholars and among those theorists working on other cultural differences is rarely site-specific.[5] Rather, it is invoked as a marker of hybrid or liminal subjectivities, such as those that would be experienced by persons who negotiate among multiple cultural, linguistic, racial, or sexual systems throughout their lives. When the border *is* spatialized in these theories, that space is almost always universal. "The Third World having been collapsed into the First,"[6] as the argument goes, the border is now to be found in any metropolis—wherever poor, displaced, ethnic, immigrant, or sexual minority populations collide with the "hegemonic" population, which is usually understood to consist of middle- and upper-class WASPs.

In this chapter, I examine two sets of aesthetic texts in which the border figures prominently as a space of fantasy and sociopolitical allegory, with the aim of challenging the project of expanding borders and the types of experiences understood by the term *border crossing* outlined above. The first group of texts is documentation relating to two performances by Guillermo Gómez-Peña, *Border Brujo* (1988–90) and *Year of the White Bear: The New World (B)order* (1992–94). Gómez-Peña, a former member of the Border Art Workshop/Taller de Arte Fronterizo (BAW/TAF), made U.S.–Mexico border issues a central theme of his work from the mid- to late-1980s. The video version of *Border Brujo* marked a shift in terms of Gómez-Peña's thematic concerns; its release in 1990 roughly coincided with the artist's decision to de-emphasize the U.S.–Mexico border region, while nevertheless retaining the border metaphor as a way to address general issues of appropriation and cultural imperialism.

The second group of texts is a subgenre of speculative fiction that has been called "contemporary urban fantasy" by one of its creators.[7] Currently there are over a dozen writers in the United States and Canada who have collaborated in creating an imaginary metropolis called Bordertown.[8] Their shared world has been elaborated in four collections of short stories and three novels; at the time of this writing, future novels were planned.[9] An active fan culture has sprung up around the Bordertown series, which ranges from raves held in Los Angeles and San Francisco warehouses, where guests recreate "The Dancing Ferret" (a Bordertown nightclub), to dance troupes in several U.S. cities that derive inspiration from Bordertown's "Horn Dance" commune (figure 36). Websites dedicated to the series exist where fans interact with one another and several of the series contributors through an e-mail bulletin board. Some write their own "fanfic" (fan fiction) or create art inspired by the series that is posted on a related website. Others run live role-playing games based on the series in their hometowns, while a text-based, real-time, role-playing software program called Anime MUSH allows Bordertown fans to role-play on the internet.[10] Bordertown's various fan subcultures may become more mainstream in the near future, as one of the Bordertown novels is presently being considered for a two-hour TV pilot, and world rights for the stories were recently negotiated.[11]

Both Gómez-Peña's work and that of the Bordertown collective conform to the type of "global border consciousness" I have outlined above; neither claims to be exclusively about the U.S.–Mexico border. If I am rather perversely trying to tie them to this particular geographical region, it is indirectly, through the common issues that these aesthetic projects share with popular mass media coverage of NAFTA and globalization. Like the news media, the former texts are grappling with ways to broach the subject of "North American identity" in light of globalization's putative threat to national identities. The synecdochic way of seeing the border outlined in chapter 3, in which the border signifies the whole of U.S.–Mexico relations in microcosm, has been quite prevalent in NAFTA and post-NAFTA media coverage. Both advocates and detractors of free trade have appropriated this model in order to cast the border

36. The Bordertown series has given rise to an active fan culture. Alan Scott's light eyes and pointed ears indicate his elvin heritage. Reproduced by permission of the photographer, ReyLynda Colquhoun, and Terri Windling, Editor/Creator of the "Bordertown" series.

as "the future" or "the cutting edge" of what would occur throughout the North American continent if NAFTA were ratified. The Bordertown stories and Gómez-Peña's recent work also place their border zones in a not-too-distant, apocalyptic future—a future that nonetheless incorporates many elements from our immediate present.

Globalizing the Border: Guillermo Gómez-Peña

In his recent work, Guillermo Gómez-Peña, *Chica-lango*[12] performance artist, has increasingly unmoored his border from the "transfrontier metropolis" of San Diego/ Tijuana, where he was a founding member of BAW/TAF in 1984. BAW/TAF was, and still is, a group of Mexican, Anglo, and Chicano/a artists who engage in collaborative multimedia and interactive arts projects about the U.S.–Mexico border region.[13] During the period of Gómez-Peña's membership, BAW/TAF artists were both present-minded and oppositional; their work responded critically to border issues such as immigration, human rights violations, and racism, and they were utopian in that they asked their audiences to "imagine a world in which this international boundary has been erased."[14] Site-specificity—not just in terms of installation, but also in terms of audience address and thematic issues—became a guiding principle of the group. Jeff Kelley described BAW/TAF's project as an "art of place":

> [A]n art of place is concerned less with the phenomenal and geological aspects of a place than with the cultural, historical, ethnic, linguistic, political, and mythological dimensions of a site. To some degree, of course, site and place are matters of interchangeable perception. Thus, we see site-specific art transformed into a place-particular practice which represents the domestication and/or socialization of the '70s site, and defines approaches to art-making in which a place, a condition, or an occasion is seen and worked as the materials of human or social exchange. A place is not merely a medium of art, but also its contents.[15]

For Gómez-Peña, as for other BAW/TAF members, the border was always much more than a line demarcating national space. Emphasizing the social and cultural dimensions of the U.S.–Mexico border over topographical ones immediately gave "border consciousness" a certain mobility. As a phenomenological category, the border was something that people carried within themselves, in addition to being an external factor structuring their perceptions.

Gómez-Peña's endeavors in performance art prior to forming BAW/TAF (e.g., with Poyesis Genética)[16] suggest that he was already working through ideas about liminal subjectivities before he attached them to the San Diego/Tijuana region. Emphasizing subjectivity as predominant over social geography, however, facilitated his later expansion of the border to encompass "the World." This shift is clearly evident in several essays he published in U.S. arts media during the period immediately prior to and following his break with BAW/TAF. In his 1988 essay "Documented/ Undocumented," for example, Gómez-Peña referred to the process of world "borderization,"[17] but he also privileged the deterritorialized perspective of the (U.S.–Mexico) border artist, which allowed him or her to act as facilitator of intercultural dialogue among ethnic groups. In his 1989 "The Multicultural Paradigm," Gómez-Peña extended the role of "border crosser" to all North Americans and all readers of his work:

> Today, if there is a dominant culture, it is border culture. And those who still haven't crossed a border will do it very soon. All Americans (from the vast continent of America) were, are, or will be border crossers. "All Mexicans," says Tomás Ybarra-Frausto, "are potential Chicanos." As you read this text, you are crossing a border yourself.[18]

Gómez-Peña's next step was to make the border global. "From Art-mageddon to Gringostroika," an essay published in 1991 in *High Performance,* found him speaking of many geographical borders, from the Americas to the Iron Curtain. But geographical borders were all but upstaged in this essay by a new, temporal threshold. Gómez-Peña wrote, "We stand equi-distant from utopia and Armageddon, with one foot on each side of the border, and our art and thought reflect this condition."[19] This apocalyptic look toward the next millennium, signified by a vertiginous time-space compression, has since become a major theme of Gómez-Peña's work, and I will discuss it in relation to the Bordertown series later in this chapter.

But first I want to discuss how Gómez-Peña's incrementally expanding border has had an impact upon his visual work. As I stated earlier, the release of the video version of *Border Brujo* in 1990 can be read as a signpost of the shift in his thinking about borders in relation to place. In some ways the video is an anomalous conclusion to his involvement with BAW/TAF, for it was released just as the collective was in the throes of reorganization and shortly before Gómez-Peña denounced border art altogether in several highly publicized articles in 1991.[20] Isaac Artenstein, a Mexican-born filmmaker well-known for his movie *Break of Dawn* (1988), about the rise of Spanish-language radio in Los Angeles, produced and directed *Border Brujo* after Gómez-Peña successfully toured the performance for two years (1988–90) in North America and Europe.[21]

The publicity for *Border Brujo* describes it as a performance "in which Guillermo Gómez-Peña transforms himself into 15 different personas to exorcise the demons of dominant cultures. In English, Spanish, Spanglish, Ingleñol, and Náhuatl-bicameral." People familiar with BAW/TAF's earlier work would note immediate continuities of theme, costume, iconography, and sets between *Border Brujo* and previous BAW/TAF projects. This was also not the first time that a BAW/TAF member had used video to record a performance.[22] For the most part, *Border Brujo* privileges documentation of Gómez-Peña's performance over experimentation with the video medium itself. Its camera movement and editing are relatively nonintrusive; other than alternation between medium shots and close-ups of Gómez-Peña, the camera only cuts for brief moments to extreme close-ups of the props that comprise the altar/set (figure 37).[23] There is one sequence in which Artenstein's camera work breaks markedly with this tendency. In the "Casa de Cambio" sequence, Gómez-Peña plays a Tijuana barker who advertises the various transformations of personal identity available to those who dare to cross the border.[24] The video rapidly cuts from camera positions to the left and right of Gómez-Peña, establishing an imaginary line that actually bisects his body. This technique represents a drastic departure from the way that U.S. and Mexican commercial cinema have used an imaginary borderline in narratives set in

37. Director Isaac Artenstein and Guillermo Gómez-Peña during the *Border Brujo* shoot. Photograph by Max Aguilera Hellweg.

the U.S.–Mexico border region, namely, as a structuring device that segregates rather than integrates opposing elements of "cultural identities" (see chapters 3 and 4 for a discussion of more conventional uses of the borderline in photography and film).

From its first intertitle, which asserts that "language is the border," *Border Brujo* preoccupies itself with the perceptual and perspectival definition of the border that I have associated with BAW/TAF. The Brujo incarnates a mosaic of parodic characters including a *mojado,* a *cholo,* a Texas redneck, and a transvestite, who are differentiated from one another by variations in costume, body movement, and speech. The idea of alternation among personae, spaces, and languages is so integral to the performance that it raises the issue of whether Gómez-Peña would really like to see borders eliminated, or whether his work is indeed dependent upon borders to uphold the oppositions that he critiques. Gómez-Peña is not out to destroy differences, as much as he attempts to effect abrupt collisions among various "subject positions," and to compel his audience to perform a similar kind of "border crossing." The gestures of religiosity and self-purification that punctuate *Border Brujo*'s segments, which include lighting candles, burning sage, the bell-ringing of transubstantiation, and most memorably, drinking from a bottle of Clairol Herbal Essence shampoo, also beg the question of just whose "dominant culture" demons Gómez-Peña is exorcising—his own or the audience's? Rather than adopting such a thematic in order to denounce the pervasiveness of U.S. mass media and commercialism, in the name of preserving some "authentic" national or local culture, Gómez-Peña turns this exorcism into an indictment of a monocultural point of view on the part of his implied audience. The Brujo's ritualistic gestures punctuate his entry into a liminal state in which the notion of an essential or stable identity is thrown into question.

The Brujo not only speaks in Spanish and English, but also in "tongues," suggesting that the spectator has access only to a fragmentary view of the complex, hallucinatory reality to which the Brujo is privy. This disproportionate relation of knowledge and power between the Brujo and his audience is established from the very beginning of the video when the Brujo says, "Allow me the privilege of reorganizing your thoughts," and it is sustained throughout the video's often claustrophobic framing and Gómez-Peña's frequent eye contact with the camera. As he mutates from character to character, the Brujo speaks as many "I's," while frequently leveling accusations at a "you" who is seemingly stable, both in terms of location and identity. Very often this "you" would appear to be a white, male cultural imperialist:

"I speak, therefore you misinterpret me";
"I am in Tijuana, you are in San Diego";
"I exist, therefore you misunderstand me";
"How ironic, mister, I represent you, yet you don't represent me."

Self-reflexive comments scattered throughout the video also imply that this "you" constitutes the video's audience. At one point the Brujo chants, "If it wasn't for the fact that I wrote this text on a Macintosh and I shot my rehearsals with a Sony 8, I would really fulfill your expectations."

Grant Kester identifies Gómez-Peña's relationship to his audience, characterized by polemical statements and direct address, as typical of what he terms the "rant" performance artists who came to prominence in the U.S. "alternative arts" scene of the mid-1980s and early 1990s. Writing of Gómez-Peña, Karen Finley, and other artists, Kester remarks that the "implied viewer . . . is often a mythical father figure conjured up out of the artist's imagination to be shouted at, attacked, radicalized, or otherwise transformed by the work of the performance."[25] According to Kester "rant" performances turn upon a tacit play between this fantasy audience composed of racist, sexist, homophobic, white men and the "real" audience, drawn from the enlightened habitués of the "alternative arts" scene. The former camp, of course, would be quite unlikely to attend such performances in the first place, which leaves the "alternative arts" audience to engage in a double identification:

> The audience of a performance by Finley or a Kruger installation knows that it isn't the "real" target of the outraged pronouncements on sexism or racial oppression. Rather they consume the work simultaneously in the first person and the third person; imagining themselves as the intended viewer while at the same moment reassuring themselves of their own ideological superiority to this point of view.[26]

Thus, haranguing a phantom audience permits Gómez-Peña to enter a bond of complicity with an audience of informed spectators. The fact that this confrontational mode of address becomes a sort of in-joke on those who are not actually present for the performance is also suggested in Gómez-Peña's critical writings on multiculturalism and cultural studies in the United States, where he subtly defines his intended audience by suggesting who it is not.[27] Chicano/a nationalists are another group besides conservative Anglos who are absent from Gómez-Peña's implied audience. In *Border Brujo,* they are not directly addressed, but rather more delicately isolated from the imaginary audience: "They say I talk to Gringos; they say I wasn't born in East L.A.; they say I left the committee by choice; they say I promote negative stereotypes of my people." By eliminating these two "extremes"—that is, Anglo and Latino/a separatists—Gómez-Peña rhetorically constructs a "middle" of sorts, which consists of those who, in his estimation, would be most receptive to hybrid cultural identities and "border crossing."

The piece's transformation from performance to video was also marked by additional features that suggest a shift in the way Gómez-Peña conceived of his mass media audience. For one thing, in the earlier in situ versions of the piece, he interacted with the audience during the performance. He would shine a flashlight on them and interrogate them in a parody of a Border Patrol agent, for example, and at the end of the performance, he collected items from various members of the audience and added them to his altar/set for future performances or buried them on the U.S.–Mexico border. The video does not portray an audience at all, nor does the camera ever cut to give a point-of-view shot from Gómez-Peña's perspective. In the live versions, Gómez-Peña often changed portions of his script to include the name of the place where he was performing and other site-specific information. Three published versions of the script,[28] for example, include a great deal of material about California, and specifically about San Diego/Tijuana. The video version, on the other hand, includes fewer references to the location of the performance, and at one point Gómez-Peña refers to "Sushi," the performance space/gallery that supported the video's production. Finally, and perhaps most important, in the video version

Gómez-Peña deleted almost all of the large chunks of the script that were in Spanish, as well as some of the more politically pointed critiques in English.[29]

Many of these outtakes were eventually recut into another much shorter piece, entitled *Son of Border Crisis: Seven Video Poems* (1990). The latter video is like an alter ego of the former. It contains more material in Spanish, and because its roughly fifteen minutes of footage are broken up into seven segments, the pace is aphoristic rather than sermonic. It even opens with an exterior shot of Gómez-Peña in front of Sushi, pitching the show to potential spectators through a megaphone. This video was released largely due to demand from Chicano/a and Latino/a film festivals in the United States, and also from festivals in Latin America and Spain, for a sample of Artenstein and Gómez-Peña's project that fit in well with the time constraints of short-subject programming.[30]

As Gómez-Peña was moving toward a solo career based in New York and gaining access to a broader "alternative art" audience through his video, he was simultaneously attacking the co-optation of the border art movement by major museums and galleries in the press.[31] A key complaint on his part was that BAW/TAF, which had in some sense brought border art to the attention of the national arts community, was now being ignored by that same community. He criticized the La Jolla Museum of Contemporary Art (now the Museum of Contemporary Art, San Diego) for raising half a million dollars in order to "bring big names from out of town" for a four-year border art project.[32] Perhaps being "deterritorialized" from the U.S.–Mexico border region itself provided Gómez-Peña with the rationale for abandoning an "art of place" in favor of the more general "New World (B)order." The border arts project to which Gómez-Peña referred was known as *Dos Ciudades/Two Cities,* and it culminated in 1993–94 with an exhibition called *La Frontera/The Border: Art about the Mexico/United States Border Experience,* jointly organized by San Diego's Centro Cultural de la Raza and the Museum of Contemporary Art. The Centro Cultural, founded in 1970 in the wake of the Chicano/a Movement, had housed and sponsored BAW/TAF during Gómez-Peña's tenure with the group, and it had long been positioned as "alternative," both in terms of funding and constituency, to the "mainstream" Museum of Contemporary Art. Though the two institutions did achieve a rapprochement during the period of the *Dos Ciudades/Two Cities* project, Gómez-Peña was among several artists who declined to have their work included in the *La Frontera/The Border* show.[33]

"The New World (B)order" is a 1992–94 performance written and directed by Gómez-Peña, and performed by Gómez-Peña and Coco Fusco, and later Roberto Sifuentes. An essay by the same name and closely following the text of the performance appeared in *High Performance,* and versions of the scripts have been published in the *Drama Review* and an anthology of Gómez-Peña's recent work entitled *The New World Border.*[34] The format of the performance is loosely based on a news or radio broadcast in which two characters, El Aztec High-Tech (Gómez-Peña) and

Miss Discovery 92 93 (Fusco) alternate in presenting their descriptions of the new world. As in *Border Brujo,* each character actually comprises many different voices and personae. "The New World (B)order" was conceived as part of a larger, year-long project relating to the quincentenary, entitled *The Year of the White Bear,* which included a trilogy of performances, as well as essays and radio broadcasts. Gómez-Peña assembled a team of Mexican, Chicano, and Caribbean artists from the East and West Coasts to collaborate on various aspects of the productions.[35] Like *Border Brujo, The New World (B)order* was adapted for television by filmmaker Daniel Salazar and was scheduled for distribution in fall 1994.[36]

Rhetorically speaking, "The New World (B)order" takes up a strategy that Gómez-Peña has identified elsewhere as common in border art. He plays with imaginary role reversals in order to "adopt a position of privilege and speak from a position of privilege even though we know it's a fictional position."[37] Gómez-Peña creates these hypothetical situations out of contradictions presently operative in U.S. political discourse. One such contradiction is the promotion of a united North America by advocates of free trade, while at the same time the continent's national populations remain juridically segregated from one another. Gómez-Peña, who has consistently called attention to the already "borderized" state of U.S. cultures, subverts the idea of an Anglo majority in North America by asking, What if NAFTA lifted barriers to immigration on the continent? What if the roles between gringos and Mexicans were reversed? Following the arrival of "Gringostroika"[38] on the North American continent,

> Geo-political borders have faded away. Due to the implementation of a *Free Raid Agreement* and the creation of a *Zona de Libre Cogercio,*[39] the nations formerly known as Canada, the United States, and Mexico have merged painlessly to create the Federation of U.S. Republics. FUSR is controlled by a Master Chamber of Commerce, a Department of Transnational Tourism and a Media Junta.[40]

Laggard, separatist gringos in turn have flocked to the former U.S.–Mexico border and have become the next wave of low-wage maquiladora and fast-food workers.

Gómez-Peña's fin de siècle continent is no utopia, despite the dissolution of the Anglo-dominated state and the adoption of Spanglish and Gringoñol as the official languages. Even as the FUSR promotes an official, commerce-oriented version of multiculturalism through its gigantic media apparatus, a flurry of separatist nationalisms demand sovereignty: "Québec, Puerto Rico, *Aztlán,* Yucatán, Panama, and all Indian nations have managed to secede from the new Federation of U.S. Republics. Independent micro-republics are popping up everywhere in the blink of an eye."[41]

Gómez-Peña also devotes considerable attention to describing the youth of "the New World (B)order," whom he divides into two camps: *robo-raza I* and *robo-raza II.* The former, "the new citizens of horizontal nothingness," are technophilic mall rats who lack the consciousness and passion to become engaged in any type of "cause."

On the other hand, *robo-raza II,* together with former artists, form part of the resistance movement known as *Arteamérica Sociedad Anónima*:

> [E]very block has a secret community center where the runaway youths, called robo-raza II, publish an anarchistic laser-xerox magazine, edit experimental home videos on police brutality (yes, police brutality still exists), and broadcast pirate radio interventions over the most popular programs of *Radio Nuevo Orden.*[42]

Robo-raza II is presented as a nonsectarian bright spot in this otherwise bleak scenario of transnationalist/nationalist binarisms. Their role as the hope for the future is underlined by Gómez-Peña's contrasting and derogatory treatment of the retrograde "Mafias" at the essay's (and performance's) conclusion. The "Mafias" are ethnic and nationalist purists, such as the "Chicano Aristocracy from East L.A." and the "Real African Nation," who "cling to the past in order to experience an optical illusion of continuity and order."[43]

In interviews, Gómez-Peña now refers to himself as a "cross-cultural diplomat,"[44] and one notes in his recent work an ever-increasing faith in the political effectivity of art and artists. From the outset, BAW/TAF had conceived of its artistic projects as working in concert with other activities such as journalism, education, and political activism; art projects were but one aspect of the group's site-specific work. In a recent essay, in contrast, Gómez-Peña argues, following a prophecy of Joseph Beuys from the 1970s, that art became politics and politics became art by the second half of the 1980s.[45] He proceeds to create a continuum of "Performance Politics or Political Performance Art,"[46] under which he assembles many artists and activists in the United States and Latin America, based upon their common use of performative strategies to achieve political goals. To this new breed of grassroots artist-politician, Gómez-Peña contrasts certain conservative forces that have on several occasions appropriated performance art and progressive popular culture icons in order to bolster state power.

The idea that the performance artist's power transcends that of the "nonaesthetic" political activist is identified in several sources with a trip that Gómez-Peña took to the former Soviet Far East as part of a binational human rights commission, where he realized that "[t]he artist as intercultural diplomat is able to cross many borders that political activists are unable to."[47] The idea is consistent with a trend in the work of many of the postmodern theorists, such as Henry Giroux, Iain Chambers, and D. Emily Hicks[48], who highlight certain professions as those which facilitate "border crossing." In texts by the latter theorists, "cultural workers," identified as artists, writers, educators, architects, and lawyers, among others, are portrayed as having "primacy"[49] in processes of social transformation, because their jobs give them a unique position from which to "dialogue" with "Others."[50]

But other reasons may help to account for the ease of such "border crossings" by professionals and intellectuals. The U.S.–Mexico border has rarely presented itself as a hindrance to artists, intellectuals, and tourists, for example, but then again, these crossings are not demographically representative of other large-scale flows of border traffic that currently characterize the region, such as that of undocumented workers northward and U.S. capital southward. The de facto emergence of the metropolis as the site of "border crossings" in the work of the postmodern theorists, in the wake of allegedly collapsed national boundaries, has in a sense made it possible for these intellectuals to conceive of crossing borders while remaining in the same place, simply by carrying out the duties of their profession.

Gómez-Peña's periodization of the art/politics merger in the late 1980s coincides with the emergence of an oppositional "artist-administrator" figure that Grant Kester has identified as characteristic of the "alternative arts" sphere in the United States during the same period.[51] Artists whose work was deemed controversial or obscene by the National Endowment for the Arts and other government-supported arts funding agencies during the Reagan-Bush era were often publicized as victims of censorship, stemming from racism, sexism, and homophobia. On a thematic level, these artists linked their own victimization at the hands of the right wing to other forms of oppression such as poverty and homelessness. According to Kester, many "alternative" artists who gained notoriety during this period, among them several in the performance-art monologue movement, based their artwork upon a declared solidarity between artist and "the oppressed," and positioned themselves as spokespersons, if not as members, of their avowed constituencies. Gómez-Peña's self-presentation as a shaman in performances such as *Border Brujo* has clearly been read by academics, journalists, and others as that of a spokesperson for all "border crossers." His descriptions of "border consciousness," for example, appear repeatedly in an article by anthropologist Roger Rouse about a transborder migration circuit of undocumented workers between Aguililla, Mexico, and Redwood City, California, but at no point in the article does Rouse quote his own informants regarding their lifestyle and consciousness.[52]

The Mass Media Border: The Bordertown Series

Gómez-Peña's recasting of the border as a global and temporal zone was in part a reaction to the border hype that was already being spread on a national level, not just by major U.S. art museums but also by mass marketing campaigns, as in Taco Bell's "Make a Run for the Border" ad campaign, which featured Latino musicians and celebrities.[53] But popular culture has produced some progressive attempts to portray border zones, such as that of the Bordertown series. In contrast to Gómez-Peña's point of departure in San Diego/Tijuana, these narratives take as their starting point Gómez-Peña's present global border perspective. That is, the border of the fantasy stories is already non-site-specific, futuristic, and urban. The authors claim that their models for Bordertown are any number of world cities where they have lived. It is difficult, therefore, to read Bordertown as an allegory of one particular geographical referent, although the type of globalism in the stories remains very U.S.–centered, as suggested by the youth cultures as well as the range of ethnicities portrayed.[54]

The creator of the Bordertown series, Terri Windling, is a writer and a painter who, through her experience as consulting editor for Ace and Tor (both sci-fi and fantasy imprints), is credited with having developed and promoted "contemporary urban fantasy" literature, and with having contributed to the boom of shared-world anthologies in the mid- to late-1980s.[55] Demographically speaking, the books in the series are aimed at sixteen- to eighteen-year-olds who watch MTV, although an active fan culture exists among adults as well. Windling and the writers of the series affirm that the development of strong characters is central to the narratives, and that the principal border of the series is to be understood as psychological rather than geo-graphical—it is the border between childhood and adulthood, between dreams and reality.[56] The stories are meant to be "narratives of empowerment" that show adolescents confronting obstacles and making decisions without the intervention of adults.

The externalization of the adolescent psyche in the physical and social environment is what interests me about Bordertown, especially since the characters are quite often explained as the products of their "environment" in the first place.[57] The stories are set sometime after "the Change," that is, the relatively recent reemergence of the Faerie kingdom (after several centuries' hiatus), which has witnessed the rise of racial animosity between elves (a.k.a. Truebloods) and humans. Elves speak Elvish among themselves, a language inscrutable to humans and largely untranslatable into English, and they speak English with an accent. They are portrayed as cool, dispassionate, and formal in contrast to sloppy, neurotic, and emotional humans. Physically, the elves are exceptionally tall, with extremely pale skin and white hair. Capable of magic and often wealthy, they appear to be the dominant race over the humans, but each race is both attracted to and repulsed by the other to some degree. The elves, for example, are often shown to be dependent upon human subcultures, which they tap for musical, literary, and artistic inspiration.[58] Humans, on the other hand, are attracted to elvin beauty and magic.

The creators of the series consciously avoid any description of Elfland for fear that it would detract from the goals of the series. Even so, as adolescents aspiring to adulthood, the portrayal of both elvin and human societies as having "good" and "bad" qualities invites readers to engage in a doubled or split identification with elements of both the human and elvin worlds. On the one hand, adolescent readers aspire to the magical power and privileges of the elvin (adult) world, but insist upon taking their own emotional makeup (humanity) along with them. On the other, they identify politically with the superior technology and goods of the human world, but find it unfair that, as humans, they are forbidden to go to Faerie. The interracial friendships and coalitions that form at the juncture of both cultures are in some way a solution to this split identification; they suggest that through cooperation and inter-dependence, one can have the best of both worlds.

Elfland and "the World" remain relatively isolated from one another with the ex-ception of Bordertown, a contact zone disparaged as culturally deracinated by both "centers" but serving as a magnet for fortune-hunters, dissidents, misfits, and run-aways from both cultures. Here, transgression of boundaries, either through smug-gling, encroachment on one another's turf, or interracial sex, is commonplace, but not generally condoned. The series focuses on one particular neighborhood called SoHo, inhabited by teenage runaways from both cultures.[59] Most of Bordertown youth culture is violent, separatist, and organized around various street gangs. This environment is especially difficult for Bordertown's "halfies," the offspring of elves and humans, who are usually forced to "pass" if they want to survive. But the heroes of Bordertown's vignettes are always those youths who dare to establish nonsectarian communities amidst the omnipresent danger of the streets. These brief utopian mo-ments usually occur at narrative closure.

Several authors have acknowledged diversity within this imaginary world, which looks largely to Anglo-Saxon and Celtic folklore as its founding texts, by introducing new ethnic geographies into the city, such as Dragontown, a Japanese neighborhood, and Tintown, a barrio, and by developing African-American, Native American, Mexican, and gay characters. One imperative remains constant throughout all of the Bordertown stories: moments of cultural understanding, be they between humans or between humans and elves, take place on a cultural plane—that is through group ac-tivities centered around bands, dance clubs, used-book stores, bohemian communes, the production and distribution of underground newspapers, and so on. As I have argued with regard to Gómez-Peña's "New World (B)order," an intellectual-lumpen alliance enacted through collaborative cultural projects is held up in the series as the antidote to racism and other types of oppression.

The Bordertown writers have tacitly refused to address the reasons for Elfland's return and the events that precipitated "the Change" in any comprehensive way.[60] We do know that Bordertown is a "trade zone," set up by elves for the purpose of commerce with humans. Elfland is repeatedly described as being situated to the World's north. The city itself is demarcated by two salient geographical features—an enormous wall separating Elfland proper from the World, and a red river whose fish are contaminated (by magic) and whose water turns humans into brain-dead junkies. Only elves are privileged to pass back and forth from Elfland to the World through a gate staffed by elvin customs agents. Humans, on the other hand, may only dream about what lies on the other side.

All of this should sound vaguely familiar to North American readers: a trade zone, humans lured to the north by promises of magic, a wall, a toxic river, immigra-tion restrictions, customs officials . . . As Bordertown becomes progressively fleshed out in each successive work, it more and more closely resembles an export-processing zone. Though the Bordertown writers have not consciously modeled their imaginary world on the U.S.–Mexico border region, their elaboration of the border as a trade zone and an area of cultural integration would probably have been unimaginable before the mid-1960s. Urban, industrialized, national borders are a relatively new and growing phenomenon in the world economic system, especially in the emerging trade blocs of North America and Europe, yet such borders are rarely represented in U.S. popular genres. Instead, the border continues to be portrayed as a no-man's-land or a war zone. The Bordertown writers recognize these traditional images of the border in their work, yet try to reinscribe this familiar dystopian space with more positive features.

Though the Bordertown stories do not explore the contradiction of free flow of goods versus restricted flow of people that is central to Gómez-Peña's "New World (B)order," husband-and-wife contributors Will Shetterly and Emma Bull have touched on this issue in two of the most recent Bordertown novels. Shetterly's *Elsewhere* deals with a conspiracy of "liberal" elf operatives, working undercover in Bordertown. One of them discloses his mission to a human friend at the end of the novel:

> "For the Lords of Faerie, the Border is an inconvenient necessity. It permits trade, and it keeps out humans, and it allows elves to pass through at only a few locations. All of these things are seen as desirable.
> "But there are those who think Faerie and the World should have greater knowledge of each other." He glanced at Wiseguy and smiled. "Strider and I are of that party."[61]

Bull's *Finder* deals with a conspiracy of another sort. A wealthy elvin mercantile family "with interests on both sides of the border"[62] is secretly pushing an illicit street drug called "passport" on human runaways. The drug's appeal is that it genetically transforms humans into elves, thus permitting them to cross the border undetected. (At one point, the narrator quips, "I couldn't think of why anyone would refer to the Elflands as if they were on a par with Cancún . . ."[63]) But the drug has an unanticipated effect. Before genetic transformation is complete, the junkies' immune systems are weakened to the point that they are highly susceptible to elvin diseases, and thus unwittingly become carriers for a rare virus that reaches epidemic proportions. As human and elf fatalities mount, the elvin population is placed under quarantine, and vicious rumors threaten even the most solid elvin-human relationships—that is, until the novel's human hero, Orient, locates the sweatshop where elvin runaways manufacture "passport" and puts an end to the dynastic merchants and corrupt cops backing the drug.

In these fantasies of role reversal, Elfland occupies the position of a neocolonialist power, and humans in turn become exploited Third World subjects. Bordertown, however, downplays national identity in favor of racial and cultural divisions. The nation-state has disappeared in the series, and the U.S. cities from which Bordertown's human runaways flee are now simply places in "the World."

Technology and Postnationalism

At one point in "The New World (B)order," Gómez-Peña self-reflexively recalls his former identity as a border artist and in so doing evokes the image of a nationally coded space, now defunct:[64]

> A techno-shrine to Juan Soldado, Holy Patron of border-crossers and migrant workers, now stands on what used to be the San Ysidro border check point. With multi-image projections, the old border saint reminds people of what once was a common yet dangerous experience, crossing from the Third to the First World, from the past to the future. Remember?[65]

His question, "Remember?" asks his audience to recall the site-specific focus that has all but disappeared from his recent work, in favor of bicoastal and multinational networks of fellow "cross-cultural diplomats." Gómez-Peña continually relies upon long-distance communication and electronic media to produce and distribute his work. The Bordertown writers, geographically dispersed throughout the United States and Canada, meet for dinner once a year to discuss problems of continuity among various episodes in the series and the directions they would like Bordertown to take; otherwise, they communicate to one another informally at conferences and via fax, phone, newsletters, and e-mail.[66]

The mode of production of each of these artistic projects differs markedly from the worlds they depict. In terms of production, this contradiction finds the artists using international publishing and museum circuits, and video distribution, precisely in order to advocate local, community-based arts movements, whose leadership they displace from themselves onto youth cultures.[67] On the thematic level, the cyberpunk hallmark of counterpointing high-tech and low-tech is met with ambivalence by the Bordertown writers and Gómez-Peña, whose respective "future worlds" are hardly more technologically advanced than present day U.S. society.[68]

For his part, Gómez-Peña has repeatedly shunned artists who are fascinated with technology for technology's sake. This tendency has two antecedents, as he explains it. The first is from the performance-art monologue movement of the late 1980s, associated with Eric Bogosian, Spalding Gray, Karen Finley, and Tim Miller, in which these artists sought to "rescue the spoken word"[69] from pyrotechnic spectacles. The second comes from a respect for the lack of access to technology under which many Chicano/a, Mexican, African-American and Native American artists must operate.[70]

In the Bordertown series, the bias against technology is even more pronounced. Elvin magic tends to make human technology go haywire, although magic itself is pretty unreliable in Bordertown. Almost every type of electric or gas-fueled device, from motor scooters to refrigerators and burglar alarms has become operable through hybridization: now they are powered by eco-safe "spell boxes." The Bordertown economy is often represented as informal (street vendors, artists, and musicians) or illegal (thieves, smugglers), and focuses on barter rather than the exchange of currency (given that elves can fabricate precious metals). The introduction to the first anthology offers several possible accounts for "the Change" by recalling the folklore concerning the disappearance of Faerie in the first place: "Some say it was industrialization and the use of iron that drove the elvin folk away, some say the spread of Christianity . . ."[71] In other words, the future return of Faerie is in some sense predicated upon the return of a preindustrial past.

The arrest of technological "modernization" in these texts is linked to the disappearance of other political and social institutions such as the state, army, and police force.[72] As I have pointed out, the first pass in creating the "New World (B)order" and Bordertown is the obliteration of the U.S. nation-state through the processes of "Gringostroika" and "the Change," respectively. The result is that the most salient remaining geographical units of analysis are cities, which increasingly resemble one another through cultural contact.

The conjunction of antitechnology, antinationalist, and futuristic discourses within these works is at first puzzling, given that in much mainstream science fiction, an antitechnology bias is often associated with reactionary political ideology.[73] Current arguments about the future of North America again help to clarify how the position of Gómez-Peña and the Bordertown writers could so recently have been recoded as a "progressive" stance. In Mexico, NAFTA was sold to the general public as a plan to modernize the country. Under the administration of former President Carlos Salinas de Gortari, the figure of pre-Revolutionary tyrant Porfirio Díaz was even recuperated as the leader who brought Mexico into the twentieth century. Mexico's century-long drive toward a modernization supposedly culminating in NAFTA has strong affinities with Gómez-Peña's fin de siècle apocalyptic vision. In the United States, "competitiveness" and "efficiency," rather than "modernization," were the buzzwords of NAFTA coverage, but as in Mexico, they were employed to justify a program of massive dislocation, privatization of state-supervised sectors, and additionally, increased research and development spending in high-tech industries. For Gómez-Peña and the Bordertown writers, all of whom are working in a historical period in which state power and technological advancement are so often coarticulated, opposition to the "official" vision of the future may find a logical counterrepresentation in an alternative world that has no United States and no advancement of technology, but has instead an efflorescence of cultural production.

Through their advocacy of cultural "border crossing" and transgression of borders, both Gómez-Peña and the Bordertown writers call attention to a major oversight of NAFTA negotiations—immigration rights. From the point of view of Gómez-Peña and the Bordertown writers, culture and immigration are closely related, since the flow of media and people is largely responsible for the diffusion of culture. Gómez-Peña's recent call for a "Free Art Agreement" challenges the fact that cultural issues were downplayed during the NAFTA debates and that cultural industries were given cursory mention in the treaty itself. All of this has been taking place against the backdrop of an ongoing drive throughout the continent to privatize cultural industries, which is bound to have its most profound effects on smaller arts organizations, the very ones most likely to promote the work of minority populations.

Theorizing "The Change": NAFTA and the Exportation of Culture

While Gómez-Peña and the Bordertown writers confront some of NAFTA's black holes, they also have one feature in common with U.S. media coverage of the treaty. All three neglect the fact that the deleterious effects of economic restructuring will be felt in some geographical areas more than in others. NAFTA is only a recent step in a three-decade-long process of continental economic integration. It is difficult to forecast how swiftly or severely the effects of this particular treaty will be felt, but among North American regions, the U.S.–Mexico border so far has witnessed the most drastic transformations as the result of North American free trade. The flight of U.S. and foreign industries to Mexico in the wake of the world financial crisis of the early 1970s and Mexico's own financial crises in 1982 and 1994 has brought to the border region heightened labor abuses, environmental degradation, and shortages of housing, water, food, and medical care.

The uneven development fostered by free trade is marked within the U.S.–Mexico "transfrontier metropolises" themselves. Social scientists have for years insisted that from a cultural perspective, the border should be viewed as a semiautonomous social system because the twin cities straddling the border have more in common with one another than with U.S. and Mexican cities of the interior.[74] But the industrialization of the border through the maquiladora program has also made the cities extremely heterogeneous economically, even as it has increased binational ties. This heterogeneity, in turn, has given rise to artistic and literary production concomitant with the boom in industrial parks,[75] although in most border cities institutional support for local artists and writers remains very modest.

Although art is produced on the border under much more comfortable conditions than TVs and other consumer products, it too, is subject to exportation, as Gómez-Peña asserted when he repudiated the genre. When an "art of place" finds itself decontextualized and distributed for mass consumption on a national or international level, it becomes all the more important to differentiate between two "borderized" cities like Matamoros and New York; often the distinction is not only spatial and national, but also divides production from consumption and distribution. The globalized border of postmodern theorists overlooks the specificity of regions such as the U.S.–Mexico border, where nation-states continue to enforce differences within urban space. Making the border the global metaphor of an oppositional politics also falls prey to facile appropriation by an equally globalizing U.S. nationalist expansionism. A recent headline in the *New York Times,* proclaiming Northern Mexico to be "America's Newest Industrial Belt" and referring to Mexico as "the 51st State" in terms of the U.S. economy, illustrates how easily the border can be assimilated by U.S.

industrial interests. There still *is* a border between "us" and "them," according to the logic of the *Times* article; it has simply been displaced southward.[76]

Collapsing the distinction between production and consumption, furthermore, has consequences for the formulation of anti-imperialist strategies. Another part of the *Year of the White Bear* project was the well-known "Two Undiscovered Amerindians Visit . . ." performance in which Gómez-Peña and Fusco inhabited a ten-by-twelve-foot cage and presented themselves as indigenous inhabitants of an island in the Gulf of Mexico. The idea for the piece was based on the colonial practice of exporting Native Americans, Asians, and Africans to Europe for "aesthetic contemplation, scientific analysis and entertainment."[77] Fusco and Gómez-Peña toured Europe, North America, and Australia and exhibited themselves in public areas, where Fusco reported that many spectators mistook them for "authentic" natives, in spite of their eclectic costumes and props such as a laptop computer.[78] Fusco and Paula Heredia subsequently produced a video about this interactive performance entitled, *The Couple in the Cage: A Guatinaui Odyssey,* in which they recorded the reactions of many unsuspecting viewers who did not realize that what they were witnessing was a performance.

Eurocentric ways of perceiving "native" populations are by no means obsolete along the U.S.–Mexico border, but the main offenders, rather than individual spectators, are nationally and internationally recognized cultural institutions. Locally based art movements linked to activist agendas, as exemplified by BAW/TAF, are still relatively rare on the U.S.–Mexico border; meanwhile, "border art" flourishes in national arts media. One cannot see this phenomenon in terms of a simplistic opposition between site-specificity and mass media, as though incursions into mass media immediately signified inauthenticity and co-optation. Indeed, many grassroots organizations currently engaged in cross-border organizing employ communications strategies similar to those used on a smaller scale by Gómez-Peña and the Bordertown writers, including video, fax, internet, and e-mail.[79] In contrast to professional artists, however, grassroots organizations do not necessarily isolate their videos, installations, and the like from the rest of their activities, as "aesthetic" artifacts.

One example of such a movement is the Strategic Organizing Alliance that has been established between the Frente Auténtico del Trabajo (FAT) of Mexico, an independent federation of unions, cooperatives, farm-worker and community organizations, and the United Electrical, Radio, and Machine Workers (UE), a U.S. union with a long history of progressive, internationalist organizing.[80] Both organizations recognize the importance of art and communications to their movement and dedicate branches of their organizations to culture and education. The UE, in fact, is the only U.S. union to employ an artist on staff, and recently the Alliance undertook a cross-border mural project featuring the work of artists Mike Alewitz, Daniel Manrique, and the Chicago Public Art Group (see *Crossborder Mural Project* in appendix). In addition, the Alliance has been responsible for significant gains in the struggle to improve living standards on both sides of the border during a period when prominent scholars in cultural studies have declared labor-based models of social activism to be passé. With support from the UE, the FAT obtained the first secret-ballot election in Mexican labor history at a GE plant in Ciudad Juárez.[81] In 1994, organizers from the FAT worked with the UE to unionize the mostly Mexican labor force of one of the most notoriously exploitative plants in Milwaukee. As one reporter commented, Ace/Co (locally known as "Slave Co.") was the largest plant in that city to go union in years.[82] The Alliance has developed long-term strategies to foment leadership skills among women workers, and together with the Teamsters, it filed the first complaints under the NAFTA labor side agreements. Its most recent campaign, launched in 1997, involves trinational organizing of workers for Echlin, an auto parts manufacturer, and seeks to implement a company code of conduct that will apply in all Echlin plants throughout the continent. These successes make it clear that cultural workers do have a role to play in such movements. Perhaps, then, the emphasis in promoting an "art of place" should be less on the formal or thematic qualities of a given work than on the supposition that performers and spectators alike are potential actors in a common social struggle once the performance or exhibition is over.

Appendix

Videos about Free Trade and Related Issues

I wish to thank Ricardo Hernández and Edith Sánchez, with whom I coedited an earlier version of this videography, published as "Videos on Free Trade," *BorderLines* 2.1 (February 1994): 13. For further video descriptions, see Sue Worthington, "Keeping the Pressure On: Tools for Organizing Beyond NAFTA," *Beyond Borders* (spring 1994): 10+; and Rachael Kamel, *The Global Factory: Analysis and Action for a New Economic Era* (Philadelphia: American Friends Service Committee, 1990): 87–88.

$4 a Day? No Way! Joining Hands Across the Border. Washington, DC: American Labor Education Center, 1991. 19 min.

All Work and No Play: NAFTA's Impact on Child Labor. Washington, DC: Child Labor Coalition/Labor Institute of Public Affairs (AFL-CIO), 1993. 9 min.

The Battle for Hearts and Minds. Ottawa: Canadian Labour Congress, 1992. 27 min.

Borderline Cases: Environmental Matters at the United States–Mexico Border. Dir. Lynn Corcoran. Oley, Pennsylvania: Bullfrog Films, 1996. 65 min.

Bottom Line. Toronto: Common Frontiers, 1990. 12 min.

Cross Border Organizing, A Response to NAFTA. San Diego: Support Committee for Maquiladora Workers, 1994. 10 min.

Crossborder Mural Project. Dir. and prod. Steve Dalber. Chicago, 1998. 34 min.

Dirty Business: Food Exports to the United States. Dir. Jon Silver. Freedom, California: Migrant Media Productions, 1990. 15 min.

Encuentro de Zacatecas: Foro internacional—la opinión pública y el TLC. Mexico City: Red Mexicana de Acción Frente al Libre Comercio, 1991. 35 min.

Fighting Back. Ottawa: Action Canada Network, 1991. 60 min.

Free Trade: Who's Gonna Pay? Minneapolis: Labor Education Service and Minnesota at Work, 1992. 30 min.

From the Mountains to the Maquiladoras. Knoxville: Tennessee Industrial Renewal Network, 1993. 25 min.

Fury in the Land. Ottawa: Canadian Labour Congress, 1992. 20 min.

Global Assembly Line. Dir. Lorraine Gray. New York: New Day Films, 1983. 57 min.

The Great Free Trade Debate: Renegotiation or Abrogation? Ottawa: Council of Canadians, 1992. 45 min.

GUESS Who Pockets the Difference? New York: UNITE, 1996. 8 min.

Hometown. Ottawa: Canadian Labour Congress, 1991. 25 min.

Interview with Santos Martínez. Windsor: Windsor Occupational Safety and Health Group, n.d. 29 min.

Leaving Home: A Road Trip into Our Free Trade Future. Berkeley: We Do the Work, 1992. 59 min.

Let's Make Canada Work for People. Ottawa: Canadian Labour Congress, 1993. 9 min.

Los que se van. Dir. Adolfo Dávila and Helena Tamayo. Tijuana: CONACULTA and COLEF, 1990. 27 min.

Massacre at Acteal: The Other Side of NAFTA. Dir. Kerry Appel. Denver: The Human Bean Co., 1998. 17 min.

Mexico: For a Few Dollars More. London: British Broadcasting Corporation/The London Observer, 1992. 50 min.

Mexico: For Sale. Dir. Dermot and Carla Begley. Altadena, California: Mexico Libre Productions, 1991. 40 min.

NAFTA Briefing by Canadian Environmental Law Association, Canadian Auto Workers, and Ecumenical Coalition for Economic Justice. Toronto: Common Frontiers, 1992. 95 min.

NAFTA: Playing with a Volatile Substance. Toronto: Cinefocus Canada, 1993. 55 min.

The New Global Economy: A View from the Bottom Up. Dir. Pam Costain. Minneapolis: Resource Center of the Americas, 1995. 23 min.

New World Border. Dir. Casey Peek. Oakland: National Network for Immigrant and Refugee Rights/Rollin' Deep Prods., 1997. 35 min.

Por empleos con salarios dignos: The Campaign for Higher Wages in the Maquiladoras. San Diego: Support Committee for Maquiladora Workers, 1997. 20 min.

River of Broken Promises. Dir. Mark R. Day. San Diego: Environmental Health Coalition, 1996. 24 min.

The Secret Side of Free Trade. Dir. Elizabeth Garsonnin. San Francisco: Public Media Center, 1993. 29 min.

South of the Border: The Maquiladoras. Chicago: Labor Beat/Chicago Access Corporation, 1989. 26 min.

Stepan Chemical: The Poisoning of a Mexican Community. San Antonio: Day Communications, 1992. 18 min.

The Ties That Bind: Stories behind the Immigration Controversy. New York: Maryknoll World Productions, 1996. 56 min.

The Time Has Come! An Immigrant Community Stands up to the Border Patrol. El Paso: Border Rights Coalition, 1996. 42 min.

Trading Our Future. Minneapolis: Fair Trade Campaign and League of Rural Voters, 1990. 20 min.

Unidos Cruzaremos Las Fronteras/Unity Crosses Borders. Tucson: Derechos Humanos Coalition/Arizona Border Rights Project, 1997. 18 min.

We Can Say No! Ottawa: Repeal the Deal/Action Canada Network, 1991. 28 min.

We Didn't Want It to Happen This Way. Washington, DC: AFL-CIO Educational Films, 1979. 30 min.

What's the Cost of Your Blouse? Dir. Sydney Brown and Betty McAfee. Northern California Interfaith Council/Open Window Images, 1992. 18 min.

Zoned for Slavery: the Child behind the Label. Dir. David Belle, Katharine Kean, Rudi Stern. New York: National Labor Committee, 1995. 23 min.

Work in Production

On the Job: The Maquiladora Worker; At Home: The Maquiladora Worker; The Maquiladoras: Our Shared Environment; Trade: Fair or Free. Dir. Jolanda and David Westerhof-Schultz. Elsah, Illinois: Veritas International, 1994–.

Notes

Introduction

1. This is the title of a performance by Guillermo Gómez-Peña and Luke Theodore Morrison. For an illustration, see Jeff Kelley, ed. of English text, *The Border Art Workshop/Taller de Arte Fronterizo (BAW/TAF): 1984–1989*, 51. See also Guillermo Gómez-Peña, "The Multicultural Paradigm: An Open Letter to the National Arts Community," 26.

2. David Harvey, *The Urban Experience*, 192.

3. Guillermo Gómez-Peña, "Death on the Border: A Eulogy to Border Art," 8–9.

4. Charles Tatum, "Introduction: Stasis and Change along the Rio Grande: Aristeo Brito's *The Devil in Texas*," in *El diablo en Texas/The Devil in Texas*, by Aristeo Brito, 16.

5. Lawrence A. Herzog, *Where North Meets South: Cities, Space, and Politics on the U.S.–Mexico Border*, xii. See also Lawrence A. Herzog, ed., *Planning the International Border Metropolis*. I will use the phrase *transfrontier metropolis* throughout this study.

6. In 1961 the Mexican government introduced the Programa Nacional Fronterizo (PRONAF), which used public- and private-sector funds to subsidize border products and build up the infrastructure of border cities, especially facilities associated with tourism. Four years later, the Border Industrialization Program was announced, thereby laying the groundwork for the maquiladora program. See John S. Evans, "Taxation and Fiscal Policy," in *The Borderlands Sourcebook*, ed. Ellwyn Stoddard, Richard L. Nostrand, and Jonathan P. West, 173; and Oscar J. Martínez, *Border Boom Town: Ciudad Juárez since 1848*, 116–17.

7. Robert Alvarez, "The Border as Social System: The California Case," 120.

8. Lawrence A. Herzog, ed., *Changing Boundaries in the Americas: New Perspectives on the U.S.–Mexican, Central American, and South American Borders*, 6.

9. Herzog, *Changing Boundaries*, 21.

10. I would like to thank Chris Lion of the Office of Inter-American Affairs, U.S. Department of Commerce, Washington DC, for providing me with information about regional trade blocs. Additional general information may be found in the following articles: Joachim Bamrud, "Uniting Forces: The Integration of the Hemisphere," and "Expanding the Markets: The Unprecedented Trade Boom."

Specific information about the CACM may be found in *Resource Center Bulletin*, spec. issue "Trade

Dreams in Central America." Information about Mercosur may be found in "The Mercosur Marriage." Information about the ACS may be found in "ACS Meeting Concludes in Trinidad."

11. Harvey, *Urban Experience,* esp. ch. 6, "Money, Time, Space, and the City," 165–99.

12. See David Harvey, *The Condition of Postmodernity: An Enquiry into the Origins of Cultural Change*; Néstor García Canclini, *Culturas híbridas: estrategias para entrar y salir de la modernidad,* ch. 7; Herzog, *Where North Meets South,* ch. 2.

13. *Resource Center Bulletin,* spec. issue "Inside Guatemala," 4; John Cavanaugh et al., eds., *Trading Freedom: How Free Trade Affects Our Lives, Work, and Environment,* 3; "CARICOM Prepares for Trade Talks."

14. For further information regarding Chile's incorporation into Mercosur and NAFTA, see "Mercosur Experiences Growing Pains"; "Desde hoy, Chile es socio comercial del Mercosur"; and "Canada, Chile Negotiate Trade Deal."

15. "Maquila Scoreboard"; see also Peter Cooper and Lori Wallach, *NAFTA's Broken Promises: Job Creation under NAFTA,* 18; Lori Saldaña, "The Downside of the Border Boom"; and Arnoldo García, "The Deepening Mexican Crisis." Lower statistics are cited in a recent graph published by the Coalition for Justice in the Maquiladoras, which highlights only "major maquiladora centers"; see "Maquiladoras in the U.S.–Mexico Border Region."

16. Clifford Krauss, quoted in George Yúdice, Jean Franco, and Juan Flores, eds., *On Edge: The Crisis of Contemporary Latin American Culture,* xiii.

17. For a meticulous chronicle of events leading up to the passage of NAFTA (1988–93) written from a Mexican perspective, see Javier Garciadiego et. al, *El TLC día al día: Crónica de una negociación.*

18. On Salinas being earmarked for WTO leadership, see Ernest H. Preeg, *Traders in a Brave New World: The Uruguay Round and the Future of the International Trading System,* 183. The early stages of these events in Mexico are outlined by Jorge Castañeda in *Sorpresas te da la vida: México 1994.* (The work was revised later that year and published under the title *Sorpresas te da la vida: México fin de siglo.*)

19. Jorge Castañeda, *The Mexican Shock: Its Meaning for the U.S.;* "Peso Devaluations Affect *Maquiladoras*"; Walker F. Todd, "Bailing Out the Creditor Class"; Ken Silverstein and Alexander Cockburn, "The Killers and the Killing."

20. For historical periodizations, see Friedrich Katz, *The Secret War in Mexico: Europe, the United States, and the Mexican Revolution,* 3–49; and Oscar J. Martínez, *Troublesome Border.* One reason why the Revolution ignited in northern Mexico, according to Katz, is that by the late 1880s the Mexican "frontier" had become a "border." That is, it had become thoroughly linked to Mexico City and to the United States by railroad, telegraph, and automobile, and the threat of Apache raids disappeared. Modernization provoked unrest among earlier settlers who were displaced in order to accommodate large cattle ranching and mining interests, as well as among certain sectors of the elite, who resented being brought into the orbit of the centralized government. Martínez sees the conclusion of the Revolution as the beginning of a new era in U.S.–Mexico relations, one in which diplomacy became the preferred form of border conflict resolution rather than state violence, filibustering, or raids.

For geographical periodizations, see Herzog, *Where North Meets South,* and John William House, *Frontier on the Rio Grande: A Political Geography of Development and Social Deprivation.*

21. History seems to be the one disciplinary exception regarding the split between the humanities and social sciences in border studies.

22. The bias toward the social and natural sciences is evident also in professional organizations that focus attention on border or binational issues. PROFMEX, the Consortium for Research on Mexico, for example, is primarily a policy-oriented organization. The Association of Borderlands Scholars does have a commitment to interdisciplinary study of the region, though its emphasis is weighted toward the social sciences; at the 1995 ABS conference, only two out of thirty-five panels were dedicated to cultural issues (see "Association of Borderlands Scholars 1995 Annual Meetings").

23. Norma Iglesias Prieto, *Entre yerba, polvo y plomo: Lo fronterizo visto por el cine mexicano*; David R. Maciel, *El Norte: The U.S.–Mexican Border in Contemporary Cinema.*

24. Aurelio de los Reyes, *Con Villa en México: Testimonios de camarógrafos norteamericanos en la Revolución, 1911–1916.*

25. Paul J. Vanderwood and Frank N. Samponaro, *Border Fury: A Picture Postcard Record of Mexico's Revolution and U.S. War Preparedness, 1910–1917*; *War Scare on the Rio Grande: Robert Runyon's Photographs of the Border Conflict, 1913–1916.*

26. The Editorial Binacional is jointly sponsored by San Diego State University and the Universidad Autónoma de Baja California.

27. Américo Paredes, *"With His Pistol in His Hand": A Border Ballad and Its Hero.* Limón is a professor in the Departments of English and Anthropology at the University of Texas at Austin, and Vila is a professor in the Department of Sociology at the University of Texas at San Antonio. For a sample of their work, see José Limón, *Dancing with the Devil: Society and Cultural Politics in Mexican-American South Texas*; and Pablo Vila, *Everyday Life, Culture, and Identity on the Mexican-American Border.*

28. Gloria Anzaldúa, *Borderlands/La Frontera: The New Mestiza.*

29. *The Old Gringo,* dir. Luis Puenzo.

30. Claire F. Fox, "Hollywood's Backlot: Carlos Fuentes, *The Old Gringo,* and National Cinema."

31. Larry Rohter, "A New Star for Studios Is Mexico."

32. *El jardín del Edén,* dir. María Novaro.

33. For more information about the movie's production and exhibition history, see Elissa Rashkin, independent scholar, "*El jardín del Edén,*" unpublished ms., Mexico City, 1995.

34. The presentation of the San Diego/Tijuana border beach in this movie conflicts with my visual impression of the area, because it avoids showing Border Field State Park on the U.S. side and the Playas de Tijuana neighborhood on the Mexican side.

35. Graciela Iturbide, *Juchitán de las mujeres.*

36. The publicity materials for *El jardín del Edén* in fact evoke key lines from Gómez-Peña's video *Border Brujo* (see chapter 5) and Gloria Anzaldúa's *Borderlands/La Frontera*: "The border is an open wound. And language is the border, too" (Anzaldúa, *Borderlands/La Frontera,* 3). I am indebted to Martin Roberts's critique of ethnographic surrealism in my understanding of this recent wave of border imagery; see his essay, "The Self in the Other: Ethnographic Film, Surrealism, Politics."

37. García Canclini, *Culturas híbridas,* ch. 7, "Culturas híbridas, poderes oblicuos," 263–328.

38. I am borrowing this phrase from an essay by Neil Smith and Cindi Katz entitled, "Grounding Metaphor: Towards a Spatialized Politics." While acknowledging that metaphor is foundational to linguistic systems, Smith and Katz argue that the new spatial theories in the humanities and social sciences should concern themselves with "the interconnectedness of material and metaphorical space" (68). They argue that the "border" is one of the more "interesting" metaphors to emerge in postmodern theoretical writing, because unlike other popular metaphors such as "mapping," "position," and "location," the "border" implies the existence of a different type of spatial organization lurking "on the edge" of absolute space. Thus, the border at least offers the possibility of pointing to relative space, even if "its critical *Aufhebung* is barely initiated" (78).

39. Neil Larsen, "Foreword," in *Border Writing: The Multidimensional Text,* by D. Emily Hicks, xx.

40. Jorge Castañeda, *Utopia Unarmed: The Latin American Left after the Cold War,* esp. ch. 14, "A Grand Bargain for the Millennium," 427–76.

41. Néstor García Canclini, *Consumidores y ciudadanos: Conflictos multiculturales de la globalización,* 190; see also 13–37. Unless otherwise indicated, all translations are mine.

42. Carlos Fuentes, "Latin America's Alternative: An Ibero-American Federation."

43. The terms *contact zone* and *transculturation* are taken from Mary Louise Pratt's study of colonial travel writing by Europeans, *Imperial Eyes: Travel Writing and Transculturation.* Pratt defines "contact

zones" as "social spaces where disparate cultures meet, clash, and grapple with each other, often in highly asymmetrical relations of domination and subordination . . ." (4). Transculturation, a concept borrowed from ethnography, describes "how subordinated or marginal groups select and invent from materials transmitted to them by a dominant or metropolitan culture" (6).

44. See, for example, Ovid Demaris, *Poso del Mundo: Inside the Mexican-American Border: From Tijuana to Matamoros*; Alan Weisman, *La Frontera: The United States Border with Mexico*; Tom Miller, *On the Border*; Douglas Kent Hall, *The Border: Life on the Line*; William Langewiesche, *Cutting for Sign*; and Augusta Dwyer, *On the Line: Life on the U.S.–Mexico Border*.

45. Carlos Monsiváis, "Interacción Cultural Fronteriza," 222.

46. Larsen, "Foreword," xx.

1. Cultural Exemptions, Cultural Solutions

1. *Cielo de abajo,* dir. Jesusa Rodríguez. Liliana Felipe was born in Argentina and currently resides in Mexico, where she has been partners with Rodríguez since the 1970s. The PRI refers to the Partido Revolucionario Institucional, the ruling political party in Mexico since 1946. (The precursor to the PRI, the PRN, was established in 1929.)

2. *Cielo de abajo,* program notes.

3. Diana Taylor's description of the play, based upon its production at Rodríguez's Teatro La Capilla in Mexico City, does not mention the part about the PRI and Televisa, which makes me wonder if this touch was added for the U.S. production. See Diana Taylor, "'High Aztec' or Performing Anthro Pop: Jesusa Rodríguez and Liliana Felipe in *Cielo de abajo*."

4. For more information about the history of La Capilla, see Jean Franco, "A Touch of Evil: Jesusa Rodríguez's Subversive Church."

5. I have chosen to use the phrase *cultural industries* in this study, following the lead of John Sinclair in his excellent essay "Culture and Trade: Some Theoretical and Practical Considerations." The phrase recognizes the Frankfurt school's contribution to the study of mass media and also distinguishes the "abstract homogeneity" of their phrase, "culture industry," from the plurality of contemporary mass media forms (31). Widespread use of the phrase *cultural industries* is associated with UNESCO initiatives in the 1970s, and it has been adopted by scholars of mass media (32–33). I also prefer *cultural industries* because it is a serviceable translation of the common phrase in Spanish, *industrias culturales*.

6. Jean Franco, "'Manhattan Will Be More Exotic This Fall': The Iconisation of Frida Kahlo," 221.

7. Franco, "Manhattan," 221.

8. Guillermo Bonfil Batalla, "Dimensiones culturales del Tratado de Libre Comercio," 157.

9. I am grateful to Officer Dennis Burke, Mexico Desk, U.S. Department of Commerce, for helping me to interpret the relevant portions of the treaty. The cultural exemption for Canadian industries is NAFTA Annex 2106 (National Trade Data Bank, *The North American Free Trade Agreement*).

Vincent Mosco argued that the Canadian cultural exemption in the USCFTA was a farce because it contained a loophole that allowed the United States to retaliate "to equivalent commercial effect" for what it perceived to be "unfair" subsidies of cultural products (Vincent Mosco, "Toward a Transnational World Information Order: The U.S.–Canada Free Trade Agreement," 63).

The first major test of Canada's cultural exemption came in 1995, when Nashville-based Country Music Television was blocked out of two million Canadian homes due to competition with a local broadcaster. Westinghouse Electric Corporation, a parent of the network, filed a complaint under the "Special 301" code of NAFTA, which provides for investigating issues of cultural protection. The dispute was settled, however, when Country Music Television reached an agreement with the Canadian broadcaster to form a single Canadian country music network. See "Canada Seeks to Protect 'Cultural' Industries"; and "U.S.–Canada T.V. Dispute Settled."

10. Department of Commerce, Office of Mexico, *Nafta Facts,* Document 0101; Document 6000; Document 6248; Document 6268; and Document 6351. In the case of commercial movies, the United States did not enforce tariffs on imported movies, but Mexico did prior to NAFTA.

11. Bonfil Batalla, "Dimensiones culturales," 167.

12. Jeff Silverstein, "Culture: An Industry Exempt from Free Trade? Canadians Fight to Keep Their Identity."

13. See José Manuel Valenzuela Arce, "Ámbitos de interacción y consumo cultural en los jóvenes."

14. García Canclini, "Las industrias culturales," 233, and *Consumidores y ciudadanos: conflictos multiculturales de la globalización.*

15. Dean C. Alexander, "Mexico's Cinema and Video Industries Show Signs of Expansion." For two excellent overviews of the U.S. movie industry's trade in foreign markets, including Latin America, see Kristin Thompson, *Exporting Entertainment: America in the World Film Market, 1907–1934*; and Janet Wasko, *Hollywood in the Information Age: Beyond the Silver Screen.*

16. García Canclini, "Las industrias culturales," 226–28.

17. Néstor García Canclini and Mabel Piccini, "Culturas de la ciudad de México: Símbolos colectivos y usos del espacio urbano," 49.

18. Paul Krugman, "The Uncomfortable Truth about NAFTA," 163.

19. García Canclini, "Las industrias culturales," 233. García Canclini is an Argentine sociologist who resides in Mexico; he is a leading figure in Latin American cultural studies and has written extensively on Mexican popular and mass cultures. Guevara Niebla is a specialist in Mexican educational administration and theory.

At the time of this writing, McAnany and Wilkinson's *Mass Media and Free Trade* had recently been published. It is an anthology similar to García Canclini and Guevara Niebla's, but it features essays by U.S., Canadian, and Mexican contributors.

20. George Yúdice, "The Cultural Impact of Free Trade in the United States," unpublished ms. (March 1995): 14–23. Forthcoming as a chapter in *We Are Not the World: Identity and Representation in an Age of Global Restructuring* (Durham: Duke University Press).

21. Carlos Monsiváis, "De la cultura mexicana en vísperas del Tratado de Libre Comercio," esp. 207–9.

22. Quoted in "The World after NAFTA, According to Paz," 57.

23. "World after NAFTA," 58.

24. Benedict Anderson, *Imagined Communities: Reflections on the Origins and Spread of Nationalism,* 50–65.

25. Monsiváis, "Cultura mexicana," 208–9.

26. The text of the original is as follows: "Pero el problema no es la virginidad de las culturas, sino la destrucción de las economías y la subordinación de la nación al rango único de productora de materias primas y exportadora de mano de obra barata" (Monsiváis, "Cultura mexicana," 208–9).

27. Ricardo Hernández and Edith Sánchez, eds., *Cross-Border Links: A Directory of Organizations in Canada, Mexico, and the United States,* 7.

28. Hernández and Sánchez, *Cross-Border Links,* 7.

29. See chapter 2. The video is titled *Foro Internacional—Opinión Pública y el TLC.* I would like to thank Berta Luján, Secretaria Técnica de la RMALC, for providing me with information produced by her organization about education, culture, and free trade.

30. Matthew Fraser, "A Question of Culture: The Canadian Solution Resolves a GATT Standoff," 50.

31. Mario Vargas Llosa, "¿La excepción cultural?"; Régis Debray, "Respuesta a Vargas Llosa"; I am aware of reprints that appeared in the Latin American newspapers, *El Comercio* (22 November 1993) and *La República* (23–25 October 1993).

32. See, for example, Christian Wiener, "Cine, subdesarrollo y libre mercado." García Canclini discusses the debate in *Consumidores y ciudadanos,* 125–26.

33. Jagdish Bhagwati, letter; Jack Valenti, letter.

34. William Safire, "Hold That GATT"; Seth Fein, letter.

35. Ralph Nader et al., *The Case against Free Trade: GATT, NAFTA, and the Globalization of Corporate Power.*

36. Ernest H. Preeg, *Traders in a Brave New World: The Uruguay Round and the Future of the International Trading System,* 154, 164, 181.

37. Suzan Ayscough, "Greenberg Says No Culture in NAFTA Deal," 46.

38. Quoted in Silverstein, "Culture," 35.

39. Margaret Atwood, "Blind Faith and Free Trade," 94.

40. La Malinche was the indigenous translator and mistress to Hernán Cortés. In Mexican historical, mythical, and popular narratives, she is often vilified and associated with treason. Carlos Fuentes's fiction provides one example of how the figure of La Malinche has appeared in conjunction with modern-day representations of the U.S.–Mexico border. Fuentes has repeatedly portrayed the border as a site of Mexican castration at the hands of the United States, and more recently as a site of U.S. masculine penetration via the maquiladora industries. His short story "Malintzín de las maquilas" recasts Malinche and other Mexican female icons of Mexican nationalism as *maquila* workers; also featured in various guises are the archetypes La Virgen de Guadalupe, La Llorona, and María Candelaria. See Carlos Fuentes, *La frontera de cristal,* 129–60.

41. Fraser, "Question of Culture," 50.

42. John Rockwell, "French Love the U.S., but Fiercely Defend Their Film Industry."

43. These statistics vary slightly among different sources. See Roger Cohen, "Culture Dispute with Paris Now Snags World Accord"; Bernard Weinraub, "Directors Battle over GATT's Final Cut and Print"; Roger Cohen, "Europeans Back French Curbs on U.S. Movies"; Chris Fuller, "Audiovisual Gums Up GATT Talks"; and García Canclini, *Consumidores y ciudadanos,* 118.

44. Preeg, *Traders,* 172.

45. Alan Riding, "Europe Still Gives Big Doses of Money to Help the Arts."

46. Nataša Ďurovičová, "Some Thoughts at an Intersection of the Popular and the National."

47. This argument is summarized in Valenti, letter; Fuller, "Audiovisual"; and Fraser, "Question of Culture." See also the article "Taking Cultural Exception," 61.

48. Fuller, "Audiovisual," 27.

49. The text of the original is as follows: "De acuerdo con la noción amplia de cultura que actualmente manejan las ciencias sociales—como el conjunto de las prácticas en las que se elaboran, procesan, y comunican los significados de la vida social—este libro abarca un espectro amplio de actividades" (Guevara Niebla and García Canclini, *La educación y la cultura,* ix).

50. According to Katharyne Mitchell, Williams traces this deployment of the term to the growth of liberal industrial society beginning in the nineteenth century, when recognition and representation of daily life became a means to "politicize and harness all aspects of life in the context of a rapidly changing and increasingly fragmented 'modern' industrial society." See Katharyne Mitchell, "In Whose Interest? Transnational Capital and the Production of Multiculturalism in Canada," 221; and Raymond Williams, *Culture and Society, 1780–1950,* 285.

51. National Trade Data Bank, *NAFTA* Article 2107.

52. Yúdice, "Cultural Impact," 3.

53. Virginia R. Dominguez, "Invoking Culture: The Messy Side of Cultural Politics," 21. The full quotation is as follows: "So culture stays with us but not, I shall argue, because it is simply a part of life. Rather, because we think and act in terms of it, and we make strategic social and political interventions by invoking it. I am calling this propensity to employ culture (to think, act, and fight with it) 'cultural-

ism.'" According to Dominguez, culturalism is the preferred form of legitimation among independent nations in the late twentieth century, having displaced counterparts from previous eras such as "'racial' theories, spiritual theories, economic/class theories and naturalist theories" (31–32).

54. Dominguez, "Invoking Culture," 21.

55. Bonfil Batalla, "Dimensiones culturales," 167.

56. Debray, "Respuesta," 16.

57. Quoted in Peter Brooks, "Never for GATT," 35. Similar statements were made by former French Minister of Culture, Jack Lang, at a 1982 UNESCO conference in Mexico; see "Taking Cultural Exception," 61; and Bonfil Batalla, "Dimensiones culturales," 168. I am grateful to Neil Larsen, whose discussions with me about his current research on the residual presence of Second International Marxism in contemporary Latin American cultural studies have informed my understanding of the GATT debates.

58. See, for example, "Taking Cultural Exception," 61; Fraser, "Question of Culture," 51; and David Lawday, "France Guns for Clint Eastwood," 72.

59. Debray, "Respuesta," 16.

60. Pierre Assouline, *Germinal: L'aventure d'un film.*

61. "Taking Cultural Exception," 61; and Lawday, "France," 72.

62. The movement for the exemption was not as strong in other European countries as it was in France. For a comparison of the climate in France, Germany, and England, see "El cine europeo se enfrenta al 'enemigo americano.'"

63. Quoted in Fuller, "Audiovisual," 27.

64. Meredith Amdur, "U.S. Broadcasters Berate GATT," 14.

65. Quoted in Weinraub, "Directors Battle," 24. See also Michael Williams, "Top Biz Talent in Culture Clash."

66. Weinraub, "Directors Battle," 24; Williams, "Culture Clash," 62. Toby Miller cites a similar controversial statement made by Lang in Mexico at the Mondiacult conference in 1982: "We hope that this conference will be an occasion for peoples, through their governments, to call for genuine cultural resistance, a real crusade against this domination, against—let us call a spade a spade—this financial and intellectual imperialism"; see Toby Miller, *The Well-Tempered Self: Citizenship, Culture and the Postmodern Subject,* 106.

67. Quoted in Weinraub, "Directors Battle," 24. Mexican film director Paul Leduc has also used the dinosaur analogy to describe the situation confronting Latin American filmmakers during the financial crises of the 1980s. While referring lovingly and nostalgically to the bygone "cinema of quality," he urges Latin American filmmakers to embrace new, less expensive technologies as a means of survival: "Dinosaur cinema has died. But long live lizard cinema. Long live salamander cinema." See Paul Leduc, "Dinosaurs and Lizards," 59.

68. "Filmmakers Lobby EC," *Variety* (25 October 1993): 76.

69. Fraser, "Question of Culture," 50.

70. Thomas Elsaesser, "Hyper-, Retro-, or Counter-Cinema: European Cinema and Third Cinema between Hollywood and Art Cinema," 122. Elsaesser explains, "If the term 'international market' draws attention to the economic realities of film production in competition for the world's spectators, the term 'national cinema' disguises another term: an auteur cinema will often be more opposed to its own national commercial cinema than it is to Hollywood film. The *'politique des auteurs'* or 'cinephilia' are based on such preferment" (122).

71. For an explanation of this principle, see Peter Passell, "How Free Trade Prompts Growth: A Primer"; and Krugman, "Myths and Realities of U.S. Competitiveness," 91.

72. Quoted in Keith Bradsher, "Big Cut in Tariffs: Movies, TV, and Financial Services Are Some of the Areas Left Out."

73. Quoted in "Taking Cultural Exception," 61.

74. Peter Passell, "Is France's Cultural Protection a Handy-dandy Trade Excuse?"

75. Ďurovičová ("Some Thoughts," 7–8) is especially eloquent on this issue.

76. In the most recent French presidential elections both left and right candidates, Lionel Jospin and Jacques Chirac, had relatively identical policies regarding state support of the arts (Riding, "Europe Still Gives," C15).

77. For a discussion of cultural industries and the state in Latin America, see Nissa Torrents, "Mexican Cinema Comes Alive," 222–29; and Randal Johnson, "In the Belly of the Ogre: Cinema and the State in Latin America," 204–13.

78. Carole Condé and Karl Beveridge, "Interventions," 21. For more information about the artists, see their *Class Work*; Linda Hutcheon, *Splitting Images: Contemporary Canadian Ironies,* 118–21; and Peter Dunn and Loraine Leeson, "The Art of Change in Docklands." I would like to thank Condé and Beveridge for discussing their work with me.

79. The status of Canadian publications remains a sensitive one. In January 1997, the World Trade Organization ruled that Canada could not try to ban U.S. magazines through measures such as excise taxes or postal subsidies for Canadian magazines; see Anthony DePalma, "World Trade Body Opposes Canadian Magazine Tariffs."

80. Condé and Beveridge, "Interventions," 24.

81. See for example, Condé and Beveridge, *Class Work*.

82. Karl Beveridge, letter to the author, 3 January 1997.

83. Lynn Schwarzer, letter to the author, 16 October 1996.

84. Maris Bustamante, *A Corazón Abierto: Naftaperformances.* The original Spanish reads "ciudadanos intercontinentales."

85. The closest she comes to addressing the connection between her work and NAFTA is in the program notes for the performance (the translation is also from the program notes): "Convenios inevitables como el TLC/NAFTA cuyas consecuencias tendremos que vivir, nos desorientan a priori porque sentimos vulnerabilidad y temor de perder nuestra tierra, nuestros pedazos aquí en la tierra, lo poco seguro que hemos acumulado, nuestros lenguajes, nuestros idiomas, nuestro tiempo. . . . Estamos simplemente frente a lo desconocido, tratemos de enfrentaro . . ." [*sic*; ellipses in original]. ("Inevitable treaties like NAFTA whose consequences we will have to always live with, first disorient us because we are afraid of losing our land, the only sure thing that we have accumulated, our languages, our times. . . . We are simply facing the unknown, let's try to face it.")

86. Guillermo Gómez-Peña, "The Free Art Agreement/El Tratado de Libre Cultura." Another version of this essay appeared in *High Performance* 63 (fall 1993): 58–63, and a third in Guillermo Gómez-Peña, *The New World Border,* 5–19. The quotes featured in this chapter are taken from the Becker anthology.

87. Gómez-Peña, "Free Art Agreement," 214.

88. For a discussion of artisanry and free trade, see Bonfil Batalla, "Dimensiones culturales," 170–72.

89. Quoted in García Canclini, "Prehistoria económica y cultural del TLC," 10. A similar quote has been attributed to Miguel Alemán Velasco (see Monsiváis, "Cultura mexicana," 208).

90. Néstor García Canclini, "Memory and Innovation in the Theory of Art," 10. By the way, Octavio Paz wrote the introduction to the *Splendors of Thirty Centuries* catalogue ("Will for Form").

91. On the subject of *fridismo,* see Franco, "Manhattan."

92. Alfred H. Barr, Jr. *Painting and Sculpture in the Museum of Modern Art, 1929–1967,* 634. John D. Rockefeller resigned as President of MOMA's Board of Trustees in 1941 in order to become Coordinator of Inter-American Affairs for the U.S. government. The following year the Inter-American Fund was established by an anonymous donor. Later in the 1960s, Joseph Hirshhorn of the Hirshhorn Museum, Smithsonian Institution, was instrumental in reviving U.S. interest in Latin American art.

93. The following passage from a 1943 MOMA exhibition catalogue is a good example of such rhetoric: "Thanks to the Second World War and to certain men of good will throughout our Western Hemisphere, we are dropping those blinders in cultural understanding which have kept the eyes of all the American republics fixed on Europe with scarcely a side glance at each other during the past century and a half. In the field of art we are beginning to look each other full in the face with interest and some comprehension" (Lincoln Kirstein, quoted in Barr, *Painting and Sculpture,* 634).

94. Miguel Cervantes, "Introducción," xxv.

95. In addition, numerous exhibitions have been held in the United States during this period that exclusively feature Latin American art. One notable exception to the hemispheric trend, in my opinion, was the exhibition entitled *South of the Border: Mexico in the American Imagination, 1914–1947,* organized at Yale University by James Oles. The exhibition examined the influence of Mexico and Mexican art on U.S. artists in a manner that established a thorough historical basis for the binational frame. See the catalogue of the same title by James Oles.

96. Gómez-Peña, "Free Art Agreement," 215–16.

97. García Canclini, "Prehistoria económica," 10. Mauricio de María y Campos also discusses Televisa in his essay, "Las industrias culturales y de entretenimiento en el marco de las negociaciones del Tratado de Libre Comercio."

98. Andrew Paxman, "Art for Sale's Sake," 17.

99. Paxman, "Art," 19.

100. Leslie Sklair, "The Maquila Industry and the Creation of a Transnational Capitalist Class in the United States–Mexico Border Region," 75. An expanded essay on this theme, entitled "Capitalism and Development in Global Perspective," appears in Leslie Sklair, ed., *Capitalism and Development.*

101. Sklair, *Capitalism,* 77.

102. Bonfil Batalla, "Dimensiones culturales," 175, n. 15.

2. Establishing Shots of the Border

1. V.I. Lenin, quoted in Neil Smith, *Uneven Development: Nature, Capital and the Production of Space,* 88.

2. The characters are introduced as follows. Sailor: "A Texas boy/Just returned from duty/With the navy in the Pacific/On leave in the port of San Diego"; Spanish Alice: "A Mexican prostitute/Working the bars in Tijuana/And looking for ways/into the USA"; Jabo: "A Juarez-born pachuco/Living in Los Angeles/Decides to go home/By way of a joy ride/Up into southern Colorado"; and Chic Blundie: "Jabo's L.A. girlfriend/An enigma/Rock-writer/And occasionally . . . Jabo himself" [Terry Allen, *a simple story (Juarez),* 7].

3. Sarah Rogers-Lafferty, "Afterword," in Allen, *simple story,* 77.

4. Rosetta Brooks, "From the Middle of Nowhere: Terry Allen's Badlands," 86.

5. "The Perfect Ship" has a white mannequin inside of it, and the video projected in that set is a long-take of a woman's legs as she walks across the bridge from the United States into Mexico.

6. Allen, *simple story,* 6.

7. Patricio Chávez and Madeleine Grynsztejn, *La Frontera/The Border: Art about the Mexico/United States Border Experience,* 38. In her catalogue essay, Grynsztejn acknowledges the work of several important artists who were conspicuously absent from the show.

8. See Sally Yard, ed., *inSITE 94: A Binational Exhibition of Installation and Site-Specific Art,* and *inSITE 94 Guide,* and Danielle Reo, ed., *inSITE 97 Guide.* The first *inSITE* exhibition featured local artists; the second featured artists from around the globe. The third seems to strive for a balance of sorts between the previous two shows; it features artists from North and South America and the Caribbean.

9. George Yúdice, "The Cultural Impact of Free Trade in the United States," unpublished ms.

(March 1995), 27. Forthcoming as a chapter in *We Are Not the World: Identity and Representation in an Age of Global Restructuring* (Durham: Duke University Press).

10. A few examples of such exhibitions include *The Decade Show: Frameworks of Identity in the 1980s* (New York: Museum of Contemporary Hispanic Art, The New Museum of Contemporary Art, and the Studio Museum in Harlem, 1990); *Art of the Other Mexico: Sources and Meanings* (Chicago: Mexican Fine Arts Center Museum, 1993); *Chicano Art: Resistance and Affirmation, 1965–1985* (Los Angeles: Wight Art Gallery, UCLA, 1991); *Mito y magia en las Américas: Los ochenta* (Monterrey: Museo de Arte Contemporáneo de Monterrey, 1991); *About Place: Recent Art of the Americas* (Chicago: The Art Institute of Chicago, 1995); and *1993 Festival of American Folklife, July 1–July 5* (Washington, DC: Smithsonian Institution, 1993). Lucy R. Lippard's book *Mixed Blessings: New Art in a Multicultural America* is also an important early contribution to this current.

11. Paul J. Vanderwood and Frank N. Samponaro, *Border Fury.* Postcard images of the border during the Mexican Revolution are discussed in chapter 3.

12. *Chulas Fronteras,* dir. Les Blanc; Aristeo Brito, *The Devil in Texas/El diablo en Texas.*

13. On Aztlán, see Rudolfo Anaya and Francisco Lomelí, eds. *Aztlán: Essays on the Chicano Homeland*; and Carlos Muñoz, Jr., *Youth, Identity, Power: The Chicano Movement.* On the Borderlands, see Héctor Calderón and José David Saldívar, eds., *Criticism in the Borderlands: Studies in Chicano Literature, Culture, and Ideology*; and Gloria Anzaldúa, *Borderlands/La Frontera: The New Mestiza.*

14. Néstor García Canclini, *Culturas híbridas: Estrategias para entrar y salir de la modernidad,* 300.

15. Richard Griswold del Castillo, Teresa McKenna, and Yvonne Yarbro-Bejarano, eds., *Chicano Art: Resistance and Affirmation, 1965–1985,* flysheets, 248, 256.

16. Griswold del Castillo et al., eds., *Chicano Art,* 35, 255.

17. Griswold del Castillo et al., eds., *Chicano Art,* 49, 286. In the early 1970s, ASCO entered into polemics with certain Chicano/a artists who favored the revival of Aztec and pre-Colombian myth as subject matter for their work; ASCO in contrast, preferred to refashion the contemporary visual languages of mass media, urban street life, and popular culture that they found in their native East Los Angeles.

Another founding member of ASCO, Harry Gamboa, Jr., has used the chain-link motif in the post-ASCO years. The climactic scene of his 1993 video, *L.A. Familia,* which deals with the disintegration of a Chicano family in Los Angeles, is staged on a chain-link enclosed pedestrian bridge spanning an eight-lane freeway. The video was included in the exhibition "Identity and Home" (Museum of Modern Art, New York, 8 November 1993–9 January 1994).

18. Roberto Rodríguez, "(Barbed) Wired for Controversy"; Nancy Traver, "NM, Artist, University Divided over Sculpture Topped with Wire."

19. For the record, many fencing materials are currently in use on the U.S.–Mexico border. They include barbed wire, chain-link, metal webbing, wire cable, and steel-reinforced concrete. Newer barriers that are increasingly being implemented in the past five to ten years are drainage ditches and corrugated steel walls constructed from military surplus landing mats. As pressure from U.S. nativist groups and the fencing proposals of right-wing politicians Pat Buchanan and Newt Gingrich have gained momentum, more imposing fencing materials are found in urban and densely crossed zones. So far the areas affected are San Diego/Tijuana, Tecate, Calexico/Mexicali, San Luis Río Colorado, Nogales, Douglas, and Naco, and a fence is currently being erected in Sunland Park/Anapra. The passage of the Illegal Immigration Reform and Immigrant Responsibility Act of 1996 calls for constructing second and third fences behind the main fence in San Diego/Tijuana.

See James S. Griffith, "The Arizona-Sonora Border: Line, Region, Magnet, Filter"; Peter Goin, "Following the Line: The Mexico-American Border"; People Against the Wall, *People against the Wall, El Paso, TX, Sunland Park, NM and Anapra, Chih.,* unpublished ms., 1996 (available from Border Rights Coalition, El Paso); and Marisa J. Demeo, "Bolstering INS Enforcement."

20. *A Conversation with Terry Allen and Dave Hickey,* video.

21. For work of this type by Bartletti, see the Oakland Museum, *Between Two Worlds: The People of the Border, Photographs by Don Bartletti*; for Hall, see Douglas Kent Hall, *The Border: Life on the Line*; and Allen, *simple story*; for Dusard, see Alan Weisman, *La Frontera: The United States Border with Mexico*; for Aguilera-Hellweg, see Museum of Contemporary Hispanic Art et al., *Decade Show,* 56–57, plate 1; for Salgado's, see Salgado, "The Border." Jeff Wall's photos were featured in the exhibition *About Place* at the Art Institute of Chicago and in a solo exhibition at the Museum of Contemporary Art, Chicago, both in 1995. Susan Meiselas's unpublished photoessay is titled, "The U.S.–Mexico Border" (1990).

22. I refer to the installations "Border Realities III, February 1987; "Fence Border line boundary," January 1987; and "Aztep," February 1986. These are illustrated in Jeff Kelley, ed. of English text, *The Border Art Workshop (BAW/TAF), 1984–1989,* 26, 43, 27.

23. BAW/TAF, *Tallér de Arte Fronterízo, 1.984–1.991,* cover.

24. For several examples of political cartoons anthropomorphizing the continents of North and South America, see George Black, *The Good Neighbor.*

25. Morris Berman, "Shadow across the Rio Grande," 90.

26. Guillermo Gómez-Peña, *The New World Border,* 2–3. *Cojones* means "balls."

27. Rolando J. Romero, "Border of Fear, Border of Desire," 38.

28. Joseph Wambaugh, quoted in Romero, "Border of Fear," 37–38.

29. Bruce Selcraig, "Poisonous Flows the Rio Grande."

30. Luis Alberto Urrea, *Across the Wire: Life and Hard Times on the Mexican Border,* and *By the Lake of Sleeping Children: The Secret Life of the Mexican Border.*

31. Urrea, *Lake of Sleeping Children,* 70. Urrea also quotes from Wambaugh's novel (6).

32. Debbie Nathan, "Love in the Time of Cholera: Waiting for Free Trade."

33. Nathan relocated to San Antonio in 1998.

34. Nathan, "Love," 15.

35. Nathan, "Love," 12.

36. Debbie Nathan, personal interviews, fall 1992.

37. Benedict Anderson, *Imagined Communities: Reflections on the Origin and Spread of Nationalism.*

38. Cathryn Thorup, "The Politics of Free Trade and the Dynamics of Cross-Border Coalitions in U.S.–Mexican Relations," 15.

39. Kim Moody and Mary McGinn, *Unions and Free Trade: Solidarity vs. Competition,* 14–15.

40. Professor Fran Ansley, University of Tennessee College of Law and the Tennessee Industrial Renewal Network, personal interview, 10 September 1993; Professor Fran Ansley, letter to the author, 17 June 1997. For further information on grassroots video in Latin America, see *Media Development,* spec. issue, "Video for the People"; and Pat Aufderheide, "Film and Video in the Cultural Struggle of Latin America," and "Latin American Grassroots Video: Beyond Television."

Transnational corporations also use video as a means of communicating with their workers. In testimony delivered before the Trade Staff Policy Committee hearings in Atlanta, Georgia, Shirley Reinhardt, a former GE worker, recalled the company's treatment of its workers right before it initiated a period of massive layoffs: "At the same time the company was threatening us, they were also sweet-talking us. I especially remember the video they made which was shown to all the workers at the plant right before the time for the union election. The video showed a lot of local spots in Morristown. It was like they were trying to say how 'at home' the company was here in our little town, what a difference they made to the whole community. (And of course they *do* make a difference.) They had also gone around and taken photographs of every worker at the plant. When they finally showed the video to us, there we were up on the screen, each one a part of the picture. In fact, the video said that we were all a part of the 'GE Family.'" (Citizens Against Temporary Services, "Testimony Prepared for the Trade Staff

Policy Committee, Office of the U.S. Trade Representative, Atlanta, Georgia, Thursday, August 29, 1991," unpublished ms. [available from the Tennessee Industrial Renewal Network], 3).

41. *The Global Assembly Line,* dir. Lorraine Gray.

42. *What's the Cost of Your Blouse?* dir. Sydney Brown and Betty McAfee.

43. *Mexico: For Sale,* dir. Dermot and Carla Begley.

44. Bruce Campbell, quoted in David Brooks, "The Search for Counterparts," 95.

45. Personal interview, 16 July 1993. The director preferred to remain anonymous.

46. *Leaving Home: A Road Trip into Our Free Trade Future,* prod. We Do the Work.

47. García Canclini, *Culturas híbridas,* 293.

48. Avalos writes, "The formation of these border laboratories was duly noted by the local media as academic events of international significance"; see David Avalos, "A Wag Dogging a Tale."

49. *We Can Say No!* dir. Mark Cameron.

50. Two documentaries broadcast on Public Television, *Global Assembly Line* and *Leaving Home,* as well as the BBC's *Mexico: For a Few Dollars More* evidently were able to shoot inside the maquiladoras; *Leaving Home* also features footage of the interior of a plant taken from a concealed, handheld video camera.

51. *Stepan Chemical: The Poisoning of a Mexican Community,* dir. Mark R. Day.

52. Stepan was one of ninety-two companies in the Brownsville/Matamoros area named in a lawsuit that was filed by twenty-seven families who had been affected by such birth defects. The case was finally settled out of court for an undisclosed sum in September 1995 ("Anencephaly Suit Settled, Many Questions Remain," 6).

53. *NAFTA: Playing with a Volatile Substance,* prod. Cinefocus Canada; *$4 a Day? No Way!* prod. American Labor Education Center.

54. *Dirty Business: Food Exports to the United States,* dir. Jon Silver. Though Irapuato is not on the border, it is interesting to note that as early as 1984 Paco Ignacio Taibo II had dubbed it a maquiladora town in his *Irapuato mi amor.*

55. Kim Moody, *An Injury to All*; Moody and McGinn, *Unions and Free Trade,* 48.

56. Several of the videos besides *Dirty Business,* such as *Leaving Home* and *What's the Cost of Your Blouse?* acknowledge the position of Mexican Americans in the North American economy, but do not engage in an analysis of their perspectives as U.S. citizens or residents.

57. Hon. Jerry Kleczka, "Special Report on NAFTA." The spin that Kleczka put on this video is difficult to distinguish from the anti–free trade campaign launched in 1997 by major produce growers and Republican Representative Sonny Bono. Bono proposed legislation called the Import Produce Labeling Act that would require all Mexican produce sold in the United States to be labeled as such. Florida growers produced their own video entitled *The True Cost of Winter Vegetables,* which recurred to familiar images of waste water and raw sewage in Mexican agricultural areas (see "Video Evidence for Import Labeling Bill").

58. Ross Perot, quoted in "The NAFTA Debate."

59. The 1992 U.S. elections witnessed a strange spectrum of positions on NAFTA, which did not neatly correspond to party lines. The extreme right wing of the Republican Party, such as Pat Buchanan and David Duke (one of whom advocated building a great wall between the United States and Mexico, and the other of whom participated in a "Light Up the Border" vigilante photo-op), shared the protectionist camp with Ross Perot and "Rust Belt" and pro-labor Democrats, while the center left and center right of the two major parties tended to support NAFTA.

For an excellent overview of the U.S. political parties' stances on free trade, written from a liberal position, see Alan K. Henrikson, "A North American Community: 'From the Yukon to the Yucatan.'"

60. Susan Buck-Morss, "Passports," 68.

61. Buck-Morss, "Passports," 75.

62. Buck-Morss, "Passports," 77.

63. J. Evetts Haley, *Jeff Milton: A Good Man with a Gun,* 378–81. For a modern story emphasizing similar themes, see Debbie Nathan's essay on the deportation hearing of Margaret Randall entitled "Adjustment of Status: The Trial of Margaret Randall," 90–108.

64. Paul Krugman, *Pop Internationalism,* 6.

65. Moreover, this way of seeing boundaries carries over to the videos' portrayal of U.S. and Canadian space. A segment of *Leaving Home,* for example charts the closure of a Zenith plant in Springfield, Missouri, and its subsequent relocation to Mexico. Shots of the plant taken from outside chain-link fence are coupled with this voice-over observation from John Piney, a former Zenith worker: "We can kind of relate to what's happening to us now because we took this work away from Chicago."

66. Quoted in Tracy Wilkinson, "Dreams Die on Mexico's Second Border," A10. The priest is Raúl Hernández of the Catholic Church's Episcopal Conference in Guatemala.

67. Quoted in Hayes Ferguson, "Seeking a Better Life—in Mexico," A10. The priest is Fr. Ademar Barilli.

3. U.S.–Mexico Border Conflict in U.S. Popular Culture

1. Carlos E. Cortés, "To View a Neighbor: The Hollywood Textbook on Mexico," 94.

2. Linda B. Hall and Don M. Coerver, *Revolution on the Border: The United States and Mexico, 1910–1920,* 20.

3. Luis Alberto Urrea, *By the Lake of Sleeping Children: The Secret Life of the Mexican Border,* 6.

4. Hall and Coerver, *Revolution,* 8.

5. Paul J. Vanderwood and Frank N. Samponaro, *Border Fury: A Picture Postcard Record of Mexico's Revolution and U.S. War Preparedness, 1910–1917,* 72.

6. Cortés, "To View a Neighbor," 109 (the film is *They Came to Cordura*). The 1960s seem to mark a shift in portrayals of Villa from the U.S. perspective. At the Columbus Historical Museum in Columbus, New Mexico, for example, there is a 1961 letter on display from the Mexican government celebrating the fact that both nations could pay homage to so great a patriot as Villa. Hollywood also produced several "pro-Villa" films in the late 1950s and 1960s such as *Villa!* (1958) and *Villa Rides* (1968) (Cortés, "To View a Neighbor," 104).

7. John King, *Magical Reels: A History of Cinema in Latin America,* 17.

8. In the exhibits at the Columbus Historical Society Museum in Columbus, New Mexico, all of these theories are mentioned. The number of U.S. citizens killed in the Columbus Raid varies according to different sources, but is usually placed in the high teens. The number of U.S. army regulars that served under Pershing also varies from six to twelve thousand, depending upon the source. I am using the figures from the Columbus Historical Society Museum.

9. This is another figure which varies widely, depending upon the source. I am using Vanderwood and Samponaro's figures, which concur with those of the Columbus Historical Museum. Hall and Coerver place the number at 110,000 (Vanderwood and Samponaro, *Border Fury,* 12; Hall and Coerver, *Revolution,* 69).

10. Vanderwood and Samponaro, *Border Fury,* 11–12.

11. Hall and Coerver, *Revolution,* ch. 7.

12. Benedict Anderson, *Imagined Communities: Reflections on the Origin and Spread of Nationalism,* 16.

13. Anderson, *Imagined Communities,* 18.

14. Patrick McGreevy, "Reading the Texts of Niagara Falls: The Metaphor of Death," 69. As the title of this essay implies, McGreevy also links this U.S.–Canadian border site with images of mortality.

15. Robert W. Larson, "Statehood." During the period between the signing of the Treaty of Guadalupe Hidalgo and admission into the union, Anglo lawyers and settlers in New Mexico systematically

sought to undermine the power of territory's Mexican American population through challenging their ancient claims to communally held lands. The last of these claims was "settled" by a Congressional court in 1903.

16. Calvin A. Roberts and Susan A. Roberts, "The End of Isolation."

17. According to Chon Noriega, the distinction between Mexicans and Mexican Americans would not be made in U.S. social practice and popular culture until the Chicano/a Movement; see "This Is Not a Border," 4.

18. The Plan de San Diego called for a race war in order to regain the Mexican territory that had been ceded to the United States. A Liberating Army of Races and Peoples, which would unite Mexican Americans, African-Americans, and Japanese under the same banner was supposed to slay every white male over sixteen in the U.S. Southwest as part of the plan. The plan was never carried out on a large scale, though it did lead to a number of border raids in the Lower Rio Grande Valley prior to the Columbus Raid and provoked a great deal of racial tension and violence in Texas. Historians have debated whether the plot was a Huertista diversionary scheme, later exploited by Carranza, or whether it was a Carrancista scheme from the beginning, and to what extent German and Japanese interests participated in it. They do agree however, that the plan was intended to use Mexican Americans as pawns against Washington rather than actually to liberate the oppressed of the region. See Charles H. Harris III and Louis R. Sadler, "The Plan of San Diego and the Mexican-United States War Crisis of 1916: A Reexamination"; Allen Gerlach, "Conditions along the Border—1915: The Plan de San Diego"; James A. Sandos, "The Plan of San Diego: War and Diplomacy on the Texas Border, 1915–1916"; and James A. Sandos, *Rebellion in the Borderlands: Anarchism and the Plan de San Diego, 1904–1923.*

19. Hall and Coerver, *Revolution,* 126.

20. James A. Sandos, "German Involvement in Northern Mexico, 1915–1916: A New Look at the Columbus Raid"; Francis J. Munch, "Villa's Columbus Raid: Practical Politics or German Design?"

21. I am using the term *modernization* following Perry Anderson's critique of Marshal Berman's *All That Is Solid Melts into Air.* Anderson invokes Marx's concept of uneven temporal and spatial capital expansion in order to question Berman's theorization of modernization as a "constant, uninterrupted, everlasting" process of development. Military-industrial organization and visual technology also influence the construction of human subjectivities and of historical experience, categories that Berman labels "modernism" and "modernity," respectively. See Perry Anderson, "Modernity and Revolution," 101.

22. Vanderwood and Samponaro, *Border Fury,* ch. 4.

23. James A. Sandos, "Prostitution and Drugs: The United States Army on the Mexican-American Border, 1916–1917."

24. Vanderwood and Samponaro, *Border Fury,* 73.

25. Cortés, "To View a Neighbor," 95–98.

26. Patricia King Hanson, ed., *The American Film Institute Catalog of Motion Pictures Produced in the United States,* vol. F1, *Feature Films, 1911–1920.* The films are *America Preparing* (documentary), *Behind the Lines, The Brand of Cowardice, Following the Flag in Mexico, The Gringo* (release date believed to be 1916), *Lieutenant Danny, USA,* and *The Love Thief.* In addition, two feature films were released in 1914 that vaguely referred to the U.S. occupation of Veracruz: *The Man O'Warsman* and *For the Honor of Old Glory; or, the Stars and Stripes in Mexico.* Unfortunately, I have not been able to locate any prints of these films; however, Margarita de Orellana's detailed plot description of *Lieutenant Danny, USA* in her book *La mirada circular* suggests that she has seen a print of the movie (see *La mirada circular: El cine norteamericano de la Revolución Mexicana, 1911–1917*).

27. The film mentioned is *Lieutenant Danny, USA.* It is difficult to generalize about these movies with information from plot summaries, but there was apparently some variation among them in terms of representations of gender and national types. In *The Love Thief,* for example, the enemy is a vindic-

tive Mexican *soldadera,* whereas in *The Gringo* and *Lieutenant Danny, USA* the love interest is a wealthy *porfirista* woman.

28. For an extensive survey of U.S. newsreel coverage of the Revolution, see Aurelio de los Reyes, *Con Villa en México: Testimonios de camarógrafos norteamericanos en la Revolución.* My observations are also based upon research of the Hearst Metrotone News Collection at the UCLA Film and TV Archive Research and Study Center, Los Angeles, California.

29. Cortés, "To View a Neighbor," 97.

30. Cortés, "To View a Neighbor," 98.

31. Hanson, ed., *Catalog.* The films are *The Border Wireless* (1918), *Fighting Through* (1919), and *His Majesty the American* (1919). The plot trajectory of this last title moves from Mexico to an imaginary, "undemocratic" European country.

32. Vanderwood and Samponaro, *Border Fury,* 7.

33. Horne's work is discussed thoroughly in Vanderwood and Samponaro, *Border Fury.* For a survey of Aultman's photos, see Mary A. Sarber, *Photographs from the Border: The Otis A. Aultman Collection.*

34. Vanderwood and Samponaro, *Border Fury,* ch. 1. For a history of photography in Latin America and Mexico, see Robert M. Levine, *Images of History;* Olivier Debroise, *Fuga mexicana: Un recorrido por la fotografía en México;* and Teresa Matabuena Peláez, *Algunos usos y conceptos de la fotografía durante el Porfiriato.*

The postcard craze hit the United States and Latin America at the same time, shortly after the turn of the century. In Latin America, though, foreigners comprised the first generation of photographers in the mid-nineteenth century. Even after photographic studios became established in major cities, a division of labor remained between native- and foreign-born photographers. The latter group tended to travel and to produce exotic outdoor shots of landscape and "primitive" peoples for export, along the theme of the "white man's burden," while the former group generally handled conventional portraiture, weddings, funerals, and urban themes. In Mexico at the time of the Revolution, the split between U.S. (and other foreign) documentary photographers and Mexican studio photographers was not as pronounced as it was in other parts of Latin America, perhaps because the positivist applications of documentary photography were encouraged in the *científicos'* promotion of modernization. Popular themes in Mexican photography during the Porfiriato included public works projects, diplomatic pomp and parades, and posed photographs of "ordinary" (i.e., lower-class or indigenous) citizens.

In my own research in the Southwest Collection at the El Paso Public Library, I noted that many of the Mexican postcards of the Revolution, like contemporary postcards, were printed in large batches, and featured generic typeset captions superimposed directly on the photograph or at its margins.

35. Vanderwood and Samponaro, *Border Fury,* ch. 2.

36. Vanderwood and Samponaro, *Border Fury,* 114.

37. The obelisk-shaped markers still remain along various stretches of the border. In El Paso, the markers also demarcate the perimeters of the Border Patrol Headquarters and the U.S. side of the Chamizal memorial park.

38. My comments in this section are based upon research in the Southwest Collection at the El Paso Public Library.

39. Vanderwood and Samponaro, *Border Fury,* 48–49. Many U.S. postcards of the Veracruz occupation also portrayed U.S. soldiers posing with Mexican women.

40. As an example of Osbon's macabre side, in one series of photographs, he returned to the site of the Battle of Agua Prieta, three months after it had occurred (according to the dates on his postcards), where he photographed the decomposed, half-buried bodies of its victims. The results are extreme close-ups of feet, skulls, and hands protruding out of the sand. Their captions combine details about the battle with descriptions of the corpses that read as though they were from a forensics manual.

41. Brown Meggs, *The War Train: A Novel of 1916*, 15.

42. Hall and Coerver, *Revolution*, 20.

43. Vanderwood and Samponaro, *Border Fury*, 113.

44. Vanderwood and Samponaro, *Border Fury*, 115.

45. I would like to thank Debbie Nathan for this information.

46. Oscar J. Martínez, *Border Boom Town: Ciudad Juárez since 1848*, 39.

47. This could be said of the photographers as well as the armed forces. Aurelio de los Reyes described the Revolution as "un eslabón más en la cadena de perfeccionamientos técnicos y narrativos de la cinematografía" ("one more link in the chain of technical and narrative perfection of cinematography"; see de los Reyes, *Con Villa*, 67).

48. The historical background of the "triple execution" series is discussed in Vanderwood and Samponaro, *Border Fury*, 68, 94–97.

49. This idea is usually associated with Stephen Heath's work on shot/reverse-shot structure in cinema and the concept of suture. See his *Questions of Cinema*. In an elaboration of Heath's ideas, Sandy Flitterman-Lewis explains, "Most commonly applied to conversation situations, the *reverse-shot* structure implies an alternation of images between seeing and seen, the *point-of-view* shot anchoring the image in the vision and perspective of one or another character (and marked by greater or lesser degrees of subjective distortion). The spectator therefore identifies, in effect, with someone who is always off-screen, an absent 'other' whose main function is to signify a space to be occupied. . . . The reverse-shot structure enables the spectator to become a sort of *invisible mediator* between an interplay of looks, a fictive participant in the fantasy of the film. For a shot of one character looking, to another character looked at, the viewer's subjectivity is bound into the text." See Sandy Flitterman-Lewis, "The Gaze," 167.

50. I am adapting the phrase "model spectators" from Umberto Eco, who refers to the "model reader." See his "Introduction: The Role of the Reader."

51. Cortés, "To View a Neighbor," 98, 109.

52. Deborah E. Mistron, "The Role of Pancho Villa in the Mexican and American Cinema." Mistron also argues that a similar suppression of Villa's historical character has taken place in the Mexican cinema, although often those attributes that are glorified in the U.S. cinema are precisely the same ones that are downplayed in the Mexican cinema.

53. "The Curse of the Jackal," prod. Rick McCallum, dir. Carl Schultz, writer Jonathan Hales. Other texts could be related to the two that I examine in this chapter, including Bill Rakocy's eccentric documentary history, *1916 Villa Raids!* and the documentary *In Search of Pancho Villa*, dir. Hector Galan.

54. Vanderwood and Samponaro, *Border Fury*, 239. Meggs's novel also explores this issue in great detail.

55. These other sources are not represented by photographic images, but rather through long passages of the text that are set off by bold black lines. In some cases the ephemera present political points of view that assert themselves through the often racist and turgid prose of the story itself. One article by John Reed, for example, argues against derisive stereotyping of Mexicans; a poster recruiting U.S. mercenaries to serve in the Villista army attests to the participation of U.S. citizens on the Mexican side during Revolution.

56. Meggs, *War Train*, 319.

57. Meggs, *War Train*, 334.

58. Compare the ending of the novel to that of the 1915 film *The Lamb*, in which a band of Yaquis kidnap two Americans, Gerald and Mary, in Arizona and take them across the border into Mexico: "Gerald locates an abandoned Mexican rapid-fire cannon and begins an assault on the Indians. After a long and heated battle, the battered but victorious Indians close in on Gerald, intending to cut out his heart, but both he and Mary are saved by American troopers" (Hanson, ed., *Catalog*, 498).

59. For an analysis of these scenes from *The Old Gringo,* see Claire F. Fox, "Hollywood's Backlot: Carlos Fuentes, *The Old Gringo,* and National Cinema."

60. I extend my thanks to Charles Wolfe and Linda Williams, who identified this movie as D.W. Griffith's *The Battle* (1911).

61. The intertitles say, "'To the Halls of Montezuma!' US Troops sweep into Mexico," and "General Pershing: We shall soon have that cowardly bandit Pancho Villa on the run." Indy tells the audience, "Tropas de Estados Unidos visitan de cortesía a Canadá" and "General . . . dice que Pancho Villa es un gran hombre" ("U.S. troops pay a courtesy visit to Canada" and "General . . . says that Pancho Villa is a great man"). The shots of the Punitive Expedition from the newsreel appear to have been fabricated in order to have Pershing played by the same actor in the newsreel as in the rest of the episode.

62. Indy experiences another *toma de conciencia* as he is leaving Hearst's hacienda. He sees a photograph of an unidentified woman and becomes transfixed by it. This image is the only loot he carries off with him.

63. A brilliant Hal Roach silent movie entitled *Why Worry?* (1923, dir. Fred Newmeyer and Sam Taylor) called attention to this spectatorial dichotomy a few years after the Revolution, at the onset of an intense and prolonged period of U.S. intervention in Latin America. The movie is about a wealthy hypochondriac Harold Van Pelham (played by Harold Lloyd) who travels to the fictional South American island of Paradiso in order to take a rest cure. An innocent abroad, Van Pelham does not realize that he has stumbled into a politically volatile situation, and his snobbery and arrogance keep him from recognizing what is going on until it is too late. The island is ruled by an age-old military dictatorship that has the support of Northern banks. Opposing the regime are bands of rebel soldiers ("riffraff") led by a gringo adventurer named Blake. The rebels mistake Van Pelham for a bank representative, and mayhem ensues.

The first third of the movie is devoted to a series of comic misrecognitions in which Van Pelham observes revolutionary violence, but believes that what he is seeing are spectacles orchestrated by the natives for his entertainment: a staggering slain man in the arms of his lover earns applause from Van Pelham, who thinks that he is seeing a native dance; Van Pelham nods to a man who has been clubbed over the head, believing that the native is bowing to him; with a moralistic sigh, he tosses a coin into the hat of a dead man, believing him to be a lazy beggar. The tables are turned in the third reel, when Van Pelham and two allies outwit the rebel army by staging a show for them. From behind a wall on the edge of town, they use simple props such as a ladder, a drum, and coconut-cannonballs to simulate the appearance of marching hoardes of soldiers. The rebels flee in fright.

64. See Timothy Dunn, *The Militarization of the U.S.–Mexico Border, 1978–1992: Low-Intensity Conflict Doctrine Comes Home*; "Policing the Border—A Military Approach"; *Resource Center Bulletin,* spec. issue, "Washington's Aid Programs to Mexico: Military and Anti-Narcotics Assistance"; and Don Baum, *Smoke and Mirrors: The War on Drugs and the Politics of Failure.*

65. Miriam Davidson, "Militarizing the Mexican Border," 406.

66. "Policing the Border," 1.

67. Caspar W. Weinberger, *The Next War.*

68. Miriam Davidson, "The Mexican Border War."

69. Guillermo Gómez-Peña, "From Art-mageddon to Gringostroika," 25.

70. Davidson, "Mexican Border War," 559.

71. Martínez, *Border Boom Town,* 22 ff, 67.

72. Rebecca Morales and Jesús Tamayo-Sánchez, "Urbanization and Development of the United States–Mexico Border," 57–58.

73. The work of sociologist Pablo Sergio Vila on border identities is exemplary in this respect; see *Everyday Life, Culture, and Identity on the Mexican-American Border.*

74. See, for example, quotations from Enrique Krauze and others throughout "Progress and

Promise"; and Robert A. Pastor and Jorge G. Castañeda, *Limits to Friendship: The United States and Mexico,* 121–22.

75. Eduardo Barrera Herrera, "Nationalism versus Capitalism."

76. Néstor García Canclini, *Culturas híbridas: Estrategias para entrar y salir de la modernidad,* 13. García Canclini opens his book with the following question: "¿Cuáles son, en los años noventa, las estrategias para entrar y salir de la modernidad? Colocamos la pregunta de este modo porque en América Latina, donde las tradiciones aún no se han ido y la modernidad no acaba de llegar, dudamos si modernizarnos debe ser el principal objetivo, según pregonan políticos, economistas y la publicidad de nuevas tecnologías." ("In the 1990s, what are the strategies for entering and leaving modernity? We pose the question in this manner because in Latin America, where traditions still have not left and modernity has not finished arriving, we doubt if modernizing ourselves should be the principal objective, as politicians, economists, and the publicity for new technologies proclaim.")

77. A marked shift is evident when one compares the free trade stance of Salinas in 1988 to the one in 1991. See, for example, Larry Rohter, "North American Trade Bloc? Mexico Rejects Such an Idea"; and Carlos Salinas de Gortari, "A New Hope for the Hemisphere."

78. For an account of this incident, see George R. Leighton, "Afterword: The Photographic History of the Mexican Revolution," 288.

79. On democratization, see Ana Cristina Laurell, "Democracy in Mexico: Will the First Be the Last?" For examples of several parodic references to Creelman's question, see n. 68.

80. For a discussion of the representation of the Porfiriato in the Mexican cinema, see Jorge Ayala Blanco, "La añoranza porfiriana," 40–47.

81. Pastor and Castañeda, *Limits to Friendship,* 121–22. The figures cited in the next two paragraphs are taken from the section of the book authored by Castañeda and are from Mexican sources.

4. Narratives of Cross-Border Migration during the Revolution's Developmentalist Phase

1. José Manuel Valenzuela Arce, "Ámbitos de interacción y consumo cultural en los jóvenes," 403.

2. Martín Luis Guzmán, *El águila y la serpiente,* 343; or *The Eagle and the Serpent,* 291.

3. For a few examples, see *La perla* (*The Pearl*; 1945, dir. Emilio Fernández), *Macario* (1959, dir. Roberto Gavaldón), and *El Gallo de Oro* (*The Golden Cock*; 1964, dir. Roberto Gavaldón).

4. Deborah E. Mistron, "A Hybrid Subgenre: The Revolutionary Melodrama in the Mexican Cinema," 48.

5. For more information about this period in Mexican film history, see Carl J. Mora, *Mexican Cinema: Reflections of a Society, 1896–1988,* 75–100; and Charles Ramírez Berg, *Cinema of Solitude: A Critical Study of Mexican Film, 1967–1983,* 12–28.

6. Sara Sefchovich, *Ideología y ficción en la obra de Luis Spota,* 223–53.

7. Daniel Cosío Villegas, quoted in Charles A. Hale, "The Liberal Impulse: Daniel Cosío Villegas and the *Historia moderna de México,*" 482.

8. Daniel Cosío Villegas, "Mexico's Crisis," 3.

9. Cosío Villegas, "Crisis," 27.

10. Enrique Krauze, *Daniel Cosío Villegas: Una biografía intellectual,* 157.

11. Hale, "Cosío," 481.

12. See Hale, "Cosío"; and Daniel Cosío Villegas, "Sobre la libertad de prensa," 313–25.

13. Charles A. Hale, "Liberalism, the Revolution, and Nationalism in Mexico."

14. Hale, "Liberalism," 10–11.

15. Hale, "Liberalism," 10.

16. For more information about the Bracero Program, see Morales and Tamayo-Sánchez, "Urbanization and Development of the United States–Mexico Border," 49–68.

17. "Bracero II: Coming Soon?" and "Anti-Immigration Bill Moves Ahead, Bracero II Dead."

18. Mark Stricherz, "Bill of Wrath."

19. Morales and Tamayo-Sánchez, "Urbanization," 60.

20. The original Spanish is as follows: "Esta tragicómica secuela de *La vida inútil de Pito Pérez,* imaginada especialmente para el cine por el novelista michoacano Romero, resultó totalmente frustrada, no sólo por la incompetencia manifiesta del director Patiño Gómez, sino por la ubicación del personaje en la frontera imposible que separa a dos cines: el anterior y el posterior al sexenio alemanista." Quoted in Norma Iglesias Prieto, *Entre yerba, polvo y plomo: Lo fronterizo visto por el cine mexicano,* vol. 2, 25.

21. *Coyotes* and *pateros* are corrupt labor contractors or smugglers of braceros.

22. I take this phrase from Ramírez Berg's discussion of the emigrant experience in Mexican cinema (*Cinema of Solitude,* 196–200).

23. Luis Spota, *Murieron a mitad del río; Espaldas mojadas,* dir. Alejandro Galindo.

24. Elda Peralta, *Luis Spota: Las sustancias de la tierra,* 117.

25. Alejandro Galindo, *El cine mexicano: Un personal punto de vista,* 146; Emilio García Riera, *Historia documental del cine mexicano,* vol. 5, 185–88; and Seth Fein, "Nationalist Anticommunism and Mexican Cinema of the 1950s," 21–22.

The prefatory statement to *Espaldas mojadas* reads as follows: "Nuestro propósito es advertir a nuestros connacionales de la inconveniencia de tratar de abandonar el país en forma ilegal, con el riesgo de sufrir situaciones molestas y dolorosas que podrían hasta crear dificultades en las buenas relaciones que venturosamente existen entre ambos países." ("Our purpose is to warn our compatriots about the inconvenience of trying to abandon the country illegally, with the risk of suffering disturbing or painful situations which could even create difficulties in the good relations that fortunately exist between both countries.")

26. David Wilt, "The Arieles, Part 4," 3. The Arieles for 1955 movies were awarded at the 1956 ceremony. It is interesting to note that CONACULTA's video version of *Espaldas mojadas* does not recognize the period of *enlatamiento* and lists the movie's Ariel awards for the year 1953; it also lists an award for "best director," contradicting Wilt's newspaper and archival research about the categories for which *Espaldas mojadas* was awarded.

27. Peralta, *Spota,* 100.

28. Peralta, *Spota,* 167.

29. Spota, *Murieron,* 13.

30. Spota, *Murieron,* 118.

31. Spota, *Murieron,* 13; and Peralta, *Spota,* 106–7.

32. Spota, *Murieron,* 11; regarding Spota's attitudes toward the United States, see Peralta, *Spota,* 97–98.

33. For surveys of movies and literature about the bracero experience, see Iglesias Prieto, *Entre yerba,* Ramírez-Berg, *Cinema of Solitude,* 190–210; David R. Maciel, *El Norte: The U.S.–Mexican Border in Contemporary Cinema;* and María Herrera-Sobek, *The Bracero Experience: Elitelore versus Folklore.*

34. Spota, *Murieron,* 25, 21, 236, 56, 123, respectively.

35. Spota, *Murieron,* 19, 236.

36. Sefchovich, *Ideología,* 221–74; see esp. 233.

37. Spota, *Murieron,* 53.

38. Spota, *Murieron,* 167.

39. Spota, *Murieron,* 150.

40. Spota, *Murieron,* 115, 140.

41. Spota, *Murieron,* 45, 187.

42. Mora, 80.

43. Mora, 82; Beatriz Reyes Nevares, *The Mexican Cinema: Interviews with Thirteen Directors,* 28–29.

44. Mora, 88.

45. García Riera, 185–88.

46. Both *Murieron a mitad del río* and *Espaldas mojadas* refer to discrimination against African-Americans as an index of the comparatively worse situation that Mexican braceros endure.

47. As an aside, both the Mexican and U.S. movie industries have historically tended to favor casting fair-complected actors over dark ones, and resorting to brown facepaint in order to emphasize racial features. This practice stopped fairly early in the Mexican cinema, but continued in the United States through the 1950s. The sight of Paul Muni in *Bordertown* (1934, dir. Archie Mayo) or of Charlton Heston in *Touch of Evil* (1958, dir. Orson Welles) suggests a prosthetic conception of Mexican nationality and racial difference from the U.S. perspective. Regarding the casting of Heston as a Mexican in *Touch of Evil*, Heston recalls, "Actually, I have Orson to thank for the fact that the part is as interesting as it was, because it was his idea to make it a Mexican detective. I said, 'I can't play a Mexican detective!' He said, 'Sure you can! We'll dye your hair black, and put on some dark makeup and draw a black moustache, sure you can! We'll get a Mexican tailor to cut you a good Mexican suit.' And they did, and it's plausible enough I suppose. I play a plausible Mexican. As a matter of fact it doesn't contribute to the stereotype of the sombrero Mexican lazing around in the shade" (quoted in Terry Comito, ed., *Touch of Evil*, 214). I cannot resist pointing out that for one brief moment of Welles's classic, one of the bad guys, Uncle Joe Grandi (played by Akim Tamiroff), poses next to a poster bearing David Silva's name (the star of *Espaldas mojadas*).

48. Similar moments occur in *Murieron a mitad del río* when Paván encounters a disaffected U.S. veteran of World War II (Spota, 173) and a *jalisciense* named Inocencio (Spota, 203). Each of these minor characters makes strong arguments about the socioeconomic factors influencing the braceros; however, their critiques are not carried any further in the narrative.

49. José Vasconcelos, *La raza cósmica: Misión de la raza iberoamericana*, 1–40.

50. Benedict Anderson, *Imagined Communities: Reflections on the Origin and Spread of Nationalism*, 16–17. The image of the "long grey line" comes from a speech by Douglas MacArthur, quoted in Anderson, 17n.

51. Jean Franco, *Plotting Women: Gender and Representation in Mexico*; and Roger Bartra, *La jaula de la melancolía: Identidad y metamorfosis del mexicano*.

52. Octavio Paz, *El laberinto de soledad*.

53. Galindo, *Cine mexicano*, 153–54.

54. Galindo, *Cine mexicano*, 153.

55. *Los mojados*, dir. Alejandro Galindo.

56. Oscar J. Martínez, *Border People: Life and Society in the U.S.–Mexico Borderlands*, 305.

57. Paz, *Laberinto*, 59–80.

58. Jean Franco has noted that Mexican mass media of the 1950s, especially the cinema, were preoccupied with making the Oedipus myth function in accordance with contemporary nationalist goals. See Franco, *Plotting Women*, ch. 7, "Oedipus Modernized," 147–74.

59. Herrera-Sobek, *Bracero Experience*, 36.

60. Though I agree with García Riera's description of the "Manichaean left" politics of this movie, my reading of this scene is less enthusiastic than his, because I think it still portrays the braceros as essentially passive. For García Riera, the scene is a subtle nod at class consciousness on the part of Galindo, since the typical Mexican movie of the time would have had the customs official or another authority figure exculpate Rafael (García Riera, *Historia documental*, 186).

61. Spota, *Murieron*, 206.

62. Sefchovich, *Luis Spota*, 272.

63. García Riera, *Historia documental*, 186.

5. Mass Media, Site-Specificity, and Representations of the U.S.–Mexico Border

1. Guillermo Gómez-Peña, "The New World (B)order," 60.

2. Terri Windling, ed., *Life on the Border*, 8.

3. Chon A. Noriega, "This Is Not a Border," 6.

4. See, for example, Héctor Calderón and José David Saldívar, eds., *Criticism in the Borderlands: Studies in Chicano Literature, Culture, and Ideology.* As stated in the introduction, the appearance of Gloria Anzaldúa's *Borderlands/La Frontera: The New Mestiza* in 1987 was instrumental in marking this shift.

5. The following is a partial list of recent scholarly work that features the border metaphor: Iain Chambers, *Border Dialogues: Journeys in Postmodernity*; Henry A. Giroux, *Border Crossings: Cultural Workers and the Politics of Education*; Henry A. Giroux and Peter McLaren, *Between Borders: Pedagogy and the Politics of Cultural Studies*; Mae Henderson, ed., *Borders, Boundaries, and Frames: Cultural Criticism and Cultural Studies*; D. Emily Hicks, *Border Writing: The Multidimensional Text*; Maggie Humm, *Border Traffic: Strategies of Contemporary Women Writers*; Scott Michaelsen and David E. Johnson, eds., *Border Theory: the Limits of Cultural Politics*; Renato Rosaldo, *Culture and Truth: The Remaking of Social Analysis*; Trinh T. Minh-Ha, *When the Moon Waxes Red: Representation, Gender and Cultural Politics*; John C. Welchman, ed., *Rethinking Borders.*

The border metaphor also appears in semiotic and poststructuralist critical theory. See, for example, Jacques Derrida, "Living On: Border Lines" and "The Parergon"; and Thomas G. Pavel, *Fictional Worlds.*

6. Giroux writes, for example, "In the postmodern age, the boundaries that once held back diversity, otherness, and difference, whether in domestic ghettoes or through national borders policed by customs officials, have begun to break down. The Eurocentric center can no longer absorb or contain the culture of the Other as something that is threatening and dangerous. As Renato Rosaldo points out, 'the Third World has imploded into the metropolis. Even the conservative national politics of containment, designed to shield "us" from "them," betray the impossibility of maintaining hermetically sealed cultures'" (Giroux, *Border Crossings*, 57–58).

7. Terri Windling, letter to the author, 24 April 1992.

8. The area is also called "the Border," "Borderland," and "Borderlands" in these texts. Contributors to the series include Bellamy Bach (a pseudonym of Terri Windling), Emma Bull, Kara Dalkey, Craig Shaw Gardner, Michael Korolenko, Ellen Kushner, Charles de Lint, Will Shetterly, and Midori Snyder. Additional contributors in the most recent anthology (see n. 9) include Patricia A. McKillip, Delia Sherman, Caroline Stevermer, Ellen Steiber, Felicity Savage, Micole Sudberg, Donnard Sturgis, and Elizabeth Kushner.

9. At the time of this writing, the following Bordertown books had been published: Terri Windling, ed., and Mark Alan Arnold, *Bordertown: A Chronicle of the Borderlands*; Terri Windling, ed., *Borderland: A Borderlands Anthology*; Will Shetterly, *Elsewhere*; Terri Windling, ed., *Life on the Border*; Terri Windling and Delia Sherman, eds., *The Essential Bordertown*; Will Shetterly, *Nevernever*; and Emma Bull, *Finder.* See also Emma Bull and Will Shetterly, *Double Feature*, for accounts of these two authors' participation in the series. Windling is also working on another novel in the series, entitled *Underhill.*

10. As of June 1998, the URL for the Borderlands website is http://www.player.org/pub/u/nathan/border/ (hereafter, I will refer to this as the "Borderlands Web Page"). Other links to authors' and fans' home pages can be found at http://www.borderzone.com. The address for Anime MUSH is: telnet://199.245.105.29:6260.

11. Terri Windling, letter to Nathan Bardsley, Borderlands Web Page, 4 February 1997.

12. The term is Gómez-Peña's neologism for half Chicano, half Chilango (i.e., Mexico City native).

13. BAW/TAF's membership varied throughout the years 1984–1989, although a core of founding

members remained. In 1989 many new artists joined the collective, and only one original member stayed. Gómez-Peña discusses the dissolution of the group's founding members in "A Binational Performance Pilgrimage" and "Death on the Border: A Eulogy to Border Art."

14. Jeff Kelley, ed. of English text, *The Border Art Workshop/Taller de Arte Fronterizo* (BAW/TAF: 1984–1989), 20.

15. Kelley, *Workshop,* 18–19.

16. Gómez-Peña, "Binational," 27–32.

17. Guillermo Gómez-Peña, "Documented/Undocumented," in *The Graywolf Annual Five: Multi-Cultural Literacy,* 130.

18. Guillermo Gómez-Peña, "The Multicultural Paradigm: An Open Letter to the National Arts Community," 21.

19. Guillermo Gómez-Peña, "From Art-mageddon to Gringostroika," 21.

20. See n. 13. BAW/TAF responded to Gómez-Peña in a manuscript entitled "Errata Historica," unpublished ms. (December 1991). David Avalos, cofounder of BAW/TAF, published his own recollection of the early BAW/TAF years, which responds to many of Gómez-Peña's claims about the demise of border art, in "A Wag Dogging a Tale/Un Meneo Perreando una Cola."

21. For more background on the production of *Border Brujo,* see Gómez-Peña, "Binational," 40–42; and Jason Weiss, "An Interview with Guillermo Gómez-Peña."

22. Other examples from this period include *Border Realities* (1986), *I Couldn't Reveal My Identity* (1988), and *Backyard to Backyard* (1988).

23. *Border Brujo*'s altar/set also emphasizes the cultural aesthetic enacted by the Brujo throughout his performance. A citation of the home altars honoring the dead, which are especially associated with the observation of *Los Días de los Muertos* in Oaxaca, México, Gómez-Peña's altar also quotes the transformations that this form has undergone in recent decades by Chicano/a *altaristas*. Perhaps most notable among this latter group of artists is Amalia Mesa-Bains, who is known for introducing icons of vernacular and mass culture to her altars, and who has also highlighted the altar's capacity to signify hope, rejuvenation, and communal memory. Gómez-Peña exploits the use of the vernacular and mass culture to its most impressive effect in *Border Brujo*'s set. The *títere, calavera,* and other border souvenirs displayed alongside emblems of U.S. mass consumption, such as a huge plastic hamburger, wryly point to the commoditization of Mexican "folk art," but these juxtapositions also assume an audience that, though spatially dispersed, is united in its thorough saturation by mass media images of Mexican and U.S. culture. See Amalia Mesa-Bains, "Artist's Statement."

24. The character of Border Brujo was "born" at a BAW/TAF installation entitled "Casa de Cambio." See Shifra Goldman's review essay of the installation in Kelley, *Workshop,* 8–9.

25. Grant Kester, "Rhetorical Questions: The Alternative Arts Sector and the Imaginary Public," 14.

26. Kester, "Rhetorical Questions," 14.

27. See Gómez-Peña, "The Multicultural Paradigm," for example.

28. Gómez-Peña, "Binational," 49–66; and Guillermo Gómez-Peña, "Border Brujo," in *Being América,* and "Border Brujo," in *Warrior for Gringostroika.* The script was often modified in performance.

29. For example, he has deleted the voice of a member of the Latin American oligarchy, a Central American war victim, and many of the transvestite's lines. He has also left out a part about affirmative action and the critique of Chicano/a nationalism and radicalism at the end of the piece, which greatly changes the tone of the ending.

30. I am grateful to Chon Noriega for providing background information about *Son of Border Crisis.*

31. Gómez-Peña subsequently relocated to Los Angeles in 1993.

32. Gómez-Peña, "Death," 9.

33. For more information, see Avalos, "A Wag Dogging a Tale," as well as Larry T. Baza and Hugh

M. Davies, "Foreword," and Madeleine Grynsztejn, "La Frontera/The Border: Art about the Mexico/United States Border Experience."

34. Guillermo Gómez-Peña, "The New World Border: Prophecies for the End of the Century," and *The New World Border,* 21–48. In the latter anthology, Gómez-Peña refers to at least twenty-five different versions of the script (22). The quotations from "The New World (B)order" that appear in this chapter are taken from the *High Performance* essay, unless otherwise noted. I quote from the essay with the understanding that the live version has varied greatly from performance to performance.

35. Weiss, "Interview," 11.

36. Gómez-Peña, "The New World Border: Prophecies," 120.

37. Kim Sawchuk, "Unleashing the Demons of History," 29.

38. Defined by Gómez-Peña as "A continental grass roots movement that advocates the complete economic and cultural reform of U.S. capitalism" (Gómez-Peña, "New," 65).

39. A play on "Zona de Libre Comercio." *Coger* is slang in Mexico for "to have sexual intercourse."

40. Gómez-Peña, "New," 60.

41. Gómez-Peña, "New," 61.

42. Gómez-Peña, "New," 63.

43. Gómez-Peña, "New," 64.

44. Weiss, "Interview," 11; see also Gómez-Peña, "New," 63.

45. Gómez-Peña, "Art-mageddon," 24.

46. Gómez-Peña, "Art-mageddon," 24.

47. Gómez-Peña, "Binational," 43; Weiss, "Interview," 10.

48. Hicks, author of *Border Writing,* is a former member of BAW/TAF and is currently a member of the border feminist performance group Las Comadres. She is a professor of Comparative Literature at San Diego State University. She was also once married to Guillermo Gómez-Peña. For a discussion of her influence on the development of Gómez-Peña's border aesthetics, see her essay "La Marquesa se mete Prozac/La Marquesa Goes on Prozac."

49. Giroux, *Border Crossings,* 224.

50. On the importance of "dialogue," with "Others," see Chambers, *Border Dialogues* 50, 76, 104–5; and Giroux, *Border Crossings,* 28–35. On reading and writing as "border crossing," see Hicks, *Border Writing,* xxiii–xxxi. See also Gómez-Peña, "Multicultural," 21, and his quotation of Carlos Fuentes, "Binational," 44.

51. Kester, "Rhetorical Questions," 13.

52. Roger Rouse, "Mexican Migration in the Social Space of Postmodernism." Similarly, Michael Kearney, who has done work on transnational Mixtec communities, also cites Gómez-Peña several times in his essay, "Borders and Boundaries of State and Self at the End of Empire."

53. Gómez-Peña, "Multicultural," 27.

54. In an ironic reversal of Gómez-Peña's trajectory, series creator Terri Windling relocated to Tucson, Arizona, several years ago and reports that the newest anthology in the series may include elements that reflect her proximity to the U.S.–Mexico border and Native American communities. Windling herself ran away from home at the age of fifteen. For a period of time she lived in Mexico City, where she worked as a street vendor. Midori Snyder and Terri Windling suggested that SoHo was modeled on squatters' neighborhoods in Mexico City, New York, Los Angeles, Boston, Amsterdam, and London (Midori Snyder, personal interview, 30 March 1993; Windling, letter to the author, 26 March 1993; Windling, personal interview, 28 April 1993).

55. A shared-world anthology is one in which parameters for an alternative universe are created by several authors who then collectively contribute stories to the series. In the case of the Bordertown group, each author is associated with a character or group of characters, but they may borrow other authors' characters with permission. The concept of shared world fiction began in the 1920s when H. P.

Lovecraft's town of Arkham inspired subsequent authors to appropriate it as a setting for their stories. In the 1970s, Robert Lynn Asprin and Lynn Abbey created "Thieves' World," a sword-and-sorcery universe used by many fantasy writers in almost a dozen anthologies. The popularity of that series gave rise to a host of other shared worlds, including "Meroven" (created by C. J. Cherryh, a contributor to "Thieves' World"), "Liavek" (created by Bordertown writers Emma Bull and Will Shetterly), and "Wild Cards" (edited by George R. R. Martin). By 1996, Windling reported that the boom in shared-world anthologies was over because the books simply did not sell as well as novels (Windling, letter to Nathan Bardsley, 4 February 1996). For a general history of shared-world anthologies, see Peter S. Beagle, "Authors in Search of a Universe."

Bordertown is not the only example of an alternative universe set on "the border." Several popular role-playing games such as *Rifts* and *Shadowrun* explicitly develop a post-apocalyptic U.S.–Mexico border region, although they adhere more closely to traditional representations of the border: it is a war zone without the "multicultural" alternative. In 1994 a Mexican anthology of science fiction stories about the border was published. The stories, some of them by well-known U.S. sci-fi authors, present a range of approaches to the theme, from those similar to the Bordertown authors to heavy-handed allegories based upon incidents in the history of U.S.–Mexico relations (Paco Ignacio Taibo II et al., *Frontera de Espejos Rotos.*

56. Snyder, personal interview, 30 March 1993. Windling, letter to the author, 26 March 1993.

57. I am referring to statements such as, "'He's got a lot of anger,' Mickey said. 'It isn't easy growing up a halfie in Bordertown'" (Shetterly, *Elsewhere,* 134).

58. Bordertown elves are differentiated in the stories from Elfland elves by their accent or by social class. In Bordertown, class and race are not always coterminous. For example, lower-class elves may dye their hair so that they can look more human. And Bordertown has its own upper-class neighborhood, Dragon's Tooth Hill, which is divided into an elf side and a human side.

59. SoHo is literally "South of Ho Street."

60. Each writer in the Bordertown series has his or her own opinion on the matter. Terri Windling said that the interdependence between elves and humans which we see on a cultural level in the stories may be based on something so basic as the elves' need for "raw materials" (Windling, personal interview, 28 April 1993).

61. Shetterly, *Elsewhere,* 229.

62. Bull, *Finder,* 295.

63. Bull, *Finder,* 162.

64. In the published script, this part continues as follows: "GP and CF: *(Horny and agitated)* The crossing from the Third to the First World; from the past to the future, remember? *El cruce, el bordo, el abismo, el sismo, la migra,* the spiderweb, the TV cameras, my old performances, your oldest prejudices, the original migration, your great mojado grandparents. Remember? *(Blackout.)*" See Gómez-Peña, "The New World Border: Prophecies," 138.

65. Gómez-Peña, "New," 64.

66. Midori Snyder, personal interview, 30 March 1993.

67. Gómez-Peña continues to express faith in young and newcomer artists in his recent work: "The teenagers have tremendous things to teach us; they have fewer hang-ups about race and gender; they are much more at ease with crisis and hybridity; and they understand our cities and neighborhoods better than we do. Surely, if there is an art form that truly speaks for the present crisis of our communities, this form is rap." ("The Free Art Agreement/El Tratado de Libre Cultura," in *The Subversive Imagination,* 221.)

68. Among the most "technologically advanced" artifacts in Bordertown are aging "pre-Change" videocassette decks, most of which no longer work because they are too close to Faerie's magic.

Gómez-Peña had previously combined popular, mass-produced icons from U.S. culture (i.e.,

Mickey Mouse, boom boxes, etc.) with handmade "folk" icons from Mexican culture (i.e, Día de los Muertos *calaveras*), as he does in *Border Brujo*. He has also commented on the need to distinguish between popular culture and mass culture for U.S. and Mexican contexts. In the United States, he argues, there is a superimposition of folklore and technology, given that popular culture usually refers to commodities such as video games and Hollywood movies, which have their origin in the United States, while indigenous and ethnic cultures are either co-opted or invisible to the mainstream. Mexico, he cautions, is moving in the same direction through the creation of large media conglomerates such as Televisa. See Marco Vinicio González, "Guillermo Gómez-Peña," 20.

In "New World (B)order," his descriptions of technology are perhaps more prominent, but they are still dystopian (i.e., the giant media conglomerate Reali-TV and *robo-raza I*'s technophilia).

69. Weiss, "Interview," 12.

70. Regarding the U.S. Latino/a arts community, Gómez-Peña has said, "We come from a culture which doesn't venerate irreflexively the principle of newness, or better said, a culture which considers that an apolitical reverence for originality carries dangerous ideological implications. What we consider 'avant-garde' or 'original' generally deals with extra-artistic concerns and precisely because of this, it never seems 'experimental enough' for the art world" (quoted in Kelley, *Workshop*, 57).

On this subject, see also Gómez-Peña's piece in Lilly Wei et al., "On Nationality: 13 Artists."

71. Windling, *Borderland*, vii. The "wild elves" depicted in the series still have an aversion to iron.

72. Bordertown does have a police force, called the Silver Suits, but they have little jurisdiction in SoHo and are portrayed as being rather ineffectual. By making *Finder*'s female protagonist, Sunny Rico, a hard-boiled gang-member-turned-cop, Bull appears to be challenging the tradition of pitting adolescent protagonists against cops and other authority figures. Sunny also speaks Elvish, which was previously impossible for humans in the Bordertown stories. In the "New World (B)order," Gómez-Peña writes, "The role of the presidents is now restricted to public relations and the role of the military has been reduced to guarding banks, TV stations and art schools" (Gómez-Peña, "New," 60).

73. Douglas Kellner and Michael Ryan, for example, have argued that technology was opposed to "family values," human intimacy, and the private sphere in several Reagan-Bush era science fiction film productions; see Michael Ryan and Douglas Kellner, "Technophobia."

Charles Ramírez-Berg pointed out in his study of aliens and Hispanic imagery that films like *The Terminator* envisioned a future confrontation between an embattled human race and superhuman technology—the corollary being that only a eugenics in the present, which would eliminate "the weaker races," can create a humanity fit for survival. See Charles Ramírez-Berg, "Immigrants, Aliens, and Extraterrestrials."

74. Robert A. Pastor and Jorge G. Castañeda, *Limits to Friendship: The United States and Mexico*, 283–313.

75. San Diego/Tijuana in particular has seen a rise in artistic production, which may be due to several factors. Buffered by poorer cities like San Ysidro and Imperial Beach, San Diego is atypically wealthy in comparison to other U.S. border cities, which gives it a relatively large art-consuming public. Secondly, the city has a history of powerful Chicano/a art movements dating from the late 1960s. Finally, both San Diego and Tijuana have universities with strong arts and humanities programs. For an overview of the San Diego visual arts scene, see David Joselit, "Report from San Diego"; and Leah Ollman, "Report from San Diego: A Change of Weather?"

76. Louis Uchitelle, "America's Newest Industrial Belt."

77. Sawchuk, "Demons of History," 27.

78. Sawchuk, "Demons of History," 22. Coco Fusco also wrote an essay in which she vividly describes her experiences while performing the piece at different venues, as well as critical reception of the project; see Coco Fusco, "The Other History of Intercultural Performance."

79. Many of those organizations are listed in Ricardo Hernández and Edith Sánchez, eds., *Cross-*

Border Links. An abbreviated and updated version of this directory came out in 1997: Harry Browne, ed., *Cross-Border Links: A Directory of Organizations in Canada, Mexico, and the United States.*

80. Many thanks to Robin Alexander, UE Director of International Labor Affairs, for her time and generosity in providing information about the history of the Alliance (personal interview, 2 December 1996). The Alliance maintains a website and posts items about ongoing developments in cross-border organizing: http://www.igc.apg.org/unitedelect (address as of June 1998). For history of the UE, see Ann Fagan Ginger and David Christiano, eds., *The Cold War against Labor.*

81. Robin Alexander, letter to the author, 19 October 1995; Dale A. Hathaway, *The FAT and the Workers' Center of Juárez,* 13–14; David Bacon, "Laboring to Cross the NAFTA Divide."

82. Terry Davis, "Cross-Border Organizing Comes Home," 29.

Bibliography

Note: When two or more essays from an anthology have been cited in the body of the book, the anthology is also listed in the bibliography under its editor.

"ACS Meeting Concludes in Trinidad." *Washington Report on the Hemisphere* 15.16 (1 September 1995): 1+.

Alexander, Dean C. "Mexico's Cinema and Video Industries Show Signs of Expansion." *U.S.–Mexico Free Trade Reporter* 4.18 (15 October 1995): 1+.

Allen, Terry. *a simple story (Juarez).* Columbus: Wexner Center for the Arts, Ohio State University, 1992.

Alvarez, Robert. "The Border as Social System: The California Case." *New Scholar* 9.1–2 (1984): 119–34. Spec. issue, "Border Perspectives on the U.S./Mexico Relationship," ed. Joseph Nalven.

Amdur, Meredith. "U.S. Broadcasters Berate GATT." *Broadcasting and Cable* 123.51 (20 December 1993): 14.

Anaya, Rodolfo, and Francisco Lomelí, eds. *Aztlán: Essays on the Chicano Homeland.* Albuquerque: University of New Mexico Press, 1989.

Anderson, Benedict. *Imagined Communities: Reflections on the Origin and Spread of Nationalism.* London: Verso, 1983.

Anderson, Perry. "Modernity and Revolution." *New Left Review* 144 (March–April 1984): 96–113.

"Anencephaly Suit Settled, Many Questions Remain." *CJM Newsletter* 5.3–4 (fall/winter 1995): 6.

"Anti-Immigration Bill Moves Ahead, Bracero II Dead." *BorderLines* 4.5 (May 1996): 7–8.

Anzaldúa, Gloria. *Borderlands/La Frontera: The New Mestiza.* San Francisco: Spinsters/aunt lute, 1987.

Arceo-Frutos, René H., Juana Guzmán, and Dr. Amalia Mesa-Bains. *Art of the Other Mexico: Sources and Meanings.* Trans. Alejandro Velasco. Chicago: Mexican Fine Arts Center Museum, 1993.

"Association of Borderlands Scholars 1995 Annual Meetings." *La Frontera* 20.1 (spring 1995).

Assouline, Pierre. *Germinal: L'aventure d'un film.* Paris: Fayard, 1993.

Atwood, Margaret. "Blind Faith and Free Trade." *In The Case against Free Trade: GATT, NAFTA, and the Globalization of Corporate Power,* by Ralph Nader et al. San Francisco: Earth Island; Berkeley: North Atlantic Books, 1993.

Aufderheide, Pat. "Film and Video in the Cultural Struggle of Latin America." *Media Development* 40.1 (1993): 30–31.

———. "Latin American Grassroots Video: Beyond Television." *Public Culture* 5 (1993): 579–92.

Avalos, David. "A Wag Dogging a Tale." In *La Frontera/The Border: Art about the Mexico/United States*

Border Experience, by Patricio Chávez and Madeleine Grynsztejn, 59–94. San Diego: Centro Cultural de la Raza and Museum of Contemporary Art, 1993.

Ayala Blanco, Jorge. "La añoranza porfiriana." In *La aventura del cine mexicano.* Mexico City: Ediciones Era, 1968, 40–47.

Ayscough, Suzan. "Greenberg Says No Culture in NAFTA Deal." *Variety* (24 August 1992): 46+.

Bacon, David. "Laboring to Cross the NAFTA Divide." *Nation,* 13 November 1995, 572–74.

Bamrud, Joachim. "Expanding the Markets: The Unprecedented Trade Boom." *Latin Trade* 4.3 (March 1996): 16A–20A.

———. "Uniting Forces: The Integration of the Hemisphere." *Latin Trade* 4.3 (March 1996): 2A+.

Barr, Alfred H., Jr. *Painting and Sculpture in the Museum of Modern Art, 1929–1967.* New York: Museum of Modern Art, 1977.

Barrera Herrera, Eduardo. "Nationalism versus Capitalism." *Media Development* 40.2 (1993): 15–17.

Bartra, Roger. *La jaula de la melancolía: Identidad y metamorfosis del mexicano.* Mexico City: Grijalbo, 1987.

Baum, Don. *Smoke and Mirrors: The War on Drugs and the Politics of Failure.* Boston: Little Brown, 1996.

Baza, Larry T., and Hugh M. Davies. "Foreword." In *La Frontera/The Border: Art about the Mexico/United States Border Experience,* by Patricio Chávez and Madeleine Grynsztejn, ix–xvi. San Diego: Centro Cultural de la Raza and Museum of Contemporary Art, 1993.

Beagle, Peter S. "Authors in Search of a Universe." *Omni* 10.2 (November 1987): 40–41.

Berman, Morris. "Shadow across the Rio Grande: Fear and Fascination—Why We Feel Both about Mexico." *Utne Reader* 55 (January/February 1993): 90.

Bhagwati, Jagdish. Letter. *New York Times,* 24 December 1993, late ed., A26.

Black, George. *The Good Neighbor.* New York: Pantheon, 1988.

Bonfil Batalla, Guillermo. "Dimensiones culturales del Tratado de Libre Comercio." In *La educación y la cultura ante el Tratado de Libre Comercio,* ed. Gilberto Guevara Niebla and Néstor García Canclini, 157–78. Mexico City: Nueva Imagen, 1992.

Border Art Workshop/Taller de Arte Fronterizo (BAW/TAF). *Taller de Arte Fronterizo, 1.984–1.991: Una documentación contínua de siete años de proyectos de arte interdisciplinarios sobre asuntos de la frontera de Mexico con Estados Unidos [sic].* N.p. [San Diego]: 1991.

Border Brujo. Video. Dir. Isaac Artenstein. Written and performed by Guillermo Gómez-Peña. Cinewest Productions, 1990. 52 min.

"Bracero II: Coming Soon?" *BorderLines* 3.5 (May 1995): 1+.

Bradsher, Keith. "Big Cut in Tariffs: Movies, TV, and Financial Services Are Some of the Areas Left Out." *New York Times,* 15 December 1993, late ed., A1+.

Brito, Aristeo. *The Devil in Texas/El diablo en Texas.* Trans. David William Foster. Clásicos Chicanos/Chicano Classics 5. Tempe: Bilingual Press/Editorial Bilingüe, 1990.

Brooks, David. "The Search for Counterparts." *Labor Research Review* 19 (fall 1992): 82–96.

Brooks, Peter. "Never for GATT." *American Spectator* 27.1 (January 1994): 34–37.

Brooks, Rosetta. "From the Middle of Nowhere: Terry Allen's Badlands." *Artforum* 31.8 (April 1993): 84–88.

Browne, Harry, ed., *Cross-Border Links: A Directory of Organizations in Canada, Mexico, and the United States.* Albuquerque: Inter-Hemispheric Education Resource Center, 1997.

Buck-Morss, Susan. "Passports." *Documents* 1.3 (summer 1993): 66–77.

Bull, Emma. *Finder.* New York: Tor, 1994.

Bull, Emma, and Will Shetterly. *Double Feature.* Framingham: NESFA, 1994.

Bustamante, Maris. *A Corazón Abierto: Naftaperformances.* Chicago: Randolf Street Gallery, 6 May 1994.

Calderón, Héctor, and José David Saldívar, eds. *Criticism in the Borderlands: Studies in Chicano Literature, Culture, and Ideology.* Durham: Duke University Press, 1991.

"Canada, Chile Negotiate Trade Deal." *Working Together* 17 (March–April 1996): 3.

"Canada Seeks to Protect 'Cultural' Industries." *U.S.–Mexico Free Trade Reporter* 5.1 (15 January 1995): 3.

"CARICOM Prepares for Trade Talks." *Washington Report on the Hemisphere* 11.14 (17 April 1991): 1+.

Castañeda, Jorge. *The Mexican Shock: Its Meaning for the U.S.* New York: New Press, 1995.

———. *Sorpresas te da la vida: México 1994.* Mexico City: Aguilar, 1994.

———. *Utopia Unarmed: The Latin American Left after the Cold War.* New York: Vintage–Random House, 1994.

Cavanaugh, John, et al., eds. *Trading Freedom: How Free Trade Affects Our Lives, Work, and Environment.* San Francisco: Institute for Food and Development Policy, 1992.

Cervantes, Miguel, ed. *Mito y magia en las Américas: Los ochenta.* Monterrey: Museo de Arte Contemporáneo de Monterrey, 1991.

Chambers, Iain. *Border Dialogues: Journeys in Postmodernity.* London: Routledge, 1990.

Chávez, Patricio, and Madeleine Grynsztejn. *La Frontera/The Border: Art about the Mexico/United States Border Experience.* San Diego: Centro Cultural de la Raza and Museum of Contemporary Art, 1993.

Chulas Fronteras. Dir. Les Blanc. El Cerrito, California: Brazos Films, 1976. 58 min.

Cielo de abajo. Dir. Jesusa Rodríguez. Based on a text by Alfredo López Austin. Adapted by Malú Huacuja, Jesusa Rodríguez, and Liliana Felipe. Chicago: The Firehouse, Latino Chicano Theater Co., 15–17 April 1994.

"El cine europeo se enfrenta al 'enemigo americano.'" *El País,* 7 October 1993, 35.

Citizens Against Temporary Services. "Testimony Prepared for the Trade Staff Policy Committee, Office of the U.S. Trade Representative, Atlanta, Georgia." Unpublished ms. 29 August 1991.

Cohen, Roger. "Culture Dispute with Paris Now Snags a World Accord." *New York Times,* 8 December 1993, late ed., A1+.

———. "Europeans Back French Curbs on U.S. Movies." *New York Times,* 12 December 1993, late ed., 24.

Comito, Terry, ed. *Touch of Evil.* Dir. Orson Welles. *Rutgers Film in Print.* Vol. 3. New Brunswick: Rutgers University Press, 1995.

Condé, Carole, and Karl Beveridge. *Class Work.* Toronto: The Communications and Electrical Workers of Canada, 1990.

———. "Interventions." In *Disrupted Borders,* ed. Sunil Gupta. London: Rivers Oram, 1993, 21–26.

A Conversation with Terry Allen and Dave Hickey. Video. Columbus, Ohio: Wexner Center Media Art Productions, 1992.

Cooper, Peter, and Lori Wallach. *NAFTA's Broken Promises: Job Creation under NAFTA.* Washington, DC: Public Citizen, September 1995.

Cortés, Carlos E. "To View a Neighbor: The Hollywood Textbook on Mexico." In *Images of Mexico in the United States,* ed. John H. Coatsworth and Carlos Rico. Dimensions of United States–Mexican Relations, 1. San Diego: Center for U.S.–Mexican Studies, University of California, San Diego, 1989, 91–118.

Cosío Villegas, Daniel. "Mexico's Crisis." In *American Extremes,* trans. Américo Paredes. Austin: University of Texas Press, 1964, 3–27.

———. "Sobre la libertad de la prensa." In *Labor periodística: Real e imaginaria.* Mexico City: Era, 1972, 313–25.

The Couple in the Cage: A Guatinaui Odyssey. Video. Dir. Coco Fusco and Paula Heredia. N.p.: Authentic Documentary Productions, 1993. 30 min.

"The Curse of the Jackal." Prod. Rick McCallum. Dir. Carl Schultz. Writer Jonathan Hales. *The Young Indiana Jones Chronicles.* Exec. prod. and story, George Lucas. ABC, 4 March 1992.

Davidson, Miriam. "The Mexican Border War," *Nation,* 12 November 1990, 557–60.

———. "Militarizing the Mexican Border." *Nation,* 1 April 1991, 406–10.

Davis, Terry. "Cross-Border Organizing Comes Home." *Labor Research Review* 23 (1995): 22–29.

Debray, Régis. "Respuesta a Mario Vargas Llosa." *El País,* 4 November 1993, 15–16.

Debroise, Olivier. *Fuga mexicana: Un recorrido por la fotografía en México.* Mexico City: Consejo Nacional para la Cultura y las Artes, 1994.

de los Reyes, Aurelio. *Con Villa en México: Testimonios de camarógrafos norteamericanos en la Revolución, 1911–1916.* Mexico City: Universidad Nacional Autónoma de México, 1985.

de María y Campos, Mauricio. "Las industrias culturales y de entretenamiento en el marco de las negociaciones del Tratado de Libre Comercio." In *La educación y la cultura ante el Tratado de Libre Comercio,* ed. Gilberto Guevara Niebla and Néstor García Canclini, 235–98. Mexico City: Nueva Imagen, 1992.

de Orellana, Margarita. *La mirada circular: El cine norteamericano de la Revolución Mexicana, 1911–1917.* Mexico City: Ediciones Era and Universidad de Guadalajara, 1987.

Demaris, Ovid. *Poso del Mundo: Inside the Mexican-American Border: From Tijuana to Matamoros.* Boston: Little Brown, 1970.

Demeo, Marisa J. "Bolstering INS Enforcement." *Network News* (spring 1997): 2.

DePalma, Anthony. "World Trade Body Opposes Canadian Magazine Tariffs." *New York Times,* 20 January 1997, D8.

Derrida, Jacques. "Living On: Border Lines." Trans. James Hulbert. In *Deconstruction and Criticism,* by Harold Bloom et al. New York: Seabury, 1979, 75–176.

———. "The Parergon. *October* 9 (summer 1979): 3–41.

"Desde hoy, Chile es socio comercial del Mercosur." *El cronista,* online via internet (1 October 1996).

Dominguez, Virginia R. "Invoking Culture: The Messy Side of Cultural Politics." *South Atlantic Quarterly* 91.1 (winter 1992): 19–42.

Dunn, Peter, and Loraine Leeson. "The Art of Change in Docklands." *Mapping the Futures: Local Cultures, Global Change.* Ed. Jon Bird et al. New York: Routledge, 1993, 136–49.

Dunn, Timothy. *The Militarization of the U.S.–Mexico Border, 1978–1992: Low-Intensity Conflict Doctrine Comes Home.* Austin: Center for Mexican American Studies, University of Texas Press, 1996.

Ďurovičová, Nataša. "Some Thoughts at an Intersection of the Popular and the National." *The Velvet Light Trap* 34 (fall 1994): 3–9.

Dwyer, Augusta. *On the Line: Life on the U.S.–Mexico Border.* London: Latin American Bureau, 1994.

Eco, Umberto. "Introduction: The Role of the Reader." In *The Role of the Reader: Explorations in the Semiotics of Texts.* Bloomington: Indiana University Press, 1984, 3–43.

Elsaesser, Thomas. "Hyper-, Retro-, or Counter-Cinema: European Cinema and Third Cinema between Hollywood and Art Cinema." In *Mediating Two Worlds: Cinematic Encounters in the Americas,* ed. Ana M. López, John King, and Manuel Alvarado, 119–35. London: British Film Institute, 1993.

Espaldas mojadas. Dir. Alejandro Galindo. Mexico City: Prod. ATA Films, Productora Atlas, Manuel Jasso Rojas, and José Elvia. 1953. 116 min.

Evans, John S. "Taxation and Fiscal Policy." In *The Borderlands Sourcebook: A Guide to the Literature on Northern Mexico and the American Southwest,* ed. Ellwyn Stoddard, Richard L. Nostrand, and Jonathan P. West, 171–75. Norman: University of Oklahoma Press, 1983.

Fein, Seth. Letter. *New York Times,* 24 December 1993, late ed., A26.

———. "Nationalist Anticommunism and Mexican Cinema of the 1950s." Paper, delivered at the conference, "The Formative Fifties Revisited: Latin American Cinema between Old and New, or Routes and Routes of Representation," University of California, Santa Cruz, and Stanford University, 28–31 May 1997.

Ferguson, Hayes. "Seeking a Better Life—in Mexico." *San Francisco Sunday Examiner and Chronicle,* 3 March 1996, A10.

"Filmmakers Lobby EC." *Variety,* 25 October 1993, 76.

Flitterman-Lewis, Sandy. "The Gaze." In *New Vocabularies in Film Semiotics: Structuralism, Post-*

structuralism, and Beyond, by Robert Stam, Robert Burgoyne, and Sandy Flitterman-Lewis. London: Routledge, 1992, 162–73.

Fox, Claire F. "Hollywood's Backlot: Carlos Fuentes, *The Old Gringo,* and National Cinema." *Iris* 13 (summer 1991): 63–86.

Fox, Claire F., Ricardo Hernández, and Edith Sánchez. "Videos on Free Trade." *BorderLines* 2.1 (February 1994): 13.

Franco, Jean. "'Manhattan Will Be More Exotic This Fall': The Iconisation of Frida Kahlo." *Women: A Cultural Review* 2.3 (winter 1991): 220–27.

———. *Plotting Women: Gender and Representation in Mexico.* New York: Columbia University Press, 1989.

———. "A Touch of Evil: Jesusa Rodríguez's Subversive Church." *Drama Review* 36.2 (summer 1992): 48–61.

Fraser, Matthew. "A Question of Culture: The Canadian Solution Resolves a GATT Standoff." *MacLeans* 106.52 (27 December 1993): 50–51.

Fuentes, Carlos. "Latin America's Alternative: An Ibero-American Federation." *New Perspectives Quarterly* 8.1 (winter 1991): 15–17.

———. "Malintzín de las maquilas." In *La frontera de cristal.* Mexico City: Alfaguara, 1995, 129–60.

Fuller, Chris. "Audiovisual Gums Up GATT Talks." *Variety,* 20 December 1993, 27–28.

Fusco, Coco. "The Other History of Intercultural Performance." *Drama Review* 38.1 (spring 1994): 143–67.

Galindo, Alejandro. *El cine mexicano: Un personal punto de vista.* 2d ed. Mexico City: EDAMEX, 1986.

García, Arnoldo. "The Deepening Mexican Crisis." *Network News* (summer 1996): 7+.

García Canclini, Néstor. *Consumidores y ciudadanos: Conflictos multiculturales de la globalización.* Mexico City: Grijalbo, 1995.

———, coord. *El consumo cultural en México.* Mexico City: Consejo Nacional para la Cultura y las Artes, 1993.

———. *Culturas híbridas: Estrategias para entrar y salir de la modernidad.* Mexico City: Grijalbo, 1990.

———. "Las industrias culturales." In *La educación y la cultura ante el Tratado de Libre Comercio,* ed. Gilberto Guevara Niebla and Néstor García Canclini, 211–34. Mexico City: Nueva Imagen, 1992.

———. "Memory and Innovation in the Theory of Art." *South Atlantic Quarterly* 92.3 (summer 1993): 424–43.

———. "Prehistoria económica y cultural del TLC." In *La educación y la cultura ante el Tratado de Libre Comercio,* ed. Gilberto Guevara Niebla and Néstor García Canclini, 3–14. Mexico City: Nueva Imagen, 1992.

García Canclini, Néstor, and Mabel Piccini. "Culturas de la ciudad de México: Símbolos colectivos y usos del espacio urbano." In *El consumo cultural en México,* coord. Néstor García Canclini. Mexico City: Consejo Nacional para la Cultura y las Artes, 1993.

García Riera, Emilio. *Historia documental del cine mexicano.* Vol. 5. Mexico City: Era, 1973.

Garciadiego, Javier, et al. *El TLC día al día: Crónica de una negociación.* Mexico City: Porrúa, 1994.

Gerlach, Allen. "Conditions along the Border—1915: The Plan de San Diego." *New Mexico Historical Review* 43.3 (July 1968): 195–212.

Ginger, Ann Fagan, and David Christiano, eds. *The Cold War against Labor.* 2 vols. Studies in Law and Social Change, 3. Berkeley: Meiklejohn Civil Liberties Institute, 1987.

Giroux, Henry A. *Border Crossings: Cultural Workers and the Politics of Education.* New York: Routledge, 1990.

Giroux, Henry A., and Peter McLaren. *Between Borders: Pedagogy and the Politics of Cultural Studies.* New York: Routledge, 1994.

Goin, Peter. "Following the Line: The Mexico-American Border." *Spazio e società* (October–December 1987): 22–37.

———. *Tracing the Line: A Photographic Survey of the Mexican-American Border.* Limited edition artist book. N.p., 1987.

Gómez-Peña, Guillermo. "A Binational Performance Pilgrimage." *Drama Review* 35.3 (fall 1991): 22–45.

———. "Border Brujo." In *Being América: Essays on Art, Literature, and Identity from Latin America,* ed. Rachel Weiss, with Alan West. Fredonia, NY: White Pine, 1991, 194–236.

———. "Death on the Border: A Eulogy to Border Art," *High Performance* 14.1 (spring 1991): 8–9.

———. "Documented/Undocumented." In *The Graywolf Annual Five: Multi-Cultural Literacy,* ed. Rick Simonson and Scott Walker. Saint Paul: Graywolf, 1988, 127–134.

———. "The Free Art Agreement/El Tratado de Libre Cultura." *High Performance* 16.3 (fall 1993): 58–63.

———. "The Free Art Agreement/El Tratado de Libre Cultura." In *The Subversive Imagination: Artists, Society, and Social Responsibility,* ed. Carol Becker. New York: Routledge, 1994, 208–22.

———. "From Art-mageddon to Gringostroika." *High Performance* 14.3 (fall 1991): 20–27.

———. "The Multicultural Paradigm: An Open Letter to the National Arts Community." *High Performance* 12.3 (fall 1989): 18–27.

———. "The New World (B)order." *High Performance* 15.58–59 (summer/fall 1992): 58–65.

———. *The New World Border.* San Francisco: City Lights, 1996.

———. "The New World Border: Prophecies for the End of the Century." *Drama Review* 38.1 (spring 1994): 119–42.

———. *Warrior for Gringostroika.* Saint Paul: Graywolf, 1993.

González, Marco Vinicio. "Guillermo Gómez-Peña." *Semanal de La Jornada* 117 (8 September 1991): 14–23.

Griffith, James S. "The Arizona-Sonora Border: Line, Region, Magnet, Filter." In *1993 Festival of American Folklife, July 1–July 5,* by the Smithsonian Institution, 35–41. Washington, DC: Smithsonian Institution, 1993.

Griswold del Castillo, Richard, Teresa McKenna, and Yvonne Yarbro-Bejarano, eds. *Chicano Art: Resistance and Affirmation, 1965–1985.* Los Angeles: Wight Art Gallery, University of California, Los Angeles, 1991.

Grynsztejn, Madeleine. *About Place: Recent Art of the Americas.* Chicago: The Art Institute of Chicago, 1995.

———. "La Frontera/The Border: Art about the Mexico/United States Border Experience." In *La Frontera/The Border: Art about the Mexico/United States Border Experience,* by Patricio Chávez and Madeleine Grynsztejn, 23–58. San Diego: Centro Cultural de la Raza and Museum of Contemporary Art, 1993.

Guevara Niebla, Gilberto, and Néstor García Canclini, eds. *La educación y la cultura ante el Tratado de Libre Comercio.* Mexico City: Nueva Imagen, 1992.

Guzmán, Martín Luis. *El águila y la serpiente.* 14th ed. 1927; reprint, Mexico City: Cia. General de Ediciones, 1956.

———. *The Eagle and the Serpent.* Trans. Harriet de Onis. Gloucester, MA: Peter Smith, 1969.

Hale, Charles A. "The Liberal Impulse: Daniel Cosío Villegas and the *Historia moderna de México.*" *Hispanic American Historical Review* 54.3 (August 1974): 479–98.

———. "Liberalism, the Revolution, and Nationalism in Mexico." Unpublished ms. prepared for the Seminario Internacional "Libertad y Justicia en las Sociedades Modernas." Sponsored by the Secretaría de Desarrollo Social, Mexico City, 3–5 June 1993.

Haley, J. Evetts. *Jeff Milton: A Good Man with a Gun.* 1948. Norman: University of Oklahoma Press, 1982.

Hall, Douglas Kent. *The Border: Life on the Line*. New York: Abbeville, 1988.

Hall, Linda B., and Don M. Coerver. *Revolution on the Border: The United States and Mexico, 1910–1920*. Albuquerque: New Mexico University Press, 1988.

Hanson, Patricia King, ed. *The American Film Institute Catalog of Motion Pictures Produced in the United States*. Vol. F1. *Feature Films, 1911–1920*. Berkeley: University of California Press, 1988.

Harris, Charles H., III, and Louis R. Sadler. "The Plan of San Diego and the Mexican-United States War Crisis of 1916: A Reexamination." *Hispanic American Historical Review* 58.3 (August 1978): 381–408.

Harvey, David. *The Condition of Postmodernity: An Enquiry into the Origins of Cultural Change*. Oxford: Basil Blackwell, 1989.

———. *The Urban Experience*. Baltimore: Johns Hopkins University Press, 1989.

Hathaway, Dale A. *The FAT and the Workers' Center of Juárez*. N.p., 1996.

Heath, Steven. *Questions of Cinema*. Bloomington: Indiana University Press, 1981.

Henderson, Mae, ed. *Borders, Boundaries, and Frames: Cultural Criticism and Cultural Studies*. New York: Routledge, 1995.

Henrikson, Alan K. "A North American Community: 'From the Yukon to the Yucatan.'" In *The Diplomatic Record, 1991–1992,* ed. Hans Binnendijk and Mary Locke. Boulder: Westview, 1993, 70–95.

Hernández, Ricardo, and Edith Sánchez, eds. *Cross-Border Links: A Directory of Organizations in Canada, Mexico, and the United States*. Albuquerque: Inter-Hemispheric Education Resource Center, 1992.

Herrera-Sobek, María. *The Bracero Experience: Elitelore versus Folklore*. UCLA Latin American Studies, 43. Los Angeles: University of California Press, 1979.

Herzog, Lawrence A. *Where North Meets South: Cities, Space and Politics on the U.S.–Mexico Border*. Austin: Center for Mexican American Studies, University of Texas at Austin, 1990.

———, ed. *Changing Boundaries in the Americas: New Perspectives on the U.S.–Mexican, Central American, and South American Borders*. U.S.–Mexico Contemporary Perspectives Series, 3. San Diego: Center for U.S.–Mexican Studies, 1992.

———, ed. *Planning the International Border Metropolis*. Monograph 19. La Jolla: Center for United States–Mexico Studies, 1986.

Hicks, D. Emily. *Border Writing: The Multidimensional Text*. Theory and History of Literature, 80. Minneapolis: University of Minnesota Press, 1991.

———. "La marquesa se mete Prozac/La Marquesa Goes on Prozac." In *Border Lives: Personal Essay on the U.S.–Mexico Border/Vidas Fronterizas: La crónica en la Frontera México–Estados Unidos,* ed. Harry Polkinhorn et al., 187–284. Calexico and Mexicali: Binational Press/Editorial Binacional, 1995.

House, John William. *Frontier on the Rio Grande: A Political Geography of Development and Social Deprivation*. Oxford: Clarendon Press, 1982.

Humm, Maggie. *Border Traffic: Strategies of Contemporary Women Writers*. New York: St. Martin's, 1991.

Hutcheon, Linda. *Splitting Images: Contemporary Canadian Ironies*. London: Oxford University Press, 1991.

Iglesias Prieto, Norma. *Entre yerba, polvo y plomo: Lo fronterizo visto por el cine mexicano*. 2 vols. Tijuana: El Colegio de la Frontera Norte, 1991.

In Search of Pancho Villa. Dir. Hector Galan. Telescript by Paul Espinosa. Story by Hector Galan and Paul Espinosa. *The American Experience*. Exec. prod. Judy Crichton. PBS, 1993.

Iturbide, Graciela. *Juchitán de las mujeres*. Mexico City: Toledo, 1989.

El jardín del Edén. Dir. María Novaro. Story by Beatriz Novaro and María Novaro. Prod. Macondo Cine Video, Instituto Mexicano de Cinematografía, Verseau International, Inc., Universidad de

Guadalajara, Fondo de Fomento a la Calidad Cinematográfica, Jorge Sánchez, and Lyse Lafontaine. Filmed on locations in California and Baja California. 1994.

Johnson, Randal. "In the Belly of the Ogre: Cinema and the State in Latin America." In *Mediating Two Worlds: Cinematic Encounters in the Americas,* ed. Ana M. López, John King, and Manuel Alvarado, 204–13. London: British Film Institute, 1993.

Joselit, David. "Report from San Diego." *Art in America* 77.12 (December 1989): 120–35.

Kamel, Rachael. *The Global Factory: Analysis and Action for a New Economic Era.* Philadelphia: American Friends Service Committee, 1990.

Katz, Freidrich. *The Secret War in Mexico: Europe, the United States, and the Mexican Revolution.* Portions trans. Loren Goldner. Chicago: University of Chicago Press, 1981.

Kearney, Michael. "Borders and Boundaries of State and Self at the End of Empire." *Journal of Historical Sociology* 4.1 (March 1991): 52–74.

Kelley, Jeff, ed. of English text. *The Border Art Workshop/Taller de Arte Fronterizo (BAW/TAF), 1984–1989: A Documentation of Five Years of Interdisciplinary Art Projects Dealing with U.S.–Mexico Border Issues (a Binational Perspective).* San Diego: Border Art Workshop/Taller de Arte Fronterizo, 1988.

Kellner, Douglas, and Michael Ryan. "Technophobia." In *Alien Zone: Cultural Theory and Contemporary Science Fiction Cinema,* ed. Annette Kuhn. London: Verso, 1990, 58–65.

Kester, Grant. "Rhetorical Questions: The Alternative Arts Sector and the Imaginary Public." *Afterimage* 20.6 (January 1993): 10–16.

King, John. *Magical Reels: A History of Cinema in Latin America.* London: Verso, 1990.

Kleczka, Hon. Jerry. "Special Report on NAFTA." Washington, DC, n.d. [1993].

Krauze, Enrique. *Daniel Cosío Villegas: Una biografía intellectual.* Mexico City: Joaquín Mortiz, 1980.

Krugman, Paul. "Myths and Realities of U.S. Competitiveness." In *Pop Internationalism,* by Paul Krugman, 87–104. Cambridge: Massachusetts Institute of Technology Press, 1996.

———. *Pop Internationalism.* Cambridge: Massachusetts Institute of Technology Press, 1996.

———. "The Uncomfortable Truth about NAFTA." In *Pop Internationalism,* by Paul Krugman, 155–66. Cambridge: Massachusetts Institute of Technology Press, 1996.

L.A. Familia. Video. Dir. Harry Gamboa Jr. Performance/text by Humberto Sandoval, Barbara Carrasco, and Diego Gamboa. 1993. 37 min.

Langewiesche, William. *Cutting for Sign.* New York: Pantheon, 1993.

Larson, Robert W. "Statehood." In *New Mexico Past and Present.* Albuquerque: University of New Mexico Press, 1971, 190–207.

Laurell, Ana Cristina. "Democracy in Mexico: Will the First be the Last?" *New Left Review* 194 (July/August 1992): 33–53.

Lawday, David. "France Guns for Clint Eastwood." *U.S. News and World Report* 115.23 (13 December 1993): 72.

Leduc, Paul. "Dinosaurs and Lizards." In *Latin American Visions,* ed. Patricia Aufderheide. Philadelphia: The International House, 1989, 57–59.

Leighton, George R. "Afterword: The Photographic History of the Mexican Revolution." In *The Wind That Swept Mexico: The History of the Mexican Revolution, 1910–1942,* by Anita Brenner. New York: Harper and Brothers, 1943. 287–92.

Levine, Robert M. *Images of History: Nineteenth- and Early-Twentieth-Century Latin American Photographs as Documents.* Durham: Duke University Press, 1989.

Limón, José. *Dancing with the Devil: Society and Cultural Politics in Mexican-American South Texas.* Madison: University of Wisconsin Press, 1994.

Lippard, Lucy R. *Mixed Blessings: New Art in a Multicultural America.* New York: Pantheon, 1990.

López, Ana M., John King, and Manuel Alvarado, eds. *Mediating Two Worlds: Cinematic Encounters in the Americas.* London: British Film Institute, 1993.

Los mojados. Dir. Alejandro Galindo. Prod. Producciones Fílmicas Agrasanchez, 1977. 92 min.

Maciel, David R. *El Norte: The U.S.–Mexican Border in Contemporary Cinema.* Border Studies Series, 3. San Diego: Institute for Regional Studies of the Californias, San Diego State University, 1990.

"Maquila Scoreboard." *Twin Plant News* 13.11 (June 1998): 45.

"Maquiladoras in the U.S.–Mexico Border Region." *CJM Annual Report, 1996.* San Antonio: Coalition for Justice in the Maquiladoras, 1996, 12–13.

Martínez, Oscar J. *Border Boom Town: Ciudad Juárez since 1848.* Austin: University of Texas Press, 1978.

———. *Border People: Life and Society in the U.S.–Mexico Borderlands.* Tucson: University of Arizona Press, 1994.

———. *Troublesome Border.* Tucson: University of Arizona Press, 1988.

Matabuena Peláez, Teresa. *Algunos usos y conceptos de la fotografía durante el Porfiriato.* Mexico City: Universidad Iberoamericana, 1991.

McAnany, Emile G., and Kenton T. Wilkinson, eds. *Mass Media and Free Trade: NAFTA and the Cultural Industries.* Austin: University of Texas Press, 1996.

McGreevy, Patrick. "Reading the Texts of Niagara Falls: The Metaphor of Death." In *Writing Worlds: Discourse, Text and Metaphor in the Representation of Landscape,* ed. Trevor J. Barnes and James S. Duncan. London: Routledge, 1992, 50–72.

Media Development 36.4 (1989). Spec. issue, "Video for the People."

Meggs, Brown. *The War Train: A Novel of 1916.* New York: Atheneum, 1981.

"Mercosur Experiences Growing Pains." *Washington Report on the Hemisphere* 15.12 (20 July 1995): 1+.

"The Mercosur Marriage." *Latin Trade* 4.6 (August 1996): 69–75.

Mesa-Bains, Amalia. "Artist's Statement." *Imagine* 3.1–2 (summer–winter 1986): 141–42.

Michaelsen, Scott, and David E. Johnson, eds. *Border Theory: The Limits of Cultural Politics.* Minneapolis: University of Minnesota Press, 1997.

Miller, Toby. *The Well-Tempered Self: Citizenship, Culture, and the Postmodern Subject.* Baltimore: Johns Hopkins University Press, 1993.

Miller, Tom. *On the Border.* New York: Harper and Row, 1987.

Mistron, Deborah E. "A Hybrid Subgenre: The Revolutionary Melodrama in the Mexican Cinema." *Studies in Latin American Popular Culture* 3 (1984): 47–69.

———. "The Role of Pancho Villa in the Mexican and American Cinema." *Studies in Latin American Popular Culture* 2 (1983): 1–13.

Mitchell, Katharyne. "In Whose Interest? Transnational Capital and the Production of Multiculturalism in Canada." In *Global/Local: Cultural Production and the Transnational Imaginary,* ed. Rob Wilson and Wimal Dissanayake, 219–51. Durham: Duke University Press, 1996.

Monsiváis, Carlos. "De la cultura mexicana en vísperas del Tratado de Libre Comercio." In *La educación y la cultura ante el Tratado de Libre Comercio,* ed. Gilberto Guevara Niebla and Néstor García Canclini, 179–210. Mexico City: Nueva Imagen, 1992.

———. "Interacción Cultural Fronteriza." In *Reglas del juego y juego sin reglas en la vida fronteriza: III Reunión de Universidades Mexicanas y de Estados Unidos, 23–25 de Octubre, 1983, Tijuana, B.C.,* ed. Mario Miranda and James W. Wilkie. Mexico City: Asociación Nacional de Universidades e Instituciones de Educación Superior, 1985, 221–27.

Moody, Kim. *An Injury to All.* London: Verso, 1988.

Moody, Kim, and Mary McGinn. *Unions and Free Trade: Solidarity vs. Competition.* Detroit: Labor Notes, 1992.

Mora, Carl J. *Mexican Cinema: Reflections of a Society, 1896–1988.* 2d ed. Berkeley: University of California Press, 1989.

Morales, Rebecca, and Jesús Tamayo-Sánchez. "Urbanization and Development of the United States Mexico Border." In *Changing Boundaries in the Americas: New Perspectives on the U.S.–Mexican,*

Central American, and South American Borders, ed. Lawrence A. Herzog, 49–68. U.S.–Mexico Contemporary Perspectives Series, 3. San Diego: Center for U.S.–Mexican Studies, 1992.

Mosco, Vincent. "Toward a Transnational World Information Order: The U.S.–Canada Free Trade Agreement." *Canadian Journal of Communications* 15.2 (May 1990): 46–64.

Munch, Francis J. "Villa's Columbus Raid: Practical Politics or German Design?" *New Mexico Historical Review* 44.3 (July 1969): 189–214.

Muñoz, Carlos, Jr. *Youth, Identity, Power: The Chicano Movement.* London: Verso, 1989.

Museum of Contemporary Hispanic Art, The New Museum of Contemporary Art, and The Studio Museum in Harlem. *The Decade Show: Frameworks of Identity in the 1980s.* New York: Museum of Contemporary Hispanic Art, The New Museum of Contemporary Art, and The Studio Museum in Harlem, 1990.

Nader, Ralph, et al. *The Case against Free Trade: GATT, NAFTA, and the Globalization of Corporate Power.* San Francisco: Earth Island; Berkeley: North Atlantic Books, 1993.

"The NAFTA Debate." *Larry King Live.* CNN, 9 November 1993.

Nathan, Debbie. "Adjustment of Status: The Trial of Margaret Randall." In *Women and Other Aliens: Essays from the U.S.–Mexico Border.* El Paso: Cinco Puntos, 1991, 90–108.

———. "Love in the Time of Cholera: Waiting for Free Trade." *Texas Observer,* 15 January 1993, 12–16.

National Trade Data Bank. *The North American Free Trade Agreement.* CD-ROM. Washington, DC: National Trade Data Bank, 10 May 1994.

Noriega, Chon. "This Is Not a Border." *Spectator* 13.1 (fall 1992): 4–11. Spec. issue, "Border Crossings: Mexican and Chicano Cinema."

The Oakland Museum. *Between Two Worlds: The People of the Border, Photographs by Don Bartletti.* Oakland: The Oakland Museum, 1992.

The Old Gringo. Dir. Luis Puenzo. Story by Luis Puenzo and Aida Bortnik. Prod. Jane Fonda and Lois Bonfiglio. Columbia Pictures, 1989.

Oles, James. *South of the Border: Mexico in the American Imagination, 1914–1917.* Washington, DC: Smithsonian Institution Press, 1993.

Ollman, Leah. "Report from San Diego: a Change of Weather?" *Art in America* 85.7 (July 1997): 35–43.

Paredes, Américo. *"With His Pistol in His Hand": A Border Ballad and Its Hero.* Austin: University of Texas Press, 1958.

Passell, Peter. "How Free Trade Prompts Growth: A Primer." *New York Times,* 15 December 1993, late ed., A1+.

———. "Is France's Cultural Protection a Handy-Dandy Trade Excuse?" *New York Times,* 6 January 1994, late ed., D2.

Pastor, Robert A., and Jorge Castañeda. *Limits to Friendship: The United States and Mexico.* New York: Vintage, 1989.

Pavel, Thomas G. *Fictional Worlds.* Cambridge: Harvard University Press, 1986.

Paxman, Andrew. "Art for Sale's Sake." *Business Mexico* 3.3 (March 1993): 17–19.

Paz, Octavio. *El laberinto de soledad.* 3d ed. 1950. Mexico City: Fondo de Cultura Económica, 1992.

———. "Will for Form." In *Mexico: Splendors of Thirty Centuries.* New York: The Metropolitan Museum of Art, 1990, 3–38.

Peralta, Elda. *Luis Spota: Las sustancias de la tierra.* Mexico City: Grijalbo, 1990.

"Peso Devaluations Affect *Maquiladoras.*" *Washington Report on the Hemisphere* 16.2 (20 February 1996): 1+.

"Policing the Border—A Military Approach." *BorderLines* 1.2 (February 1992): 1+.

Pratt, Mary Louise. *Imperial Eyes: Travel Writing and Transculturation.* London: Routledge, 1992.

Preeg, Ernest H. *Traders in a Brave New World: The Uruguay Round and the Future of the International Trading System.* Chicago: University of Chicago Press, 1995.

"Progress and Promise." *Los Angeles Times,* 22 October 1991, spec. section.

Rakocy, Bill. *1916 Villa Raids!* 2d ed. El Paso: Bravo, 1991.

Ramírez-Berg, Charles. *Cinema of Solitude: A Critical Study of Mexican Film, 1967–1983.* Austin: University of Texas Press, 1992.

——. "Immigrants, Aliens, and Extraterrestrials: Science Fiction's Alien 'Other' as (Among *Other* Things) New Hispanic Imagery." *CineAction!* 18 (fall 1989): 3–17.

Reo, Danielle, ed. *inSITE 97 Guide.* San Diego: Installation Gallery, 1997.

Resource Center Bulletin 28 (summer 1992). Spec. issue, "Inside Guatemala."

——37 (fall 1994). Spec. issue, "Trade Dreams in Central America."

——26 (winter 1991). Spec. issue, "Washington's Aid Programs to Mexico: Military and Anti-Narcotics Assistance."

Reyes Nevares, Beatriz. *The Mexican Cinema: Interviews with Thirteen Directors.* Trans. Carl J. Mora and Elizabeth Gard. Albuquerque: University of New Mexico Press, 1976.

Riding, Alan. "Europe Still Gives Big Doses of Money to Help the Arts." *New York Times,* 4 May 1995, C15.

Roberts, Calvin A., and Susan A. Roberts. *New Mexico.* Albuquerque: University of New Mexico Press, 1988, 137–60.

Roberts, Martin. "The Self in the Other: Ethnographic Film, Surrealism, Politics." *Visual Anthropology* 8 (1996): 79–94.

Rockwell, John. "French Love the U.S., but Fiercely Defend Their Film Industry." *New York Times,* 29 November 1993, late ed., C11+.

Rodríguez, Roberto. "(Barbed) Wired for Controversy." *Black Issues in Higher Education* 13.19 (14 November 1996): 10–11.

Rohter, Larry. "A New Star for Studios Is Mexico." *New York Times,* 1 January 1990, 31+.

——. "North American Trade Bloc? Mexico Rejects Such an Idea." *New York Times,* 24 November 1988, late ed., D1+.

Romero, Rolando J. "Border of Fear, Border of Desire." *BorderLines* 1.1 (September 1993): 36–70.

Rosaldo, Renato. *Culture and Truth: The Remaking of Social Analysis.* Boston: Beacon, 1989.

Rouse, Roger. "Mexican Migration in the Social Space of Postmodernism." *Diaspora* 1.1 (spring 1991): 8–23.

Safire, William. "Hold That GATT." *New York Times,* 9 December 1993, late ed., A31.

Saldaña, Lori. "The Downside of the Border Boom." *Los Angeles Times,* 22 August 1996, B9.

Salgado, Sebastião. "The Border." *Rolling Stone* 776/777 (25 December 1997–8 January 1998): 129–32.

Salinas de Gortari, Carlos. "A New Hope for the Hemisphere." *New Perspectives Quarterly* 8.1 (winter 1991): 4–9.

Sandos, James A. "German Involvement in Northern Mexico, 1915–1916: A New Look at the Columbus Raid." *Hispanic American Historical Review* 50 (February 1970): 70–88.

——. "The Plan of San Diego: War and Diplomacy on the Texas Border, 1915–1916." *Arizona and the West* 14 (spring 1972): 5–24.

——. "Prostitution and Drugs: The United States Army on the Mexican-American Border, 1916–1917." *Pacific Historical Review* 49.4 (November 1980): 621–45.

——. *Rebellion in the Borderlands: Anarchism and the Plan de San Diego, 1904–1923.* Norman: University of Oklahoma Press, 1992.

Sarber, Mary A. *Photographs from the Border: The Otis A. Aultman Collection.* Photographic prints by Charles H. Binion. El Paso: El Paso Public Library Association, 1977.

Sawchuk, Kim. "Unleashing the Demons of History." *Parachute* 67 (July–September 1992): 22–29.

Sefchovich, Sara. *Ideología y ficción en la obra de Luis Spota.* Mexico City: Grijalbo, 1985.

Selcraig, Bruce. "Poisonous Flows the Rio Grande." *Los Angeles Times Magazine,* 25 October 1992, 30+.

Shetterly, Will. *Elsewhere.* New York: Tor, 1991.

——. *Nevernever.* San Diego: Jane Yolen–Harcourt Brace, 1993.

Silverstein, Jeff. "Culture: An Industry Exempt from Free Trade? Canadians Fight to Keep Their Identity." *Business Mexico* (April 1992): 35.

Silverstein, Ken, and Alexander Cockburn. "The Killers and the Killing." *The Nation,* 6 March 1995, 306–11.

Sinclair, John. "Culture and Trade: Some Theoretical and Practical Considerations." In *Mass Media and Free Trade,* ed. Emile G. McAnany and Kenton T. Wilkinson, 31–60. Austin: University of Texas Press, 1996.

Sklair, Leslie. "Capitalism and Development in Global Perspective." In *Capitalism and Development,* ed. Leslie Sklair. London: Routledge, 1994, 165–88.

Smith, Neil. *Uneven Development: Nature, Capital and the Production of Space.* 1984; reprint, Cambridge, MA: Basil Blackwell, 1990.

Smith, Neil, and Cindi Katz. "Grounding Metaphor: Towards a Spatialized Politics." In *Place and the Politics of Identity,* ed. Michael Keith and Steve Pile. London: Routledge, 1993, 67–83.

Smithsonian Institution. *1993 Festival of American Folklife, July 1–July 5.* Washington, DC: Smithsonian Institution, 1993.

Son of Border Crisis: Seven Video Poems. Video. Dir. Isaac Artenstein. Written and performed by Guillermo Gómez-Peña. Cinewest Productions, 1990. 15 min.

Spota, Luis. *Murieron a mitad del río.* 1948; reprint, Mexico City: Grijalbo, 1987.

Stricherz, Mark. "Bill of Wrath." *Nation* 266.7 (11 May 1998): 6–7.

Taibo II, Paco Ignacio, et al. *Frontera de espejos rotos.* Mexico City: Ediciones Roca, 1994.

——. *Irapuato mi amor.* Mexico City: Editorial Macehual, Editorial Leega, and Información Obrera, 1984.

"Taking Cultural Exception." *Economist* 328.7830 (25 September 1993): 61.

Tatum, Charles. "Introduction: Stasis and Change along the Rio Grande: Aristeo Brito's *The Devil in Texas.*" In *El Diablo en Tejas/The Devil in Texas,* by Aristeo Brito, trans. David William Foster. Clásicos Chicanos/Chicano Classics, 5: 1–20. Tempe, AZ: Bilingual Press/ Editorial Bilingüe, 1990.

Taylor, Diana. "'High Aztec' or Performing Anthro Pop: Jesusa Rodríguez and Liliana Felipe in *Cielo de abajo.*" *Drama Review* 37.3 (fall 1993): 142–52.

Thompson, Kristin. *Exporting Entertainment: America in the World Film Market, 1907–1934.* London: British Film Institute, 1985.

Thorup, Cathryn. "The Politics of Free Trade and the Dynamics of Cross-Border Coalitions in U.S.–Mexican Relations." *Columbia Journal of World Business* 26.2 (summer 1991): 12–26.

Todd, Walker F. "Bailing Out the Creditor Class." *The Nation,* 13 February 1995, 193–94.

Torrents, Nissa. "Mexican Cinema Comes Alive." In *Mediating Two Worlds: Cinematic Encounters in the Americas,* ed. Ana M. López, John King, and Manuel Alvarado, 222–27. London: British Film Institute, 1993.

Traver, Nancy. "NM, Artist, University Divided over Sculpture Topped with Wire." *Dallas Morning News,* 2 March 1997, 47A.

Trinh, T. Minh-Ha. *When the Moon Waxes Red: Representation, Gender and Cultural Politics.* New York: Routledge, 1991.

Uchitelle, Louis. "America's Newest Industrial Belt." *New York Times,* 21 March 1993, late ed., sec. 3, 1+.

"U.S.–Canada T.V. Dispute Settled." *U.S.–Mexico Free Trade Reporter* 5.11 (15 June 1996): 5.

United States Department of Commerce, Office of Mexico. *Nafta Facts.* Document 0101. Washington, DC: U.S. Department of Commerce, February 1994.

——. *Nafta Facts.* Document 6000. Washington, DC: U.S. Department of Commerce, February 1994.

———. *Nafta Facts.* Document 6248. Washington, DC: U.S. Department of Commerce, December 1993.

———. *Nafta Facts.* Document 6268. Washington, DC: U.S. Department of Commerce, December 1993.

———. *Nafta Facts.* Document 6351. Washington, DC: U.S. Department of Commerce, January 1994.

Urrea, Luis Alberto. *Across the Wire: Life and Hard Times on the Mexican Border.* New York: Anchor-Doubleday, 1993.

———. *By the Lake of Sleeping Children: The Secret Life of the Mexican Border.* New York: Anchor-Doubleday, 1996.

Valenti, Jack. Letter. *New York Times,* 3 January 1994, late ed., A22.

Valenzuela Arce, José Manuel. "Ámbitos de interración y consumo cultural en los jóvenes." In *El consumo cultural en México,* coord. Néstor García Canclini, 384–414. Mexico City: Consejo Nacional para la Cultura y las Artes, 1993.

Vanderwood, Paul, and Frank N. Samponaro, *Border Fury: A Picture Postcard Record of Mexico's Revolution and U.S. War Preparedness, 1910–1917.* Albuquerque: University of New Mexico Press, 1988.

———. *War Scare on the Rio Grande: Robert Runyon's Photographs of the Border Conflict, 1913–1916.* Barker Texas History Center Series, 1. Austin: The Texas State Historical Association, 1992.

Vargas Llosa, Mario. "¿La excepción cultural?" *El País,* 12 October 1993, 11–12.

Vasconcelos, José. *La raza cósmica: Misión de la raza iberoamericana.* 1924; reprint, Paris: Agencia Mundial de Librería, 1929.

"Video Evidence for Import Labeling Bill." *NAFTA and Inter-American Trade Monitor* 4.9 (5 May 1997): n.p.

Vila, Pablo. *Everyday Life, Culture, and Identity on the Mexican-American Border.* Ph.D. diss., University of Texas, Austin, 1994.

Wasko, Janet. *Hollywood in the Information Age: Beyond the Silver Screen.* Austin: University of Texas Press, 1995.

Wei, Lilly, et al. "On Nationality: 13 Artists." *Art in America* 79 (September 1991): 124+.

Weinberger, Caspar W. *The Next War.* Washington, DC: Regnery Publications, 1996.

Weiner, Christian. "Cine, subdesarrollo y libre mercado." *Arco crítico* 3.4–5 (June 1994): 42–43.

Weinraub, Bernard. "Directors Battle over GATT's Final Cut and Print." *New York Times,* 12 December 1993, late ed., 24.

Weisman, Alan. *La Frontera: The United States Border with Mexico.* Photos by Jay Dusard. Tucson: University of Arizona Press, 1986.

Weiss, Jason. "An Interview with Guillermo Gómez-Peña." *Review: Latin American Literature and Arts* 45 (July–December 1991): 8–13.

Welchman, John C., ed. *Rethinking Borders.* Minneapolis: University of Minnesota Press, 1996.

Why Worry? Dir. Fred Newmeyer and Sam Taylor. Story by Sam Taylor. With Harold Lloyd and Jobyna Ralston. Prod. Pathé Exchange, Inc., and Hal Roach. 1923.

Wilkinson, Tracy. "Dreams Die on Mexico's Second Border." *Los Angeles Times,* 1 January 1994, A1+.

Williams, Michael. "Top Biz Talent in Culture Clash." *Variety,* 20 December 1993, 62.

Williams, Raymond. *Culture and Society, 1780–1950.* Harmondsworth: Penguin, 1961.

Wilson, Rob, and Wimal Dissanayake, eds. *Global/Local: Cultural Production and the Transnational Imaginary.* Durham: Duke University Press, 1996.

Wilt, David. "The Arieles, Part 4." *The Mexican Film Bulletin* 3.4 (November 1996): 3.

Windling, Terri, ed. *Borderland: A Borderlands Anthology.* 1986. New York: Tor, 1991.

———. *Life on the Border.* New York: Tor, 1991.

Windling, Terri, and Delia Sherman, eds. *The Essential Bordertown: A Traveller's Guide to the Edge of Faery.* New York: Tor, 1998.

Windling, Terri, and Mark Alan Arnold, eds. *Bordertown: A Chronicle of the Borderlands.* New York: Signet–New American Library, 1986.

"The World after NAFTA, According to Paz." *New Yorker* 69.44 (27 December 1993): 57–58.

Worthington, Sue. "Keeping the Pressure On: Tools for Organizing Beyond NAFTA." *Beyond Borders* (spring 1994): 10+.

Yard, Sally, ed. *inSITE 94: A Binational Exhibition of Installation and Site-Specific Art.* San Diego: Installation Gallery, 1994.

———. *inSITE 94 Guide.* San Diego: Installation Gallery, 1994.

Yúdice, George. *We Are Not the World: Identity and Representation in an Age of Global Restructuring.* Durham: Duke University Press, forthcoming.

Yúdice, George, Jean Franco, and Juan Flores, eds. *On Edge: The Crisis of Contemporary Latin American Culture.* Cultural Politics, 4. Minneapolis: University of Minnesota Press, 1992.

Index

Created by Eileen Quam

About Place (exhibition), 36
Ace/Co., 138
ACS. *See* Association of Caribbean States
Action Canada Network (ACN), 21
Aerial reconnaissance, 74
Aguilera-Hellweg, Max, 49
Alambristas, 46
Alemán, Miguel, 98, 99, 101–2
Alewitz, Mike, 137
Allen, Terry: *a simple story (Juarez),* 41–44, *42, 43, 44, 45,* 50, 67
Almodóvar, Pedro, 28
Alvarez, Robert, 2
Andean Pact, 3
Anderson, Benedict, 56
Anime MUSH (software program), 120
Anzaldúa, Gloria: *Borderlands/La Frontera,* 8
Art: museum influence on national culture, 35–36; of place, 136, 138; and politics, 129–30; sponsors in Mexico, 38. *See also* specific artists and exhibitions
Art Institute of Chicago (Chicago, Ill.), 36
Artenstein, Isaac, 123, *124*
Asco, 47
Association of Caribbean States (ACS), 3
Atwood, Margaret, 22–23
Ávila Camacho, Manuel, administration of, 98, 99
Azcárraga Milmo, Emilio, 37–38

Barbed wire. *See* Fences
Barr, Alfred H., 36
Bartletti, Don, 49; *Uneasy Neighbors,* 53
BAW/TAF. *See* Border Art Workshop/Taller de Arte Fronterizo
Begley, Carla: *Mexico: For Sale,* 59
Begley, Dermot: *Mexico: For Sale,* 59
Beneix, Jean-Jacques, 27
Berkman, Alexander, 66
Berman, Sara Jo: *Border Realities II,* 56
Bertolucci, Bernardo, 28
Betty Blue (film), 27
Beuys, Joseph, 129
Beveridge, Karl, 30–31; *Free Expression, 30,* 30–31; *Shutdown, 31,* 30–31
Bhagwati, Jagdish, 21
Blanc, Les, 46
Blockades: in border cities, 5
Bonfil Batalla, Guillermo, 25–26, 39
Border Art Workshop/Taller de Arte Fronterizo (BAW/TAF), 49–50, 120, 122, 123, 129, 137
Border Industrialization Program, 18, 100
Borders: and boundaries, 70; as communal space, 119; as contact zone, 13; vs. frontier, 144n20; as global, 123, 130; imagery, 2, 43–44, 46; as metaphor, 1–2, 11, 60, 119, 145n38; and national identity, 105; and North Americans, 123; photographers on, 78, *78,* 84; as polyvalent, 3; space/place duality, 2;

theatricalization of conflict, 92–94; universal-
ization of crossing, 13
Bordertown series, 120, *121*, 130–33, 134–35;
fan culture, 131
Boundaries: and borders, 70
Bracero program, 12, 100–101. *See also*
Maquiladora industries
Break of Dawn (film), 123
Brito, Aristeo: *El diablo en Texas,* 46
Brittan, Leon, 28
Buchanan, Patrick, 22
Buck-Morss, Susan: "Passports," 65
Bull, Emma: *Finder,* 133
Bush, George: on trade, 4
Bustamante, Maris, 32; *Naftaperformances,* 32

CACM. *See* Central American Common Market
Campbell, Bruce, 59
Campeón sin corona (film), 106
CARA catalogue. *See Chicano Art and Resistance*
exhibition catalogue
Cárdenas, Cuauhtémoc, 5, 59
Cárdenas, Lázaro, 93, 98
Carignon, Alain, 23
Carranza, Venustiano, 71
Castañeda, Jorge: *Utopia Unarmed,* 11
Central American Common Market (CACM), 3
Centro Cultural Arte Contemporáneo (Mexico
City, Mex.), 37
Centro Cultural de la Raza (San Diego, Calif.),
44, 127
Chain-link. *See* Fences
Chicago Public Art Group, 137
Chicano Art and Resistance exhibition catalogue,
47
Cholera, 53–55
Chulas Fronteras (film), 46
Cielo de abajo (play), 15, 16
Cinema. *See* Film
Citizens Materiél Assistance, 92
Coerver, Don M., 70
Colosio, Luis Donaldo, 5
Colquhoun, ReyLynda, 121
Columbus (New Mex.) raid (1916), 70–76; and
overseas invasion of United States, 74; recent
treatments of, 86–94
Condé, Carole, 30–31; *Free Expression, 30,*
30–31; *Shutdown, 31,* 30–31

Consumerism: and identity, 11
Contact zone, 13
Cortés, Carlos E., 69, 76, 86
Cosío Villegas, Daniel, 98–99; *Historia moderna
de México,* 99
Couple in the Cage, The (video), 137
Crètien, Jean, 5
Cultural exemption: Canadian, 22–23, 146n9;
defined, 12; and economics, 23; French,
23–24, 26–28; history of, 19–24; in NAFTA,
21
Culture/cultural industries: cultural solutions, 17;
defined, 24–25; Eurocentric, 137, 163n6;
European, 23, 24–29; and free trade, 17,
18–22, 26; French, 26–27; imperialist, 26;
and NAFTA, 17, 18–19, 39, 136–38; North
American, 29–37; and state, 16; transculturation, 13; transnational culture brokering, 18;
U.S. products in Mexico, 18

Day of the Dead iconography, 36
Debray, Régis, 12, 25–27
Depardieu, Gérard, 28
Díaz, Porfirio, 69, 72, 94. *See also* Porfiriato
Dirty Business (video), 62–64
Diva (film), 27
Dominguez, Virginia, 24–25
Dos Ciudades/Two Cities (art project), 127
Ďurovičová, Nataša, 23
Dusard, Jay, 49

Economics: devaluation of Mexican currency,
5–6; and trade in Latin America, 3
Editorial Binacional, 8
Ejército Zapatista de Liberación Nacional
(EZLN), 5
Elfland, 131–33
Elsaesser, Thomas, 28
Enterprise for the Americas Initiative, 4
Espaldas mojadas (film), 12, 101, 106–15,
117–18; publicity stills, *110, 111, 113*
¡Esquina bajan! (film), 106
Establishing shots, 46, 67
Eurocentrism, 137, 163n6
Ezell, Harold, 100

Faerie kingdom, 131–33, 135
Familia de tantas, Una (film), 106

Feigen, Ed, 62
Fein, Seth, 22
Felipe, Liliana, 15
Femme Nikita, La (film), 27
Fence: as border image, 46–50, *48, 49, 50, 51, 52, 55*, 61
Film: border cinema, 7–8; border imagery in, 46, 76; on Columbus raid, 70–76, 86; and free trade, 27–29; French subsidies, 23–24; Mexican, 97, 106–7, 114–15, 117; on Mexican Revolution, 76–77, 85–86, 95; quotas, 28; U.S., in Mexico, 17–19. *See also* specific films
Finley, Karen, 125
Fonda, Jane, 8, 9
$4 a Day? No Way! (video), 62
Franco, Jean, 16
Frears, Stephen, 28
Free trade: art, 37; and border regions, 3–4; and cultural industries, 17, 19; debates, 12; and film, 27–29; global, 22. *See also* North American Free Trade Agreement
Frente Auténtico del Trabajo (FAT), 137–38
Frontera, La/The Border (exhibition), 44–45, 127
Fuentes, Carlos, 9, 11
Fusco, Coco, 127, 137

Galindo, Alejandro, 12, 101, 106–7, 114; *Cine mexicano,* 114. *See also Espaldas mojadas*
García, Rupert, 47
García Canclini, Néstor: *Consumidores y cuidadanos,* 11; *Cultura híbrida,* 11; on culture, 24; *Educación y la cultura ante el Tratado de Libre Comercio, La,* 18; on *Mexico: Splendors of Thirty Centuries* exhibition, 36; on modernization, 94; on Televisa, 37; on U.S. movies in Mexico, 17
García Riera, Emilio, 100–101, 107, 118
General Agreement on Tariffs and Trade (GATT), 4, 12; opposition to, 18, 21–24, 26, 29; proponents of, 27–28; Uruguay Round, 22
Germinal (film), 27
Global Assembly Line, The (video), 58
Globalization, 17; borders and, 123, 130; and culture, 26; and free trade, 22, 120; and U.S. expansionism, 136
Goin, Peter, 49; *Tracing the Line,* 49, *49, 50, 51, 52*

Goldman, Emma, 66
Gómez Montero, Sergio, 8
Gómez-Peña, Guillermo, 1, 11, 13, 32–35, 122–30, *124; Border Brujo,* 120, 123–27, *124;* "Documented/Undocumented," 122–23; "Freefalling toward a Borderless Future," 51; "From Art-mageddon to Gringostroika," 123; "Multicultural Paradigm," 123; "New World (B)order," 119, 127–28, 134, 135; *Son of Border Crisis,* 127; *Year of the White Bear,* 120, 137
Greenberg, Harold, 22
Group of Three, 3
Guest worker programs, 100. *See also* Bracero program
Guevara Niebla, Gilberto: on culture, 24; *Educación y la cultura ante el Tratado de Libre Comercio,* 18
Guzmán, Martín Luis: *Águila y la serpiente, El,* 97–98

Hale, Charles, 99
Hall, Douglas Kent, 49
Hall, Linda B., 70
Haozous, Bob, 47
Harvey, David, 1
Hearst, William Randolph, 76, 90
Hecox, F. C.: "American Sightseers near Madero's Camp," *82*
Heredia, Paula, 137
Hernández, Esequiel, 92
Herrera-Sobek, María, 117
Herrón, Willie, 47
Herzog, Lawrence, 3
Hicks, D. Emily: *Border Writing,* 11
Hills, Carla, 29
Horne, Walter H., 84; picture postcards by, *85, 86*
Huppert, Isabelle, 28

Identity: of border dwellers, 13; communal, 26; and consumerism, 11; Mexican national, 105, 115–16; North American, 120
Iglesias Prieto, Norma, 7
Imagery: border, 2, 43–44, 46; lower body and Mexico, 51–54; Mexican Revolutionary, 6, 50–51; Porfirian, 6; scatological, 52
Immigration. *See* Migration

Inferiority crisis, Mexican, 106
inSite (exhibition), 45

Jardín del Edén, El (film), 9–10
Juicio de Martín Cortés, El (film), 106
Jurassic Park (film), 27

Kahlo, Frida, 36
Kantor, Mickey, 28
Kelley, Jeff, 122
Kester, Grant, 125–26, 130
Kleczka, Jerry, 64
Konchalovsky, Andrei, 28
Krugman, Paul, 18; *Pop Internationalism,* 66

La Jolla Museum of Contemporary Art (San
   Diego, Calif.), 127. *See also* Museum of
   Contemporary Art
Labor: agreements and NAFTA, 138; and
   transnationalism, 57–58
Laboratory metaphor, 60–61
Lamb, The (film), 158n58
Lang, Jack, 28
Larsen, Neil, 11, 14
Latin America: economics and trade in, 3; as in-
   dependent republics, 11
Leaving Home (video), 59–60, 61
Lenin, V. I., 41
León de la Barra, Francisco, 72
Liberty (serial film), 76
Light Up the Border, 92–93
Limón, José E., 8
Lucas, George, 87

Maciel, David R., 7
Malinche, 23, 116, 148n40
Manrique, Daniel, 137
Maquiladora industries, 2, 100, 136
Martínez, Oscar J., 82, 115
Meggs, Brown: *War Train,* 87–89, 90
Meiselas, Susan, 49
Metropolitan Museum of Art (New York, N.Y.),
   35–36
Mexican Americans: portrayals of, 72
Mexican Revolution (1910–20): border events,
   69, 70; imagery, 6, 50–51, 70; mass media
   coverage, 69–70; films on, 76–77, 85–86, 95;
   and modernization, 74; in northern Mexico,

144n20; photography during, *73, 75,* 77,
   78–81, *78, 79, 80;* photography of witnesses,
   81–85, *82, 83, 84, 85;* postcard industry during, 77; refugee camps, 72–73, *75*
Mexico: bourgeoisie in, 98; Ciudad Juárez, *60,*
   63; devaluation of currency, 5–6; and lower
   body imagery, 51–54, 79; U.S.–Mexico state
   line, *73*
Mexico: Splendors of Thirty Centuries (exhibition),
   35–36
Migration: anti-immigration sentiments, 5,
   64–65, 92–93; in border writing, 12; fear of,
   64–65; immigration rights and NAFTA, 135;
   patterns, 2; push/pull factors, 117
Milton, Jeff, 66
Mistron, Deborah, 86
Mito y magia en América: Los ochenta (exhibition),
   36
Mitterrand, François, 26
Mobilization on Development, Trade, Labor, and
   the Environment (MODTLE), 21
Modernization: and Mexican Revolution, 74; and
   NAFTA, 135; and PRI, 94
Mojados, 46
Mojados, Los (film), 115
Monsiváis, Carlos, 12, 14, 19–20
Montoya, Malaquías, 47; *Undocumented, 48*
Mora, Carl, 106
Mulroney, Brian, 5
Museo de Arte Contemporáneo (Monterrey,
   Mex.), 36
Museum of Contemporary Art (San Diego,
   Calif.), 44, 127
Museum of Modern Art (New York, N.Y.), 36
Mutual Film Corporation, 71

Nader, Ralph: *Case against Free Trade,* 22
NAFTA (video), 62
Nathan, Debbie: "Love in the Time of Cholera,"
   53–56
National Council of Agricultural Employers, 100
National Endowment for the Arts (NEA), 130
Noriega, Chon A., 119
North American Free Trade Agreement (NAFTA):
   and border art, 45; and cultural industries, 17,
   18–19, 39, 136–38; and globalization, 120;
   and immigration rights, 135; interest in, 7;
   labor agreements, 138; and modernization,

135; oppositional movements to, 18–19, 21–22, 29–37; and Porfiriato, 94–95; reactions to, 19–20; as U.S. foreign policy, 18; and U.S.–Mexico border, 2, 3, 4, 12; videos about, 58–64, 66

Obregón, Álvaro, 72
Old Gringo, The (film), 8–9, 90
Operation Blockade, 5
Operation Wetback, 100
Osbon, Cal, 78–80, 83–84; picture postcards by, *73, 78, 80*

Paredes, Américo: *"With His Pistol in His Hand,"* 8
Partido de la Revolución Democrática (PRD), 5, 58–59
Partido Revolucionario Institucional (PRI), 5, 19, 94
Patiño Gómez, Alfonso, 101
Patria (serial film), 76
Paz, Octavio, 12; on free trade, 19; *Laberinto de soledad, El,* 114, 116; on national identity, 116; on privatization, 16
Peck, Gregory, 8
Pei, I. M., 26
Peralta, Elda, 102
Performance art, 15, 129. *See also* specific artists
Perot, Ross, 22
Pershing, John J., 70, 71, 74–75
Photography: border, 49, *73*; during Mexican Revolution, *73, 75,* 77, 78–81, *78, 79, 80*; of Mexican Revolution witnesses, 81–85, *82, 83, 84, 85*; point-of-view shots, 85, 158n49; of refugee camps, 73–74, *75*; reverse-shot structure, 158n49. *See also* specific photographers
Pito Pérez se va de bracero (film), 100–101
Place: art of, 136, 138; and space duality in borders, 2
Plan de San Diego, 72
Politics: and art, 129–30
Polkinhorn, Harry, 8
Pollution: of Rio Grande/RíoBravo, 52
Porfiriato: cinematic, 114; imagery of, 6; return of, 69, 94–95, 97–106. *See also* Díaz, Porfirio
Postcards: photography during Mexican Revolution, 77, 78–85, *78, 79, 80, 82, 83, 84, 85*

Pratt, Mary Louise, 13
PRD. *See* Partido de la Revolución Democrática
Preeg, Ernest H., 22
PRI. *See* Partido Revolucionario Institucional
Privatization, 16
Programa Nacional Fronterizo (PRONAF), 143n6
Prostitutes: employment during Punitive Expedition, 75–76
Punitive Expedition (1916), 70–76; fictional accounts of, 86–87; and modernization, 74; prostitutes employed during, 75–76; theatricality of, 83

Racism: toward Mexicans in film, 76
Red Mexicana de Acción Frente al Libre Comercio (RMALC), 21
Refugee camps: during Mexican Revolution, 72–73, *75*
Repatriation Program, 100
Revueltas, José, 99, 101
Reyes, Aurelio de los: *Con Villa en México,* 8
Reyes, Rogelio, 8
Ricardo, David, 29
Rio Grande/RíoBravo: fascination with, 54; imagery of, 62; pollution of, 52
River: as border image, 50
Roach, Hal, 159n63
Rodríguez, Jesusa, 15, 16, 37
Rodríguez, Primitivo, 59–60
Rogers-Lafferty, Sarah, 41–42
Romero, Rolando J., 52
Rosaldo, Renato, 163n6
Ruiz Massieu, José Francisco, 5

Safire, William, 22
Salgado, Sebastião, 49
Salinas de Gortari, Carlos, 5
Salinas de Gortari, Raúl, 5
Samponaro, Frank N., 8, 77, 81; *Border Fury,* 77
Schnorr, Michael: *Border Realities II,* 56; *Burning Fence, 57; Fence "Border line boundary,"* 55
Schwartzer, Lynn, 32; *Images of Labor, 32, 33, 34*
Scorsese, Martin, 28
Scott, Alan, *121*
Scott, Hugh, 72
Sefchovich, Sara, 98, 103–4, 117
Serra Puche, Jaime, 35

Serreau, Coline, 28
Settlement patterns, 2
Shared-world anthologies, 131
Shetterly, Will: *Elsewhere,* 133
Sifuentes, Roberto, 127
Site-specificity, 119, 122, 134, 137
Sklair, Leslie, 38
Southern Cone Common Market (Mercosur), 3
Space: communal, 119; and place duality in borders, 2; public space and European culture, 23
Spielberg, Steven, 28
Spota, Luis, 101–2; *Costumbres de poder, Las,* 103; *Murieron a mitad del río,* 12, 101–6
State: and cultural industries, 16
Stepan Chemical (video), 62
Strategic Organizing Alliance, 137–38
Subject formation: basis of, 26; of border dwellers, 13
Swing, Joseph M., 100

Taco Bell, 52
Taft, William, 72
Taller de Arte Fronterizo. *See* Border Art Workshop/Taller de Arte Fronterizo
Tatum, Charles, 1
TCC. *See* Transnational capitalist class
Teatro La Capilla, 15
Technology: and postnationalism, 134–36
Televisa, 37–38
Temporary Agricultural Worker Act (1998), 100
Thorup, Cathryn, 57
Toubon, Jacques, 23
Trade liberalization. *See* Free trade
Transculturation, 13
Transfrontier metropolises, 2, 136
Transnational capitalist class (TCC), 38
Transnational culture brokering, 18
Transnationalism, 7, 57–58
Trujillo Muñoz, Gabriel, 8

United Electrical, Radio, and Machine Workers (UE), 137–38

U.S.–Canada Free Trade Agreement (USCFTA), 17
U.S. Cavalry, 74
Urbanization: in U.S.–Mexico border, 3
Urrea, Luis Alberto, 53; *By the Lake of Sleeping Children,* 70
Uruguay Round. *See under* General Agreement on Tariffs and Trade

Valenti, Jack, 21–22, 24, 29
Vanderwood, Paul J., 8, 77, 81; *Border Fury,* 77
Vargas Llosa, Mario, 12, 21, 25, 26
Videos: border imagery in, 46; of NAFTA era, 58–64, 66
Vila, Pablo, 8, 13
Villa, Pancho: in film, 71; masculinity of, 79; raid on Columbus, New Mex., 70–76
Viva Villa! (film), 90

Wall, Jeff, 49
Wambaugh, Joseph: *Lines and Shadows,* 52
War on Drugs, 92
WARBOYS, 92
We Can Say No! (video), 62
Wenders, Wim, 28
Wexner Center for the Arts (Ohio State University), 41
What's the Cost of Your Blouse? (video), 58
Why Worry? (film), 159n63
Wight Art Gallery (University of Calif.–Los Angeles), 47
Williams, Raymond, 24
Wilson, Pete, 100
Windling, Terri, 121, 131, 165n54
World Trade Organization, 5

Young Indiana Jones Chronicles, The (television series), 85, 87, 89–91, 97–98
Yúdice, George, 18, 24, 45

Zapata, Emiliano, 59
Zedillo, Ernesto, 5

Claire F. Fox is assistant professor of Spanish and Portuguese at Stanford University. Her essays have been published in *Discourse, Social Text,* and *Iris.* Her current research and teaching interests include pan-American movements, cinema and its sister arts in post-Revolutionary Mexico, and the impact of free trade on the Latin American cultural industries.